The Sociolinguistics of Digital Englishes

The Sociolinguistics of Digital Englishes introduces core areas of sociolinguistics and explores how each one has been transformed by the current era of digital communication and the Internet. Addressing the changing dynamics of English(es) in the digital age, this ground-breaking book:

- discusses the spread of English and its current status as a global language;
- demonstrates how key concepts such as language change, speech communities, gender construction and code-switching are affected by digital communications;
- analyzes examples of the interaction of Englishes and social media such as Facebook, Twitter and Urban Dictionary; and
- provides questions for discussion and further reading with each chapter.

Accessible and innovative, this book will be key reading for all students studying sociolinguistics and digital communication or with an interest in language in the globalized multimedia world.

Patricia Friedrich is Associate Professor of Rhetoric and Composition/Linguistics at Arizona State University, USA.

Eduardo H. Diniz de Figueiredo is Assistant Professor of English at Universidade Federal do Paraná, Brazil.

"This is a book we have badly needed. *The Sociolinguistics of Digital Englishes* is about language, culture, society, world Englishes, digital media, and the modern global world. It is an excellent introduction to each area and to their integration. But is also full of deep insights and path-breaking ideas. It is rare that anything this usable as a textbook is this smart."

James Paul Gee, *Arizona State University, USA*

"This well-researched, pioneering book will help build sociolinguistic knowledge about the Internet rights/responsibilities of users of English."

Francisco Gomes de Matos, *Universidade Federal de Pernambuco and ABA Global Education, Recife, Brazil*

The Sociolinguistics of Digital Englishes

Patricia Friedrich and
Eduardo H. Diniz de Figueiredo

Routledge
Taylor & Francis Group

LONDON AND NEW YORK

First published 2016
by Routledge
2 Park Square, Milton Park, Abingdon, Oxon OX14 4RN

and by Routledge
711 Third Avenue, New York, NY 10017

*Routledge is an imprint of the Taylor & Francis Group,
an informa business*

British Library Cataloguing in Publication Data
A catalogue record for this book is available from the British Library

Library of Congress Cataloging-in-Publication Data
Friedrich, Patricia, author.
   The sociolinguistics of digital Englishes / Patricia Friedrich and
Eduardo H. Diniz de Figueiredo.
      pages cm
   Includes bibliographical references and index.
   1. English language—Data processing—Social aspects. 2. Digital
media—Social aspects. 3. Internet. 4. Sociolinguistics. I. Figueiredo,
Eduardo H. Diniz de, author. II. Title.
   PE1074.5.F75 2016
   420'.285—dc23
   2015032716

ISBN: 978-1-138-02580-6 (hbk)
ISBN: 978-1-138-02579-0 (pbk)
ISBN: 978-1-315-68118-4 (ebk)

Typeset in Goudy
by Apex CoVantage, LLC
Printed in Great Britain by Ashford Colour Press Ltd,
Gosport, Hants

For Carolina, Tomas, and Clara

For Aline, Eveline, Eduardo, Fabricio, Flavio, Vinicius, Ana Clara, and the little ones whom we hope are yet to come

Contents

Preface

In teaching and studying sociolinguistics, we have come to rely on a number of very good books and resources that help language enthusiasts and linguistics students understand the dynamics of languages, of varieties, and in our case especially, of English in our communities and the world at large. However, in utilizing such resources, we, the authors, have come to realize that not many references and teaching resources include the new modes and media of communication represented by digital communication and especially by Internet use. This led us to think up this book, for which the basic premise is that digital media serve as wonderful, rich examples for the teaching of sociolinguistic concepts – because, while the scope and reach of digital media are greater, the dynamics are the same as those that languages have experienced all through history. Linguistic innovation, language change, power and prejudice, attitudes toward language, and the formation of speech communities can all be described and discussed vis-à-vis digital communications the same way that they can be described in relation to other forms of interaction. What is more, these new modes and genres are already a significant part of our lives and thus cannot go unacknowledged.

Still, an important part of our goal is to teach sociolinguistics: the interdisciplinary aspect of linguistics that combines formal knowledge of linguistic features and an understanding of social and anthropological phenomena that influence and are influenced by languages themselves. In that sense, these pages are filled with discussions about culture, community, human institutions, values, beliefs, and rituals. We cannot understand languages in context, or in our case English, without making these connections.

Each chapter then focuses on a few related aspects of the dynamics of English(es) in this digital age. We have aimed for a conversation that is academically rigorous but informally written. We use "English" and "Englishes" interchangeably in recognition of the multiplicity and diversity of this language that has come to be used far and wide in the world and also in the Internet universe. The reader will notice our frequent references to world Englishes knowledge and scholarship; we believe that once a person has engaged with a world Englishes approach, it is hard to ignore the contribution it brings to the understanding of how the language(s) operates in society, especially when the focus is on the

English language as a tool for wider communication. Our frequent referencing of world Englishes scholarship and theory is deliberate and, we hope, useful. On the other hand, we refrain from too much explanation of Internet media itself, focusing instead on the dynamics of language there because we believe the reader is likely very knowledgeable of social media, email, chats, texting, and other digital technology. What we can add is an understanding of linguistic processes that go on when people communicate through those media and how they mirror or add to what happens in the so-called real world. One of the important additions is that for the first time in history, written and oral modes of communication don't necessarily stand in opposition (or in complementary form) to each other in terms of conventions, dynamics, and practices, and such a new development needs to be studied in all of its sociolinguistic richness.

At the same time, we have witnessed the spread of English on a global scale, and the language has become the most widespread international code of communication in a way that has never been witnessed before (Crystal, 2003; Mufwene, 2010).

So in this book we will, in an easy-to-read narrative style, bring together a description and analysis of the sociolinguistics of English(es) on the Web, focusing on the germane topics of sociolinguistics in the context of world Englishes and the digital age. We will pursue sociolinguistically crucial concepts such as speech community, code-switching/mixing, heteroglossia, dialectal variation, language choice, multilingualism, domains of use, language shift, mother tongue, intelligibility, imperialism, linguistic ecology, language purism, displacement, register, identity, socialization, language ideology, pragmatics, standardization, and style in the context of world Englishes (Kachru, 1992) and Internet communications. While other languages may appear in the book, they appear *in relation* to English. Therefore, we are able to address elements such as minority languages, pidgins and creoles, and lingua franca vis-à-vis expanding global (and virtual) communications and Englishes.

The book first incorporates descriptions of key concepts, departing from a traditional (and more theoretical) standpoint, to then explore how each one of them has been transformed by the current era of globalization, particularly in regards to the spread of English and its current status as a global language, and the expansion of digital media. Thus, we move from the linguistically general (languages) to the more specific (Englishes), and from the more theoretical (concepts) to the more applied (language as it is realized in digital domains). We believe this will allow our readers to both learn essential elements of sociolinguistics and world Englishes, and to then apply them to the virtual world. While each chapter starts with a summary of the most important points, each ends with discussion questions that can be used for pedagogical purposes in classrooms. The concepts found in bold letters are those we would like our readers to remember. We suggest that the readers refer to the index whenever they want more information on a concept to see where else in the book it is addressed and to whom it is attributed.

The examples of text that you see in the book are, unless otherwise noted, our own creations inspired by the interactions we often find on the Internet. That is, we have done our best to mimic the dynamics of real interactions through our own originally created samples of text. For that reason, we are not claiming that the examples are sweeping generalizations about the shape of all online interaction; they simply illustrate the point at hand every time they appear. While we studied many open and public sites on the Internet to capture their linguistic dynamics, we decided on this strategy to preserve the privacy of those who interact online (even if their texts are freely accessible). Although many researchers have found methodologically sound ways to investigate these new media, we believe we also need more studies and further discussions regarding methodology so that those who interact online can have their discourses protected and treated in the most ethical way possible.

We hope the readers enjoy the discussions in the book and become curious enough about English, language dynamics, and their impact on our lives to look for other sources of knowledge and other conversations.

References

Crystal, D. (2003). *English as a global language*. Cambridge: Cambridge University Press.

Kachru, B. (Ed.) (1992). *The other tongue: English across cultures*. Champaign, IL: University of Illinois Press.

Mufwene, S. S. (2010). Globalization, global English, and world English(es): Myths and facts. In N. Coupland (Ed.), *The handbook of language and globalization* (pp. 31–55). Malden: Wiley-Blackwell.

Acknowledgements

A book is never the work of one person alone, or in this case two. It also takes colleagues, peers, institutions, readers, and families to get an idea turned into a readable text. For that reason, there are a few collaborators we would like to acknowledge and thank. First of all, thanks go to Routledge for helping us shape this project and for believing in this idea. We would also like to thank the School of Humanities, Arts, and Cultural Studies and The New College of Interdisciplinary Arts and Sciences at Arizona State University (ASU), Universidade Federal do Paraná, and the Instituto Federal de Educação, Ciência e Tecnologia de Santa Catarina for the support and understanding we received. Many thanks go to Kameron Taylor for helping us with Internet research, and to several ASU sociolinguistics students, who were willing to hear parts of this text and comment on its contents. We are also indebted to those who were always calling our attention to this or that event, hoping that they could be of sociolinguistic interest (and oftentimes they were). To the colleagues who are world Englishes scholars, we owe a great deal of our understanding of the dynamics of Englishes. Finally, many thanks go to our families for their unwavering support of us and of our writing. We hope our readers, after reading this book, will arrive at a better appreciation of language phenomena as they play out in the world and will use such knowledge to benefit their communities.

Patricia Friedrich, Peoria, Arizona, USA
Eduardo H. Diniz de Figueiredo,
Curitiba, Paraná, Brazil
December, 2015

Acknowledgements

Chapter 1

Introduction

Language, Englishes, and technology in perspective

This chapter will help you understand that:

1 Language use is a social activity, and humans are part of networks and speech communities.
2 Englishes spread through several different waves of influence, including during the industrial revolution, in the post-World War II period, and with the development of the Internet.
3 Linguistic change and technological advancement have often had a close historical connection.
4 The Internet caused us to fuse oral and written modes of communication and thus adopt new norms and strategies for effective interaction.
5 Dialects, both in the real world and the digital world, can be construed to be as large as a nation and as small as a person.
6 The English language has spread so far that it has become both many Englishes and a global language.
7 New communication technologies tend to bring about fears regarding the future of language.
8 Questions about standard language are better addressed if we take into consideration issues of power and attitude; Internet standards are no exception.

Language: A prequel

The details surrounding the origin of human languages are much disputed in linguistic circles. We often joke that the absence of recording devices (and apps!) makes it very hard for us to indicate with any precision the exact moment humans started to engage in oral communication. Several researchers claim humans have used language for at least many thousands of years, while others date language as existing even earlier.

The human capacity to produce language depends on both brain function and, in the case of oral communication, suitability of the **speech apparatus**, that is, the group of organs and structures involved in speech such as the mouth, the tongue, and the larynx with its attached vocal cords. Hence, not only does the brain need to be ready for language, but also the parts of the body involved in speech have to have certain characteristics to be able to produce the complex sounds of **natural languages**. Natural languages stand in contrast to artificial ones: while the former emerge unplanned and unpremeditated given the communicative needs of a population and the natural evolution from ancestor languages, the latter are created "on purpose" for a given end. Such is the case of computer-programming languages used for coding purposes, or Esperanto, a romance-based language created in the 1880s by Ludwig Lazarus Zamenhof and envisioned to become a lingua franca and an element of international understanding.

Were artificial languages to be used in the world within the same parameters of natural languages, they would be subject to the same dynamics of change, competition, and invention. That is, natural and artificial languages alike, once linked to the societies they serve, behave in patterns that can be described by sociolinguistics, that is, the study of language in society, and can be predicted and observed. A big part of the central argument in this book is that we can change the language, the medium, and the users, and yet core language dynamics remain the same regardless, allowing us to make certain predictions about the behavior of language use in context. For example, it is observable that when a group of users of one language moves to an area/country where another language is used, the second generation of users born in the new place tends to be the one to lose the original language by more uniformly adopting the new one (the first generation is often bilingual). Likewise, we can predict that youth language will usually have a transformative power and a central role in language innovation. Finally, sociolinguists can predict that language change will happen to any living language. Only dead languages such as Latin do not change any longer.

As for writing, many of us will have seen pictures of the early drawings found in caves and carved in stone. Evidence of (written) counting dates back to about 9,000 years ago, while the development of writing itself is currently dated around 3500–3000 BC, pending, of course, a momentous discovery of even earlier evidence. We have come to live in a highly literate society (the fears that "standards" are declining notwithstanding), and as we will see in this book, writing has taken over several functions of synchronic communications, which were traditionally more often associated with oral modes.

No matter how we look at it, it is clear that language (the ability for it) and languages (as distinct entities) have been around for a long time; language is also a defining feature of our humanity, the aptitude for verbal communication further inserting us in a community of our peers and giving us an additional ability to be part of a collective, in which we can express our wants, our feelings, our fears, and our aspirations.

Human beings are part of **speech communities**, that is, groups of people who share similar linguistic varieties and use language for specific purposes. In our professions (those we can call **communities of practice**; Lave and Wenger, 1991), social circles, families, and hobbies, we develop certain language skills and features to better communicate with those around us, and we can speculate that fine-tuning our language to serve the society in which we live has been an element of our linguistic life from the early stages of human oral communication.

But to begin this book, we will skip most of such formative years. We will also jump over the development of the ancestors of English, especially Proto-Indo European (PIE), the reconstructed common antecedent of all of the Indo-European languages, likely spoken from around 3700 BC. We will leave out many years of invasions of Britain by Angles, Saxons, Frisians, and Jutes, and subsequent incursions by Normans, too. We will flash by the continual waves of Latin and French influence, the history of contact with Old Norse, even if in modern times we find opportunity to study the results of such instances of **language contact** (for more on the history of English, refer to Gramley, 2012).

We will do all of this jumping ahead because, while the history of language and the advent of Old and Middle English are fascinating and important, we are in this book interested in studying the intersection of language and contemporary technology, and especially what happens when we put the English language and digital media together, especially on the Internet. We are interested in providing a description of digital communication fitted into a sociolinguistics framework and a world Englishes perspective.

As for technology itself, we will also skip over an intriguing history, which includes the first tablets for counting, invented much earlier than our ubiquitous digital tablets, and whose earliest example available dates back to about 300 BC. The tablet anteceded the abacus, which in turn is the early inspiration for our modern computers. These histories, of language and technology, have always had points of intersection, and in this book, we are bringing them together again. After all, what is sociolinguistics if not a systematic study of how language interacts with the most important social aspects of life in a given place and time?

In a way, this work is the result of our asking the following question: given the sociolinguistics of English(es) in the "real world," what happens to this flexible, adaptable, resulting-from-multiple-influences language when we observe its dynamics in the "virtual world"? Our main effort is neither to condemn nor to endorse digital uses of English, but rather, since they are a significant part of our current sociolinguistic reality, to observe, describe, and try to attribute linguistic meaning to them. If, at times, such attribution sounds subjective, it is because it is; we are aware that complete objectivity (especially when it comes to issues in the humanities and social sciences) is not possible (or even desirable). We are human beings observing human behavior, so in a manner of speaking, we are researchers and the researched at the same time. On the other hand, we are critical of a few specific phenomena, such as trolling and flame wars, because they do not contribute to communication and understanding; we do, however, need to understand the sociolinguistic aspects of them to avoid them where possible and educate self and others as needed.

A complete appreciation of this or any broad topic is no easy task. The more we know, the more we realize there is to know. In our time, the sources and the raw material for linguistic investigation are interminable. Since the advent of the Internet, any exhaustive coverage of an issue is in the very least exhausting and more likely impossible. If the subject matter is the Internet itself, we can pretty much assume that every time we look, our object of study will have already changed and multiplied several times. We do not think that invalidates any systematic study: quite the opposite, because technology changes the way we live, and it is important to document such change before things adjust once more! And because we are claiming linguistic dynamics are pretty stable, the knowledge we gain from investigations of the present can help us interpret what happened in the past and envision what can happen in the future.

So our primary goal is not to comprehend the whole of the Internet in relation to English use, but rather to document and look at certain sociolinguistic phenomena that we normally observe in the world around us and see if the dynamics, the processes, and the terms we use elsewhere can be applied to some of the trends we now experience virtually. If we focus on *language dynamics*, what we find does not have to be self-limiting; it will inform us about the mechanisms through which language and societies change beyond the particular environment in question. Do people use English creatively when they communicate online? Absolutely. Does the language change as a result of that? Without a doubt. Does English influence, and is it influenced by, other languages it meets online? Most certainly.

When we observe a linguistic phenomenon, such as the ones we observe on the Web, and report on what we see (i.e., the ways people use language and the way they interact), we are usually within the realm of linguistic **descriptivism**. For instance, if we take inventory of the specific linguistic features of the discourse of a given **speech community** (e.g., gamers, sports enthusiasts, technology majors), we are within the realm of description. A speech community, as Gumperz (1968:381) points out, is "any human aggregate characterized by regular and frequent interaction by means of a shared body of verbal signs and set off from similar aggregates by significant differences in language usage." Descriptivism involves observing and analyzing, without passing too much judgment, the habits and practices within speech communities, focusing on language users and uses without attempting to get them to modify their language according to standards external to the language itself. Descriptive linguistics aims to understand the ways people use language in the world, given all of the forces that influence such use. **Prescriptivism** lies at the other end of this continuum and is usually associated with stipulating rules and norms for language use. When we utter rules such as "Do not end a sentence with a preposition" or "Do not split your infinitives," we are engaging in linguistic prescriptivism; when, on the other hand, we explain that "Out of 10 blog posts analyzed, 9 contained sentence structures

Table 1.1 The difference between descriptivism and prescriptivism

Descriptivism	Prescriptivism
e.g., *Soda, soda pop*, and *pop* are all found in American English and tend to be geographically distributed.	e.g., When referring to a kind of fizzy drink, people should use the word *soda*.
e.g., Some words that are considered "uncountable" in American and British English are often pluralized in Indian English (for instance, *staffs*)	e.g., You should never pluralize uncountable nouns.

ending in prepositions," we are in the realm of descriptivism. See Table 1.1 for additional examples of descriptivism and prescriptivism.

Like every language user, English users fall within different points of this continuum depending on both their personal/professional beliefs about language and on the situation of communication in question. A teacher of academic writing, for example, probably engages with prescriptivism more often and to a greater degree while grading compositions and providing feedback to students than when chatting online (although oftentimes, language teachers report revising and editing their comments before and after posting). If that is the case, the teacher is in a way indicating that she/he has a good level of awareness of **purpose and audience**. That is, the purpose and audience of academic compositions usually require greater standardization than informal chats. Every user of language is already engaged in some level of adaptation to the context of communication, even those people who are not very aware of doing so. That is, we all have a socially acquired knowledge of what linguistic elements work better in different environments, in a way learning by experience, avoiding those choices that were not successful in the past, and investing in those that gave us the results we wanted.

For instance, if we notice the language forms we use for talking to our grandparents, our teachers, our kids, and a close friend, we will realize that they vary in vocabulary, syntax, style, and a number of other linguistic features. A certain degree of trial and error, as well as awareness of purpose and audience, gets us to such differences. Chances are that our utterances were better received when they complied with people's perceptions of what was called for in those situations, and thus we learned to use them the way we do through reinforcement. To an extent, rules of grammar and rules of usage were externally prescribed to us through stimulus and response: use a standard form in a test and you get a high grade; break the rules and the grade will go down. Speak too formally at an informal social gathering, and you can stifle the conversation; use fresh, context-appropriate slang and people will respond positively, smile, and look relaxed. Because sometimes users of languages forget that external standardization markers and internal linguistic rules are different things, we will often in this book remind you that whether we look at languages prescriptively or descriptively, these languages have an internal system and consistency regardless of external prescribed norms; languages are, therefore, **rule-governed**, even when such internal consistency differs from the more educated norm, what we call the **acrolect**. As Brinton (2000:6) puts it, "Language consists of signs occurring not in a random collection, but in a system." Any system will have patterned dynamics and rules even if these differ from one system to another.

For example, the Englishes that present frequent double negatives are as rule-governed as those that do not. From a descriptivist perspective, they are simply a variation from the standard, which in English is associated with single negatives. Were we speaking of a different language, the situation might be reversed. In Brazilian Portuguese, for example, double negatives (*Eu não vi nada*/literally, "I did not see nothing") are found in the standard, while single negatives in some constructions (e.g., *Vi não* instead of *Não vi não*, as a negative answer) are markers of regional variation. Another great example is given by Gramley (2012:251) and refers to the alternative form *ax* (for ask), which is found in some American varieties of English. While the first reaction of some English users is to condemn such use as being "wrong," as Gramley rightly points out, in Old English, the verb could be found in both the forms *ascian*, pronounced /sk/, and *acsian*, pronounced /ks/. Therefore, it is reasonable to assume that in purely linguistic terms, either form could have survived as the "standard." It is issues of attitude toward and prestige of varieties that help determine what variety is currently the default form. However, Englishes behave according to internal rules, even when these rules are not exactly like the ones externally prescribed.

Because awareness of variation and diversity is a crucial aspect of sociolinguistics, we will use "English" and "Englishes," often interchangeably. We cannot conceive of English in the singular anymore, given the **polycentric** nature of this language. Once one is aware of the presence and dynamics of world Englishes, it is impossible to go back to a monocentric view of the language. While American English and British English are important English **varieties** or **dialects**, they are not the only forms of the language available to learners and users. **Indian English**, **emerging Englishes**, and **world Englishes** will all be household terms by the time you finish reading this book, if they are not already.

The Internet is still predominantly English-based. This is a dangerous statement to make, because Chinese could soon replace English in terms of the number of users, and other languages such as Spanish, Portuguese, French, and German are also significantly present. In fact, Portuguese is already the third most-used language of Facebook (as reported in the *Portuguese American Journal* on November 18, 2012[1]), arguably one of the three most popular social media sites of worldwide appeal. So let us qualify that remark. English (still) does what no other language at present can do to the same extent; it works as the most used **lingua franca** of our time, a language of wider communication between speakers who do not share a first language. That is, English serves as a medium of communication not only between people whose native language is English, but also, and very prominently, between people who have other languages for a **mother tongue**. In the latter case, individuals might have only English in common, so they bridge their different original **linguistic**

backgrounds through English. It is therefore a fallacy to imagine that English online (and in the "real" world[2]) is used mostly when at least one of the people in communication is a native speaker of it. Quite the opposite, many interactions in English don't involve native speakers at all. English is also used at all levels of **proficiency**, in instances of **code-mixing** and **code-switching** (when it appears in combination and/or alternation with other languages), and both in **standard** form and very rich **dialectal variations**. Just like in the real world, in the virtual world even the presence of what is one predominant lingua franca does not eliminate linguistic diversity and diversity of expression.

We can imagine then that English is also used among people whose relationship to the language defies traditional labels such as **native, first**, and **second language** use. In an era of increasing global communication and increased fluidity, we should question these old labels anyway. Complex linguistic dynamics are increasingly the case in post-colonial English contexts, in which native users of such varieties as Malay English and Indian English, for example, coexist with users of English at all levels of competence. In these contexts, **multilingualism**, that is, the ability to communicate in multiple languages, is also the norm rather than the exception.

A person in a multilingual society might, for example, speak one language at home, be instructed in a regional language at school, and eventually use another language once they enter the workforce. Certain companies, for example, keep English as a work language so that information, such as meeting minutes, can freely circulate between branches in different countries. Nevertheless, colleagues might go out for coffee with their co-workers and switch back to their native languages.

A complex relationship with English and other languages is also the case among users of English, such as the authors of this book, who are not, traditionally speaking, native users of English, but who for all practical purposes perform professional activities and activities in specific **realms of use** primarily or easily (or even better) in the language. Many users of English at present fall within this category, especially because different people might have different linguistic preferences depending on the realm of use in which they use the languages. In that sense, a person may do Math calculations in one language, pray in another, write professionally in yet another, and code-mix when they speak with friends. So the realm of use, the aspect or area of life and work for which a particular language or language variety is chosen, may one day become a more significant variable in **language choice** than geography (if it is not already in some cases), and the Internet is contributing to this trend. Because of the possibilities brought forth by virtual communications, a person does not have to be at a particular physical space to use a particular language.

English and the industrial revolution

The evolution and change of a language are intimately connected to social phenomena, such as political climate, **attitudes** toward different language varieties and their speakers, existing **language policy**, and economic factors such as what social groups have financial power and how they use that power. The period start-ing in the late eighteenth century, and having its effects felt through the end of the nineteenth century and well into the twentieth, was crucial for the spread of the English language.

During that time, the development of steam power fueled production and industrialization, which in turn became precursors to the technological revolu-tion of the twentieth century – the one that would give us so many electric and electronic devices, and ultimately the computer. This was also a time of popula-tion growth and **urbanization**. Urban centers are known catalysts for the change in linguistic varieties and for **dialect leveling**, that is, the assimilation, mixing, and evening out of dialectal variation (see Gramley, 2012). Concomitantly, the colonial ventures, which had been initiated centuries before, increased, mak-ing the number of English speakers much greater and further spreading English across the globe. This historical station is important for the purposes of this book because eventually colonial Englishes would develop into world Englishes variet-ies, which are currently an important source of linguistic innovation and creativ-ity, the kind of creativity we write about in this book. While views diverge in the matter of the extent of linguistic imposition and language **replacement/displace-ment** in these environments (we will not dispute the reality of imposition here), we believe that the creativity and capacity to adapt English to local needs makes users of English in these former colonial contexts wonderful innovators and lin-guists, and that is the fascinating capacity that we want to emphasize. Note we are using the terms displacement and replacement here to indicate the process by which languages and the linguistic communities that use those languages are sometimes forced out of their original geographies or realms of use – for example, when the original Welsh population was forced out of parts of Britain by invading groups who (also) brought language with them. Displacement is sometimes used with another meaning; it can refer to the ability of human languages to refer to the past or make projections about the future (and other abstractions). For more on this later meaning, see Yule (2010:12).

Through the field of **world Englishes** itself, we have been able to become further acquainted with and study multiple varieties of English in their contexts of use. These varieties are widely documented and represented on the Internet, in their more formal structure (the **acrolect**), the more everyday form (the **mesolect**), and the least-prestigious form (the **basilect**). Because we use digital technologies to communicate at all levels of formality (from professional messages to chats with friends), we can find a continuum of dialectal variation, with each point in such continuum influenced by such variables as education, geography, and knowledge of purpose and audience. Since we can think of the Internet as providing an envi-ronment where geographical borders are much less significant and the boundaries between varieties much more porous, it is not uncommon for varieties to coexist and intertwine in creative ways.

Dialectal variation has always existed. It can be of social, geographic, age, interest, allegiance, and many other natures, individually and combined. Because of that aspect of language, a dialect description can encompass as big a range as a whole country or region (e.g., American English, British English) or restrict itself to a single person in the form of his/her **idiolect** (i.e., the equivalent of a linguistic fingerprint, an individual's own variety resulting from the person's education, interactions, tastes, and identity, which are like no one else's). The more contact exists between people who use different varieties, the more aware we become of these dissimilarities, but also paradoxically, the more we go through the process of **dialect leveling** mentioned previously. Throughout history, access to transportation, migration, as well as urbanization have been powerful catalysts of these processes. So have language attitudes and **language prejudice**, although, as Finegan and Rickford (2004:289) explain in an introduction to contributor Lippi-Green's chapter, of the latter we are "much less conscious and much less concerned." On the other hand, linguistic isolation causes a variety to develop in its own way, possibly removed and through a different path from those of originally related but geographically dispersed dialects.

During the industrial revolution, for example, steam power application meant transportation to further corners, accomplished faster and for a greater number of people. At the same time, the spread of printed media through which language is also disseminated increased exponentially. During that time, more and more people moved to urban centers such as London, bringing their dialects with them, dialects that mixed and influenced one another in the process, what we call **linguistic hybridity** (much like we see dialects influencing one another in the virtual world now).

This dynamic process of access to language had been seen before in the history of English: Alfred the Great (king between 871 and 899), for example, had realized the power of books in spreading language already in the ninth century, and he commissioned the translation of many religious texts. Although he lived in a land surrounded by Old Norse (the language of the invading Danes), Alfred managed to keep English alive by disseminating those translated texts to monasteries near and far. A book at that time was not in the strict sense the same kind of technological token that our e-books and digital readers are, but its reproduction foreshadowed what was to come with the printing press and now with our contemporary technologies. From the relative distance of his kingdom of Wessex, Alfred managed to be a major force in the maintenance and spread of English throughout England (Gramley, 2012). The scale was, to be sure, much different from what we see today; however, the dynamics and the rationale were similar: document it, send it away, engage in communication through it, and see language thrive and spread.

The power of the written word and new technological developments had already been key to the propagation of English following the invention of the printing press in the late 1400s. That one piece of technology was crucial in the dissemination of texts. Before it, documents were handwritten and then copied by scribes who were hard to find and mostly dedicated to working with religious texts, given their religious affiliations. The process was slow and did not yield many copies. Literacy was low, and books were scarce. Oftentimes, monasteries and other institutions, which now and again carried single existing copies of books, were pillaged and burned. Knowledge and language documented in these texts was lost forever. But after the printing press, many copies could be produced fast. Literacy improved dramatically, and texts of a non-religious nature became more common and accessible too. Documentation and survival of samples became more likely. Standardization increased.

So the relationship between language spread and technological advances has been a close one in various moments in history, and the relationship between English, this flexible, adaptable language, and technology can teach us much about the dynamics of language change. Perhaps not all linguistic turning points have been as extreme as the moment in which we currently live, but they were all very significant and fascinating indeed.

English and late modernity

After World War II (1939–1945), the United States experienced an economic and technological boom. When a country's power increases, its language(s), especially that/those with official or default official status, also experience(s) a boost. The English language came to inhabit further educational and popular realms, especially in the Western world, and in some instances gradually replaced French as an international language of communication (for more on the alternation between lingua francas, see Crystal, 2003).

Concomitantly with the growing presence of English in international realms of communication, and while the war raged on, John Atanasoff and Clifford Berry, a professor and his graduate student, were developing the first digital computer at Iowa State University (1939–1942). The code-breaking work of Alan Turing in Britain was also taking us in that direction. Their invention, once dismissed only to be later picked up again, would change the way the world calculates, processes information, and communicates. It would completely change the way we live, and it would take languages like English along for the ride, ultimately helping change them too.

English and post-modernity

While post-modernity can mean different things to different people, in this book it refers both to the period starting after the 1970s and to a way of viewing the world, language, and symbolic meaning as fragmented, unstable, ideologically driven, opinion-based, and subjective.

The modern world had been one of concreteness, positivism, and belief in encompassing truths and in production. After World War I and World War II, the world started to change: it became more fragmented, and people started to resist master narratives, which have gradually been replaced by individual stories, by the kind of understanding that is woven together through pieces of memory and experience. It is no wonder that memoirs, for example, have become a particularly thriving literary subgenre in a world somewhat defined by individualism and attention to self (see Friedrich, 2015).

We find many examples of this compartmentalization of the world and our perception of it in the computer: the individual narrative of the blogs, the opinion-driven posts of social media users and commentators on news sites, and the democratization of "knowledge" in online encyclopedias and wikis. The Internet user is carefully self-constructed from pieces of his/her identity, and building such identity is part of the Internet's appeal. And what we experience are snippets of reality: a status update, a photo, a segment of a speech or a clip of a streamed TV program, at times altogether or in quick sequence. The world after the computer is paradoxically a smaller one and a more fragmented, never-ending space. While we can communicate instantaneously across geographical and linguistic boundaries, we have become increasingly aware that what we access, know, or use in terms of information is a minor part of an inaccessible whole. Just as it is the case with language that no one can know "the whole language," in the virtual universe no one can know "the whole story."

When children in the 1970s and 1980s conducted library research for a school project, for example, they were restricted to the contents of their bookshelves and the encyclopedia section of their libraries. The notion might have been an illusion then too, but there was silent acknowledgement of the difficulty in accessing knowledge beyond what could be found through books and other media immediately around oneself. Even if students were aware of other resources of immediate relevance, getting them was often too difficult and time-consuming. For practical purposes, what was immediately available to people, what was printed in a book or written in the newspaper, had to be instrumentally taken as "the truth."

As our interactions have become more and more computer-mediated and our access to knowledge theoretically unlimited, we have further realized the partial, subjective, and ever-changing nature of what we know. To try and exhaust the possibilities of research or our information-seeking behavior could mean working forever on the same project, so we subjectively choose when to consider something finished. We have also felt freer to break linguistic rules and to be inventive, after almost 400 years of advancing the idea of a **written standard** for language (i.e., since the invention of the printing press, the push has always been to standardize). By doing so, we are causing the pendulum of prescriptivism to swing in the opposite direction. We abbreviate, use acronyms (though these are not an Internet or new invention), and use "wrong" spellings on purpose – and in the process, we cause English, as well as other languages, to morph. Variation in the present results in linguistic change in the long run.

English and technology

Given the above, we venture to say that the pendulum of standardization, which has swung in the direction of attempted **uniformization** and **stratification** for hundreds of years since the invention of the printing press, is now moving in the opposite direction, with many people now engaged in "creative spelling" and individualized language use, an invention fueled by the merging of oral and written language modes that virtual communications allow. Prescriptivism is still in existence, of course. But the greater variety of language manifestations online, taken by some people to signal the lowering of expectations and a decrease in literacy and in language standards, might actually be an indication of a phenomenon of a different nature. After all, the more you know the rules, the more you can break them meaningfully (for more on texting and breaking rules, see Crystal, 2009). So when an Internet user writes "S33 U" instead of "See you," it is pretty clear that they are not confused, but rather attempting to imprint their own contribution to linguistic expression, even if it is in a simple sentence (writing "your welcome" instead of "you're welcome" is a different story; more about this distinction will be discussed later).[3]

Perhaps it is the democratization of language online that scares so many people into believing languages are disintegrating. Anyone is welcome to write a blog and attempt to get readers, to write a novel and self-publish it in e-book format, or share opinions through social media. While celebrated by those who find, sometimes for the first time, an entryway to producing their own texts, this lack of "gate keeping" can be unnerving to others, while to others still it can signal a complete breakdown of linguistic standards. We remind the reader, however, that fears over the deterioration of English have been documented since Shakespearean times, and yet we are still here and able to communicate in English(es).

David Crystal (2001:2) comments on the effect the printing press had on society and the fears that such a piece of new technology brought with it at the time of the former's invention (around 1450).[4] He also mentions that each new technological communication tool after that brought with it renewed anxieties about its place in the world. Taking as the departing point the era of the printing press, Crystal also writes that

> Around 400 years later, similar concerns about censorship and control were widespread when society began to cope with the political consequences of the arrival of the telegraph, the telephone, and broadcasting technology.
> (Crystal, 2001:2)

It is no surprise, therefore, that the changes that language and society continue to go through because of the Internet would bring debates and apprehension too. However, it is possible, we believe, to consider a more optimistic view of literacy online. Within a system where anyone can "write and publish" (and people actually do), where reading materials are widely available in many languages and represent different varieties, we can estimate that literacy is actually continuously going up rather than down.

Let's entertain this hypothesis for a minute: to become better writers, we all need to write often, to practice (the same goes for reading). "Non-mainstream" writing opportunities (from blogs to fan fiction) abound on the Internet and provide any novice, amateur, or more advanced writer a chance (and a motivation) to practice and to receive feedback from peers. If we measure the success of these genres by the same standards that we apply to professional, peer-reviewed and edited formal modes, we are likely to arrive at a gloomy view of literacy. However, if we look at these expressions as being multiplied and updated versions of student compositions, learning tasks, and literacy exercises, we might be willing to consider that more people are applying writing, for longer periods of time, to perform more varied tasks. To us, that means increased literacy and possibly greater **communicative competence** (see page 137; the ability to apply adequate linguistic forms, strategies, and sociolinguistic and grammar knowledge to different situations of communication) rather than linguistic decay.

This is not to say that English has not changed or that these writing "experiments" will not modify language in ways that prescriptivists might disapprove or that even the average language user will not find daunting at first. But the truth is that over time, all languages get transformed. They change because the societies they serve change too. A short, cursory trip from Old English, through Middle English, to Modern English will illustrate just how much this language has indeed changed (and what sounds "educated" to us; for example, Shakespearean English might have been taken quite differently synchronically, at the time of The Bard).

Incidentally, can we even begin to comprehend the changes that society has gone through in the last 1500 years? If we consider the range of social change over time, linguistic change will immediately sound less intimidating and more in tandem with the changes in other spheres of life. Whereas the balance between the forces of stabilization and the forces of change are healthy and necessary (i.e., in the short run, we do want to continue to be able to understand one another!), in the end, change – at certain periods quicker, at others slower – always wins. Watch movies from the 1950s and notice how much language has changed even in this historically short period of time, and you will understand what we mean.

World Englishes and technology

When a language expands at the velocity and to the extent that English has, it will develop local norms for local uses, a phenomenon that further evidences the connection between language change and social needs as discussed earlier. Would you say "My cousin always *jealoused* her sister?" If you live in Nigeria, you might. How about "So smart *lah* you?" If you speak English in Malaysia, you likely do. And what of using the word "equipment" as "equipments" in its plural form? In India, many people say and write it, as well as the very useful "prepone," the opposite of *postpone*, as in "modifying the time of a meeting to an earlier date."

World Englishes are a result of this constant process of adaptation to local circumstances and the ascertaining of values, beliefs, and identity of the people who use them. Even when languages are first introduced through a top-down process, as was the case with colonization, once they **nativize**, they transform themselves and interact with the existing local languages to perform all of the functional and symbolic roles that languages perform. Within the process of **nativization**, functional roles are usually those more associated with practical and immediate communicative needs (e.g., buy bread at the market or communicate with a business partner), whereas symbolic ones have more to do with what a language signals about you to others (e.g., to have a tee shirt written in English might symbolize being "cool"). **Nativized varieties** or **indigenous varieties** (Kachru, 1983) themselves can be symbols of resistance, of solidarity, of friendship, and of local identity (symbolic) at the same time that they help people of different backgrounds interact in trade, education, and other public domains (functional).

Before digital communications, it was harder for those of us who did not travel widely to experience some of these local varieties and to interact with speakers of such varieties: to a great extent, they were used for intranational communication, and as such, stayed primarily within local realms of use. Now, access to such varieties is much easier, and users of these dialects are also able to broadcast their creative expressions, from movies to novels and newspaper articles, to a much larger audience, causing readers and listeners to potentially incorporate features of these varieties into their own **linguistic repertoire** (Gumperz, 1968). But this happened to "big varieties" too, of English and of other languages. In the 1990s, for example, Brazilian Portuguese arrived in Portugal on a large scale through very popular soap operas, the broadcasting of which was made possible by the wide availability of TV programs via satellite dishes. At that point in time, Brazilian Portuguese – a nativized variety that arrived on the American continent through colonization and proceeded to change, given its linguistic contact with native and later African languages – started to significantly influence vernacular European Portuguese. Through movies, American English performs a similar influential role on other Englishes around the world.

Traditionally in world Englishes, varieties have been described as belonging to the Inner Circle, Outer Circle, and Expanding Circle (Kachru, 1983 and after). The **Inner Circle** of English encompasses countries where English is acquired as a native language and holds status of official or default official language. Inner Circle countries include, for example, England, the United States, Canada, and Australia. **Outer Circle** countries are mostly those where English was primarily introduced through colonization, where it coexists with other languages, and where it holds official status (many times alongside other languages). In Outer Circle countries, English (also) fulfills intranational purposes, that is, people use English within the country to communicate across linguistic lines. Examples of such countries include India, Malaysia, and Nigeria.

Finally, the **Expanding Circle** of English encompasses the rest of the world, all countries to which English continues to expand to different degrees, and for which it performs different functions. In Expanding Circle countries, English is primarily used for communications with users abroad and for functions that involve the international community, for example, international business and study, diplomacy, media, and commerce. Brazil, Mexico, and China are all countries of the Expanding Circle.

The Concentric Circles were originally conceived to explain the historical direction and shape of the spread of English, and they continue to be of significance to us for that very reason, even if the Internet has come to smudge and complicate any geographical notion of linguistic lines. However, what we can still see, despite the Internet and the seemingly ubiquitous presence of the computer, are the effects of the politics of access on English and on communication.

The politics of digital communications

At this writing, according to the Central Intelligence Agency (CIA) World Factbook,[5] the largest number of Internet users at the latest estimation is in China (389,000,000 users), followed by the United States, Japan, Brazil, and Germany (all between 245,000,000 and 65,125,000 users). Compare those to the numbers of users in Somalia (106,000), the 159th country in number of users, and we can see how uneven access to the Internet still is. Of course we are dealing with raw numbers for highly (numerically) unequal populations, but that only strengthens the argument of uneven access. Japan, for example, boasts access by over 80% of its population, while in Somalia less than 7% of the population have access to the Internet (roughly one in every 16 people). It is known that unequal access to the Internet has economic repercussions. For example, unequal access both correlates with and exacerbates economic underdevelopment. As Mark Warschauer (2008:141) argues:

> There is no doubt that unequal access to computers and the Internet is, to a large extent, an effect of poverty. It is not surprising that only 0.6% of the population of Malawi uses the Internet when the average annual income level in the country is barely the cost of a personal computer (Internet World Stats 2006). However, lack of access to ICTs is also believed to be a causal factor in impoverishment.

So when we speak of the democratization of the world because of the Internet, we are actually speaking of the democratization of the world for the portion of the population that indeed has access to the Internet. We can make an analogy here with English use in the Expanding Circle: while in general terms English can be said to be present, used, and available throughout the globe, proficiency and access are extremely uneven, especially in the Expanding Circle, and opportunities to learn and benefit from such learning will be distributed irregularly too. The process is somewhat self-perpetuating: less access to technology means fewer communicative and educational opportunities, which in turn results in fewer resources necessary for access to technology.

The politics of English in the Internet era

Being that a large portion of online communications, online texts, and online activity is mediated through English, it seems reasonable to say that those who do not have access to English will miss out on information and opportunities.

Scientific production, for example, is primarily written in English, the language considered the default lingua franca of science. Even the more conservative estimators calculate that most scientific articles (in the natural sciences, for example) are written in English (see Ammon, 2001). This, of course, has implications not only for access to the information contained in scientific texts but also for the production of such texts (i.e., non-English users will find it hard to make their research available internationally) and the establishment of international reputations. The fear often expressed by those who oppose such hegemony of English relates to perceived dangers of cultural homogenization, linguistic **replacement**, and **displacement**. Given the close relationship between cultural expression and language, these views should be carefully and seriously considered in any discussion of the politics of language.

From computing to communicating

If we could single out one quote that inspired us to write this book, we would choose the words of Steve Jobs in his 1995 "lost interview":

> It's really sort of the realization of our original dream, that the computer would not be a machine for computation, but would be metamorphosed into a tool for communication. And with the Web, that's finally happening. I think the Web is going to be profound in what it does to our society. The Web is going to be the defining technology, the defining social moment for computing.
>
> (Sen, Segaller, and Gau, 2012)

We agree that, for better or worse, the Internet has indeed been a defining technology in human interaction, and language often interacts with such tools, both modifying and being modified by them (notice our early examples of the printing press, the telegraph, the telephone, and the television). When future historians describe eras of the past, they will likely demarcate an era that ends with the advent of the Internet and one that starts with it, the same way we do for Western history and the printing press.

A quick look at the naming of new technology-related items, a small area compared to the actual reach of language innovation brought about by technology, will show just how much this process is true. Not only have new terms been created for that which was previously nonexistent (e.g., blog, computer mouse, modem), but also such words often break from the confines of a single language to influence other languages, mirroring what happens in non-Internet realms of use. Take the example of the creation of **neologisms** (i.e., newly created words or expressions) in English for computer-associated terms and their usage in other languages. The invention of the computer, as described earlier, is closely associated with English-speaking environments, so it is not surprising that English contributes terms in this domain of use. Note the examples in Table 1.2 and observe that

Table 1.2 Neologisms and loanwords for computer technology terms in several languages

Mouse	In Portuguese, *mouse*, pronounced /mauzi/ but spelled the same, "computer mouse"
Wireless/wifi	Wifi widely used throughout Latin America to refer to wireless communications
To click	In some varieties of Spanish, *cliquear*, "to click" (as on a link) or *hacer clic*, with the same meaning In Russian, кликнуть *kliknut*, "to click" In Italian, *cliccare*, "to click"
Flash drive	In Russian, Флешка *fleshka*, "flash drive"
Blogger	In Portuguese, *blogueiro*, "blogger"
To login	In Portuguese, *fazer o login*, "to do the login" (as a noun)
To google[1]	Used as a verb, in Japanese, *guguru*, "to search online" Used as a verb, in Croatian, *proguglati*, "to search online" In Russian, рогуглить *proguglit*, "to search online"
To format	In Swedish, *formatera*, "to format" In Italian, *formattare*, "to format"
To download	In Bahasa Indonesia, *men-download*, as an informal version of *mengunduh*, "to download" In Croatian, *daulodati/downlodati*, "to download"
To upload	In Bahasa Indonesia, *meng-upload*, as an informal version of *mengunggah*, "to upload"

[1] Used as a verb, "to google" has been in the *Oxford English Dictionary* since 2006.

oftentimes these **loanwords** (i.e., words borrowed from another language) adapt to the phonology and grammar rules of the receiving language.

If we look closely, we will realize that some of these terms are **neologisms**, even in English, or are words that have had their meanings stretched, have specialized, or have been reapplied to new situations of communication. *Mouse* is one such example, as are *to format* and *to google*. Because of the structure of English, changing the grammatical category of a word (e.g., from noun to verb) is quite simple and oftentimes does not require any change in the form of the word (simply a tweak in usage and collocation in a sentence).

When words are transported into other languages, however, the process will sometimes require the nativization of the English term through the necessary prefixes and suffixes, or other mechanisms, of that language. An example of this phenomenon of **affixation** is *deletar* in Portuguese (all infinitive verbs end in vowel + r), in which the internal rules of the language are applied upon the entrance of the new lexical item into the language. Another example, in Bahasa Indonesia, is *meng-upload*, in which the prefix me- (in its different realizations depending on the sound that follows) is added to make the borrowing into a transitive verb (to upload "something"). At other times, the reverse process will occur: in *dar um reset*, for example (literally, "to give a reset," also in Portuguese), what is originally a verb in English, to reset, is used as a noun. So while languages of wider communication oftentimes contribute lexical items to other languages, the "receiving" language usually adapts the borrowing to fit its communicative needs and its grammar. Language change is the only constant.

And so, as we hope this chapter has shown, while change is normal and certain, people can become a little worried when change happens, especially when change happens fast and might mean learning new or relearning old skills. To quote Crystal (2001:62) once more,

> They [people] are realizing that their established knowledge, which has enabled them to survive and succeed in spoken and written linguistic encounters hitherto, is no longer enough to guarantee survival and success on the Internet.

It has been well over a decade since Crystal made this assertion, and yet it holds true still today: each new form of Internet communication – each new meme, emoticon, and 140-character tweet – tests our linguistic and symbolic boundaries and abilities. The predictions we can make about what is to come involve the following: it will contain further innovation, it will delight some and unnerve others, and language (as an entity), despite the worst-case-scenario fears, will survive.

Questions for discussion

1   What situations of communication online do you think are likely better performed by a more formal and a more informal style of language?
2   Give examples of the same linguistic phenomenon treated more prescriptively and more descriptively. For example, what would prescriptivists and descriptivists potentially say about *RSVP'ing*, *BRB*, and *logging in*?
3   Do you think people are more, less, or equally literate in the Internet age? What arguments and evidence would the defenders of each of these views likely use?
4   What Internet literacy practices do you take part in? How have they helped or hindered your overall literacy?
5   How might access to the Internet impact English use and proficiency? How might knowledge of English impact access to information?
6   How do Internet phenomena evidence the potential for languages to be ever changing?
7   Can you list some terms that are a direct result of the development of the Internet? Do you know of any borrowings in additional languages you might use?
8   In a few words, describe your view of language change in light of virtual communications.

Notes

1 See http://portuguese-american-journal.com/report-portuguese-is-the-third-most-used-language-on-facebook-socialbakers/.
2 We will be comparing and contrasting everyday reality and virtual expression often. At times we will refer to their environments as "real world" and "virtual world." We would like these to be read simply as shortcuts: in no way do we mean to say that virtual reality is not real.
3 In this book, we also challenge some prescriptive rules by, for example, starting sentences with conjunctions since that gives them a more informal, conversational quality. When to break such grammar rules can be a good point for discussion in the classroom.
4 In the east, in Korea and China, precursors of the printing press were invented centuries before the printing press was invented in the west.
5 See https://www.cia.gov/library/publications/the-world-factbook/.

References and suggested further reading

Ammon, U. (2001). Editor's preface. In U. Ammon (Ed.), *The dominance of English as a language of science* (pp. v–x). Berlin & New York: Mouton de Gruyter.
Brinton, L. J. (2000). *The structure of modern English: A linguistic introduction, Volume 1.* Philadelphia, PA: John Benjamins Publishing.
Crystal, D. (2001). *Language and the Internet.* Port Chester, NY: Cambridge University Press.
Crystal, D. (2003). *English as a global language.* Port Chester, NY: Cambridge University Press.
Crystal, D. (2009). *Txtng: The Gr8 Db8.* Oxford: Oxford University Press.
Finegan, E., & Rickford, J. R. (2004). *Language in the USA: Themes for the twentieth century.* New York: Cambridge University Press.
Friedrich, P. (2015). *The literary and linguistic construction of obsessive-compulsive disorder: No ordinary doubt.* London: Palgrave MacMillan.
Graddol, D. (2006). *English next.* Plymouth, UK: The English Company and Latimer Trend & Company Ltd.
Gramley, S. (2012). *The history of English: An introduction.* New York: Routledge.
Gumperz, J. J. (1968). The speech community. In D. L. Sills (Ed.), *International encyclopedia of the social sciences* (pp. 381–386). New York: Macmillan.
Kachru, B. B. (1983). *The Indianization of English: The English language in India.* Oxford: Oxford University Press.
Lave, J., & Wenger, E. (1991). *Situated learning: Legitimate peripheral participation.* Cambridge: Cambridge University Press.
Sen, P., Segaller, S., & Gau, J. (Producers), & Sen, P. (Director) (2012). *The lost interview* [Documentary film]. United States: Furnace, Public Broadcasting Service, Oregon Public Broadcasting, and John Gau Productions.
Warschauer, M. (2008). Whither the digital divide? In D. L. Kleinman, K. A. Cloud-Hansen, C. Matta, and J. Handesman (Eds.), *Controversies in science & technology: From chromosomes to the cosmos* (pp. 140–151). New Rochelle, NY: Liebert.
Yule, G. (2010). *The study of language.* New York: Cambridge University Press.

Chapter 2

Language, society, and changing networks

This chapter will help you understand that:

1 The concepts of language, society, and culture are closely interrelated.
2 With the Internet, we are redefining our social and linguistic networks, and finding greater possibilities of cross-cultural communication.
3 The Internet has changed the way we communicate in English as well as in other languages, through processes such as the emergence of new genres, the shifting dynamics of the written/spoken language dichotomy, and the coining of new terms.
4 In the case of English more specifically, there are several particularities that need to be taken into consideration, given its major lingua franca role.
5 The Internet has raised the possibility of individuals to have more power, as it has enabled them to have easier contact with others worldwide, share their stories with a large number of people, organize themselves into groups, and modify things in the world.
6 Languages change historically and vary in our own time period.
7 Digital communication has challenged pre-conceived notions of language, especially in terms of the common associations between writing and standard language, and language and nation.
8 Languages are not the exclusive property of native speakers, but are rather owned by all of those who use it for their own purposes, and the Web has brought new considerations in this regard.

In chapter 1, we saw that **language** needs to be understood not only in relation to its cognitive complexity – i.e., in regard to the knowledge of sounds, words, structures, meanings, and so forth, and their mental processing by individuals (Fromkin, Rodman, and Hyams, 2013) – but also as a social entity, one that is used for interactions among people in diverse groups. Language can be influenced by attitudes, technologies, political forces, and economic factors, to name a few. Language is used for social purposes, with functions such as communicating ideas, bonding with others, expressing feelings, and giving information. Moreover, as explained by discourse analyst James Gee (2011), language allows us not only to say things, but also to be a specific type of person and to do things in the world, like building relationships and establishing boundaries between people, nations, and places. Languages do all that while carrying a hefty dose of symbolic meaning (more details about these identity-related issues will be presented in chapter 5).

The aim of sociolinguistics, therefore, is to a great degree to study the relationship between language and society, as well as language and culture, since the concepts of *culture* and *society* are closely related. By **society,** we generally mean one of two things: a) an overall, indeterminate group representing people in general (as in *"Drugs represent a danger to society"*) or b) a more specific group of people who are bonded by something they have in common – be it a territory (*"The European society"*), a common interest (*"The society of bird watchers"*), or an affiliation to a particular institution (*"The Chinese Music Society of North America"*). In both cases, especially in the second one (which is also the one more commonly used in sociolinguistics as a whole, since it is more closely defined and less broad), the group of people in question is generally believed to share a **culture** – which we define as a system of symbols (visual, auditory, behavioral, and so on) that is constructed and transmitted socially (for more on culture, see chapter 8). When understood as such, the notion of culture encompasses both simple and complex aspects of a society, ranging from the common perception that cultures are represented by food, flags, arts, fashion, and festivals, to the more sophisticated notion that they also involve concepts of time, worth, feelings, and categorizations of people, places, objects, animals, etc. Moreover, language often cannot be dissociated from culture, as it is a symbolic system itself (with particular meanings and representations), and a way through which other systems are both encoded and transmitted (see Risager, 2006, for moments when the two concepts can be separated). That is, language is both an element of culture and a vehicle for its manifestation.

In chapter 1, we also saw how English has become a global language of communication – having repeatedly been used to perform the function of a major worldwide **lingua franca** (i.e., a language of communication among speakers of different languages), and how such development has always been closely related to technological advancements that have taken place throughout history. In particular, we saw that the development of digital media and its global spread throughout the past few decades have led English to an even further expansion, since it has been the language that has accompanied most of these changes. Moreover, we looked into the political issues that this expansion entails, in terms of both the development of digital communications and the spread of the English language itself.

These understandings of language, society, culture, and English as a lingua franca are crucial for the comprehension of how the Internet has influenced communication as a whole, and communication in English more specifically. In the present chapter, we will seek to explain such changes, paying special attention to the development of interactions in the context of cyberspace and cyberculture. Thus, we begin this discussion by presenting aspects of social and linguistic networks in the Internet era, as well as the new dynamics and genres that have emerged with the Web. We will then look at linguistic choice, and language change and innovation in the context of virtual communication. We will later raise and address some of the new questions about politics, ideology, and democracy that the online universe also brings us. Finally, we will focus on how English, or Englishes, not only expand geographically but also digitally in a way that we had not witnessed previously with any other language. Digital communications have allowed communities of language users dispersed geographically to connect in ways never possible before, and this possibility has opened the door to many questions relating to language.

How the Internet has changed the way we communicate

When we think about communication in the era of the Internet and digital technology, we need to take many elements into consideration. One of them is that the Web has changed *the frequency* and *the form* of what we communicate. For instance, it is now common for many people to use social media to let others know, in more or less detail, their accomplishments; tastes in movies, music, sports, and so forth; opinions about many different subjects (ranging from a sitcom on TV to political issues); and to publicly share their lives in ways that were not done before. Many times people create an online image that lets others know how they want to be perceived.

We have also changed *when* we communicate. Online news portals and social media statuses are often updated at a much faster speed than that of written newspapers, meaning that on-time knowledge about ourselves, others, and what is taking place in the world is now not only possible, but for many of us, it is expected. Of course, speed can at times cause inaccuracies too, as when a rumor rather than a solid piece of news is reported, only to be withdrawn later, or when language inaccuracies that would otherwise be caught by editors and proofreaders end up on websites and news reports.

Changing networks

Equally important is the fact that *with whom* we communicate is often changing. The concept of **social network**, a term that was introduced into sociolinguistics mainly by scholars James Milroy and Lesley Milroy (1985), refers to the web of relationships a person has and/or establishes with others through social ties such as friendship, affinity, and so on. It also speaks of the level of involvement this person develops with different communities. Some of a person's bonds, for instance, may be close-knit, such as generally happens among family members, while others may be more loose-knit, as in the case of acquaintances. Before the development of such a concept in sociolinguistics, many studies grouped individuals based on categories such as social class, following the potentially misleading assumption that all members of a particular class (or other group) were homogeneous in terms of linguistic choices and overall language use. Likewise, while geography influences one's idiolect, the more an individual moves from one location to the next, the more that individual's linguistic variety becomes a hybrid rather than an expression of the place where they were born and the place where they first acquired language. In other words, while sociolinguistic studies still rely on ideas of class, geography, and age, for example, to explain social phenomena, those elements are taken in relative rather than absolute terms. The notion of social network, on the other hand, emphasizes that these choices are not necessarily based on one's class, but rather on the bonds one establishes with different people from different classes, genders, ethnicities, and the **linguistic network** that one develops from such ties.

Nonetheless, the conception of social network may still be limited (Romaine, 2000) given that its effectiveness and precision in explaining how speech patterns are created and developed depend on how well the idea can be fitted into a more general theory of social behavior and human action. For example, conflicts may exist between an individual's different types of networks (e.g., one's family values vs. the values of one's school/work community), and some networks can be more powerful than others in terms of imposing their norms upon language users. Still, the understanding of social and linguistic networks, and their use in sociolinguistic research, has brought more complexity to the understanding of language use and helped to explain linguistic choices more precisely. Networks can also be thought of as being elastic and of different sizes depending on the number of participants who share linguistic, cultural, and social beliefs and practices.

In the Internet era, the concept of social network has gained much force due to at least a few factors. For one, the term "social network" itself has been used widely to describe different websites where users connect to one another in webs of relationships, being able to share their thoughts, images, profiles, and so on with all their contacts, as well as with those to whom their contacts are connected. Note that such connections may actually exist only virtually, as many members of Internet social networks will never get to know each other in "real life." In addition, the Internet has given us a chance to visually construct our networks. The tools now available allow for the grouping of those we know according to interest, level of acquaintance, profession, and language, all of which are elements that abstractly helped us define our networks before but that might have been invisible to us.

In linguistic terms, such webs of connectivity have brought several significant implications. Many individuals are (or seem to be) now connected (even if just virtually) with a much larger number of people than ever before, which means that their social and linguistic networks are much vaster than those of people from past eras. When people play multiplayer online games, post videos and/or comments on social media, or talk to others in chat rooms, they have the chance to engage and develop relationships (close- or loose-knit) with individuals from all over the planet. Hence, the possibilities for **intercultural communication** (i.e., communication among people from different cultural backgrounds, many times with different assumptions and understandings of the world and of language use) have greatly increased. It is now actually quite common for people in places as distant as Argentina and Indonesia, Japan and Brazil, or India and Norway to connect and build relationships with each other through online media without ever having actually met in person. In fact, in a recent study on the motivations for people to use social virtual worlds (such as Second Life) and/or game-oriented virtual worlds (which refer to games such as World of Warcraft), Hassouneh and Bregman (2014) showed that meeting people from *around the world* was one of the key factors that led people to start using these types of environments.

Many of these cross-cultural encounters need to take place in a lingua franca; while it is true that there are several lingua francas being used world-wide, and that each different type of situation may call for a different one,[1] it is still also true that English remains the most widespread one of them, both in "real life"[2] and in the virtual world of the Internet (as we have already discussed in chapter 1). As explained by Thorne, Black, and Skyes (2009), in the case of network-based games, many of the new digital vernaculars that are emerging in online environments have incorporated English as their lingua franca. Actually, until recently game companies had generally outsourced the translation of their games into languages other than English (Bernal-Merino, 2015), which also attests to the prevalence of this language in this particular type of medium.

Thus, with the Web, we experience an increasing number of social and linguistic networks, with people from many different sociolinguistic and cultural backgrounds engaging in interactions with each other, and many times using English as their language of communication – not only in games, as made evident in the previous examples, but also in websites, blogs, chat rooms, and so forth; as we have also explained previously, in most cases this use of English involves at least one nonnative speaker of the language (in fact, several times, all of those involved are nonnative English speakers). Such interactions, then, include what House (2003:557) calls "the most important ingredients of a lingua franca: nego-tiability, variability in terms of speaker proficiency, and openness to an integra-tion of forms of other languages." Negotiability, or **meaning negotiation**, means the process in which users try to convey their ideas and thoughts, and understand each other clearly through strategies such as asking for clarification, paraphras-ing, restating what was said/written in a different way, and asking for confirma-tion. Variability in speaker proficiency, in its turn, means that different users will have different proficiency levels when using the language for communication, which implies an even higher need for negotiation. As for integration of forms, the phrase relates to the use of other languages in English speaking/writing in acts of code-switching and code-mixing, for example, as will be further explained in chapter 3.

Lingua franca interactions and their characteristics are obviously not new or exclusive to Internet communication. However, the number of different options enabled by the Web creates new, unique scenarios for language use, and personal as well as linguistic contact. In other words, the Internet has had an important role in defining the range of possible connections among individuals and groups from different backgrounds, which in its turn has had an influence on people's linguistic networks – and English has been, at least until now, in the center of this new context.

Furthermore, with the growth of the Web and its **cyberspace** (that is, the virtual space created with the use of computer communication), we are living through the development of **cyberculture,** which relates to the cultural practices, beliefs, instruments, and so on that have been formed along with this new space of virtual communication on a global scale (more on cyberculture as a general concept and on diverse cybercultures will be provided in subsequent chapters). As with many other cultural manifestations, the development of a cyberculture has brought its own language habits and trends, such as the widespread use of emoticons and emojis, pictures that denote facial expression or tone of voice; some new abbreviations (such as BRB or B4N, *be right back* and *bye for now,* respectively in English); and certain vocabulary – the word *cyber* itself (with the meaning of computer-generated) being a good example.

Note that the use of abbreviations and letters with symbolic meanings is not a new phenomenon that began with the Internet (consider, for example, XOXO and IOU); however, certain abbreviations we see today were created specifically for online contexts, and even when present elsewhere, many of them emerged as favorites due to the limited number of characters offered by some websites and/ or technological devices, or by the perception that in synchronic forms of com-munication, saving time is very important (BRB, B4N, lol/lawl, TTYL, and BFF are some examples). Within cyberculture itself, the formation of various cultural subgroups and social networks is based not on territory, institutional affiliation, or the sharing of a first language, but rather on common interests and desires (e.g., online gamers, bloggers, fan fiction writers), all of which have their own linguistic repertoires and unique uses of language in general and of English more specifically. These have further contributed to the specialization of acronyms and other shortcuts, many of which will only be decodable by members of particu-lar linguistic communities. Gamers, for example, use many acronyms that are specific to that realm of use and that may mean nothing to people outside those particular networks.

We can say, therefore, that the Internet has changed the way we communi-cate by bringing new possibilities of connecting with different people around the world, of forming social and linguistic networks that were practically unimagi-nable in the past. We can also conclude that the role of English as a lingua franca has been enhanced by this new reality; first, because English has been at the core of the development of digital technology and of the expansion of the Web, and second, because the increase of social networks on a global scale – as well as the growth in the actual sizes of many of these networks – has increased the need for a common language of communication, and English was in the right place at the right time for that. What we will see in some of the sections that follow is that this augmentation in its lingua franca role has had other consequences for the English language itself, considering that it has come in closer and more frequent contact with other languages and that it has been claimed by many users (a large number of whom are nonnative speakers) for their **linguistic repertoire** in ways that have changed the language itself. Finally, while the scope and the medium of English use have been revamped by its digital modes, the dynamics of language use have mirrored those of the real world, with functional and symbolic meanings keeping the language alive and ever changing despite the difference in media.

Changes in oral and written modes

The changing networks that we have just described already have a significant impact on the Web and the way we interact, but such influence is only one of the many implications the Internet has had on communication if we also consider the shifting roles of oral and written forms of communication, the emergence of new genres, and the consequences these phenomena have had for the English language and other languages of wider communication. When we think and talk about language, we usually consider it as taking two basic forms: **oral language** (which involves speaking and listening) and **written language** (which involves writing and reading). Once, listening and reading were also paired together as **receptive skills**, while speaking and writing were considered **productive skills**, but we tend not to refer to these skills in this way anymore, because we know that much participation from the listener/reader needs to take place for the message to be decoded. In addition, the listener and the reader contribute to meaning formation in a very active way. These basic distinctions, moreover, are not enough for us to provide a full understanding of the different ways in which language is put to use in our everyday lives. To understand the complexities involved in each one of these modes, in their interaction, as well as in their contribution to our understanding of the world and of ourselves, we need a more complex model of how they interact.

For many centuries, oral and written modes of communication were kept somewhat apart by such features as time of response, processing, and the possibilities of answer and feedback that they enabled. That is, we had generally assumed that oral communication was instantaneous and written communication delayed. Until not so long ago, we spoke face-to-face to people and got: 1) an immediate response; 2) a chance to clarify miscommunication on the spot; and 3) the possibility of feedback not only through language itself, but also through facial expressions and tone of voice. Even technology-mediated communication often worked in those ways, with the telephone (until the development of the answering machine) providing opportunities for instant communication and feedback. On the other hand, as far as writing communication is concerned, we used to write letters and then wait several weeks for an answer. We wrote books and usually got no response at all, except for the occasional words of a literary critic in a newspaper or magazine. We read stories and had no way of providing feedback to the writer (we could write letters to their publishers, but often we never knew if they made it to their intended recipients).

Furthermore, until very recently, we had no way of recording history and spreading messages to distant parts of the world with precision unless it was in written form. As argued by English writer H.G. Wells, it was writing that

> . . . made the growth of states larger than the old city states possible. It made a continuous historical consciousness possible. The command of the priest or king and his seal could go far beyond his sight and voice and could survive his death.[3]

Older technology did not really change that pattern: telephones provided opportunities for oral, instant communication between people located in different places, and tape recorders allowed for the documentation of oral messages, but it was not until the fax machine that written communication response became more immediate (although still bound by a relatively formal style).

With the emergence of the Internet, oral and written modes were not separate anymore. In chapter 1, we discussed how Steve Jobs once explained that those in the computer industry expected the computer to become an instrument of communication (rather than one of computing only), and that the Web was the defining technology for this to happen. At the time of that interview, in 1995, however, it is possible that not even Jobs himself (or other influential people in the area) had envisioned what has happened since then. To put it simply: if in the past there existed clear differences between oral and written communication in terms of instantaneity, reach, and possibilities of interaction, today such differences no longer seem to exist. We now talk and write to strangers; provide feedback to writers, artists, and companies; post opinions; work as informal journalists; start social movements; and, especially, merge oral and written modes in new, creative, but also challenging ways. Arguably for the first time in history, written and oral modes of communication do not necessarily stand in opposition to each other in terms of conventions, dynamics, and practices: they now conflate.

A simple example of this shift in dynamics is the chat, which is perhaps the most obvious, straightforward crossover of writing and oral communication. With the chat – which gained much popularity in the 1990s – we can write for immediate response, with the possibility of clarifying misunderstandings. Not only that: we also developed emoticons to compensate for the lack of tone of voice and facial expression in written communication, and to help us express feelings and emotions in visual ways as if we were speaking. Thus, it is possible to say that the chat is a good illustration of what Crystal (2001) has called *netspeak*, a term that refers to a new kind of language used on the Web, one that is neither writing nor speaking per se. In fact, Crystal compares netspeak to both writing *and* speaking, and concludes that it is a "third medium" (p. 52), one that is "better seen as written language which has been pulled some way in the direction of speech than spoken language which has been written down" (p. 51). Although in netspeak, writing and speaking are brought together, we cannot simply equate it to a sum of these two parts, as new functions are performed and new forms achieved by this hybrid.

It is true that the reach of a spoken conversation had already broken boundaries with older technology like the telephone; likewise, television had offered the possibility of broadcasting presentations to large audiences. However, with those particular devices, there were many more limitations: on the telephone, one would generally talk to a single or a few people at most at one time, speakers could generally not see each other, and it was rare to have someone be a mere spectator of a conversation. In addition, written modes were not present. When it came to the television, it was not bidirectional, and there was no opportunity for interaction or discussion beyond the immediate family/friends network. On the other hand, with the Internet, streamed talks, for example, can be broadcast anywhere and anytime; they also show us how spoken language (in this case, a presentation), which was generally limited by space/time constraints in the past, no longer has such limits. New media have brought us information that was likely inaccessible before the advent of the Internet; and now many of us can learn from people we would likely never have had a chance to interact with before the emergence of the Web. We ask them questions, provide feedback, and combine the oral mode of presentation with written comments or chat elements.

Literary scholar Mikhail Bakhtin (1986) has asked us to consider the use of language as closely linked to human activity in general. That is, when we produce language – be it spoken or written – we do so in a **social context**, under certain conditions, and with particular goals in mind. We do not produce language in a vacuum. The language we produce in a particular situation is related to the activity we are performing, including the conditions under which it is performed, and the goals we have while performing it. Activities we carry out usually have a form of language that matches them – and this language, together with the activity of which it is a part, is something that we call **genre**. In sociolinguistics, then, we generally say that a genre is the particular type of language we use – with its specific distinctiveness – when performing an activity in a certain context.

There are many examples of genres in oral and written language. Think, for example, about the language you use when you tell a joke, narrate a story to a friend, give an oral presentation, or interview for a job. Although all of these activities usually require the use of oral language, the way such language is organized and used in each of them, as well as the terms and level of formality we choose, is very different. In fact, each one of these examples is a type of **oral genre**. In every one, you shape what you say and how you say it based on the specific activity you are performing. The same happens in the case of **written genres**: writing a letter to a friend, a quick note to a family member, a formal letter of complaint, or a statement of purpose to enter college are all distinct activities that involve different uses of language. That is, the specific **purpose** and **audience** of a particular text determine the form the language will take. This is true in English as well as in any other natural language.

The Internet has made possible the emergence of new genres, such as the *email*, the social network *post*, the *tweet*, the *wiki entry*, the *blog*, the *videolog*, the *instant message*, the *chat room interaction*, the *Web conference*, and so forth. At first sight, it may seem that these are simply the online versions of other genres that already existed in the past. For instance, some may argue that the email is simply an Internet version of a letter, or that a blog is the digital version of a personal journal or diary. Such view, however, disregards some of the issues of frequency, mode of delivery, and feedback expectation that we mentioned above: an email has its own characteristics that distinguish it from a letter, including the possibility of sending a message to many people at the same time (thus having a broader purpose and wider audience) and of hiding some of the recipients (thus making the role of different parties in the conversation different); the option of including instant videos, documents, images, and sound as attachments (thus further conflating modes); and the opportunity of using emoticons and immediate spell check. Moreover, the instantaneity of message delivery and the number of messages one may need to write in a day have led many to use a quicker and more direct form of writing, without many of the features that are generally expected of a letter. In a similar way, the blog – which is generally thought of as an online journal – has a number of characteristics and possibilities that distinguish it from a written journal or diary – the first and perhaps most important of which being the fact that it is public, making it more journalistic in nature than the private diary.

To put it in other words, blog writing and email composing, as well as many other types of online communication (such as the ones we previously mentioned), are new activities that have risen with the advent of the Internet, with their own sociolinguistic features, which make them new distinct genres in their own right rather than online versions of genres that already existed. In some cases, these new online genres have begun to compete with some of the old ones, making the latter out of date and leading fewer people to use them in their everyday lives. We can, in this sense, speak of a rearrangement of genres in light of new communication modes.

In some instances, we may even argue that we are witnessing a process of **language displacement**, where the new genre is dislodging the old one and assigning it to secondary, less influential positions. For example, it is now much more common to see people using email and other forms of online documents than letters for written communication, with the latter being used only in more specific cases.[4] This process mirrors others in language, including those to which linguistic forms are subjected. Linguistic forms are often engaged in a progression of rearrangements. For example, in the case of synonyms (we could say words with similar meanings just like we have genres with similar functions), the tendency is for one word to dominate and the other(s) to specialize (by level of formality, degree, or domain of use, etc.). In that respect, we have *beautiful* and *pretty* (where the second is a gradation of the first), *happy* and *content* (with different levels of formality and different degrees of happiness), and *cook* and *chef* (presenting different levels of formality, different attitudes toward the occupation, as well as possibly different realms of use). So linguistic displacement works on many levels, individual and communal, big and small, from new genres displacing old ones to individual words displacing synonyms, and different languages expanding to new domains of use (Romaine, 2000:44) while displacing others (for example, a job that requires that the person use English instead of their native tongue).

What the study of genres on the Internet teaches us once more is that language phenomena (displacement, new genre creation, hybridization according to purpose and audience) are, in terms of content, specific to the context. However, underlying this context-content combination, we find the same dynamics that we have observed for centuries. Many of the new genres that have emerged in cyberspace have changed the way we read and write. For example, digital forms of communication have multiplied the instances where **verbal language** (i.e., communication that uses words – whether written or spoken) and **nonverbal language** – where words are not used, as it happens in pictures, drawings, gestures, paintings, music, and so forth – merge together, forming a multitude of **multimodal texts**, where words, images, sounds, and other types of language are combined to convey our messages, contributing together for the success of the interaction. In addition, most online reading presents many **hyperlinks**, links within a text that can direct you to different sections of that text or to different texts altogether, giving more mobility to the reader to navigate within and across texts as he/she pleases. It is actually not uncommon for people to start reading an article on a news website or an online encyclopedia or even a literary story online, and then be taken on a completely different route from the linear reading path by clicking links or hyperlinks – something that brings **nonlinearity** to the reading experience (see, for example, Coiro, 2003).

Such changes to communication have not been exclusive to the English language. Still, when we look at English more specifically, there are at least two factors that are worth discussing. For one, if we consider many of the changes described here on a *global scale*, we will still see the role of English as that of a strong, worldwide lingua franca. For instance, it is true that we can, and do, use the Web to talk and write to strangers in real time or to work as informal journalists and start social movements in many different languages, but the reach of many of these actions (especially when we think of such reach globally) depends on a common language of communication, and English is still central in that case (although the growing number and developing accuracy of instant online translators may soon change such a scenario). For example, when Brazilian citizens went to the streets in June 2013 to protest against several political and economic struggles faced by the country, the protests were organized and took place mainly in Portuguese; but when there was a need to ask for international support, several videos (created by Brazilians) directed at the international public were posted online – and most of them (if not all) were *in English* or contained posters in English because of its lingua-franca status and the perceived association of the language with status and power. In addition to the belief that using English will extend one's reach and advance communication with an ever-widening population, we have to acknowledge that the language has been at the core of the development of digital technology, and therefore many of the tools that have enabled the new genres on the Web, like social media and blog platforms, were originally created in it. This strong role the language has had in the development of digital technologies and texts has led to an increase in the influence of English over other languages, especially in relation to vocabulary concerning cyberspace phenomena and tools. It is to this and other similar occurrences that we will turn to next.

Language change and variation, neologisms, and computer lingo

For sociolinguistics, one of the pillars in the study of language dynamics is **language change**. In brief, language change refers to the transformations that occur in a language due to linguistic or many times non-linguistic (e.g., social, geographical, economic, migratory, etc.) factors. An example of a linguistic factor that can cause language change is **the principle of least effort** (Ferrero, 1894), whereby speakers may reduce the articulation of certain linguistic forms, progressively leading to new forms that become acceptable. This happened in the Portuguese use of the term "*você*" (one of the forms to say *you* in the language, used especially in Brazil), which has been gradually reduced from "*Vossa Mercê*" (a formal treatment originally used for people of royal status in colonial times) into "*vossemecê*," then "*vosmecê*," and finally "*você*" (and in some regions of Brazil, more often in the **vernacular**, one can now hear even further reductions of the word, such as "*ocê*" and "*cê*"). That is the same kind of dynamic that we find in the reduction of *What's up?* to *Whazup?* and finally *Whatup?* in the US. As for non-linguistic factors that can cause language change, William Labov (1966) documents how *attitudinal issues* (rather than linguistic ones) were related to the increase in the usage of non-prevocalic "r" (i.e., when the "r" sound appears in environments that do not precede a vowel, as in *star, fur, war, bird*, for example) in the speech of upper-middle-class speakers in New York City (this non-prevocalic "r" had become a prestige feature in that city after World War II). That is, New York City speakers from the urban middle class had consciously chosen to adopt the non-prevocalic "r" based on its perceived social prestige.

Labov is actually responsible for establishing a distinction between two types of language change: a) change from above, or above the level of conscious awareness; and b) change from below, or below the level of conscious awareness.

Basically, these two types of change relate to whether or not the members of the speech community in question are aware that they are altering the language. A classic example of change from above is the case of the New York City non-prevocalic "r" presented here, in which members of the speech community were highly aware of the prestige of this feature. Change from below, on the other hand, takes place in an unconscious fashion.[5]

The study of language change is closely related to that of **language variation**, which refers to the fact that two or more different forms (phonetic, lexical, or grammatical) may be used concomitantly in a language, either within or across individual speakers, to express the same thing. When such variation occurs across different speakers of the same language, we say that it is a case of *interspeaker variation*; when it occurs within the same speaker, we say that there is *intraspeaker variation*. Interspeaker variation is generally related to a number of factors, such as differences between speakers' regional origins, cultural backgrounds, age, gender, and ethnicity. Intraspeaker variation, in its turn, may be associated with a speaker's **accommodation** of his/her speech to that of the speaker's interlocutors. As explained by sociolinguist Howard Giles and others (see Giles et al., 1973), in what is known as **accommodation theory**, language users may adapt the way they speak based on those to whom they are talking in order to reduce the differences that may exist between them.

A phonetic example of **language variation** in English is the case of the pronunciation of the word *February*. While it is common to hear this word being uttered with the first "r" replaced by the palatal approximant "j" ['fɛbjuˌɛri], it is also still the case that the same word is pronounced without this substitution: ['fɛbruˌɛri]. Other words with similar structure, such as *dictionary* and *library*, exhibit some kind of variation. If you conduct a small survey of the pronunciation of words such as *crayon*, *pecan*, and *caramel*, you are likely to find a good amount of variation, especially if your interlocutors grew up in different areas. In terms of lexicon, we have many terms that are used to talk about the same object, such as *soda* and *pop*, *elevator* and *lift*, and *sneakers* and *gym shoes* or *tennis shoes*. Again, it is possible to find clusters of use by such criteria as geography and age. As for grammatical variation, the case of double negatives that was mentioned in chapter 1 – as in "*I didn't do nothing*," which is a variation from the abstraction we call *standard English* – is a good example of a form with a linguistic function (i.e., it communicates while showing membership in a specific linguistic community).

The relationship between language change and language variation is an important one in sociolinguistics, because it points to a similar phenomenon (that of the use of different forms within the same language) from different perspectives. While language change refers to such alterations across time or **diachronically** (i.e., from how it used to be in the past to how it is in the present), language variation relates to what happens in a given point in time or **synchronically** – thus, we may say that language change is **diachronic**, whereas language variation is **synchronic**. It is the case, therefore, that language variation and change are generally seen as complementary to one another. When we look at how a language has changed over time, it is generally useful, and in fact crucial, to understand how it varied at a specific time. For example, when we look at the Portuguese example of "*você*" presented earlier, we may say that there has been a change from colonial to present time, from "*Vossa Mercê*" to "*você*." At the same time, we may also say that there probably was variation between "*Vossa Mercê*" and "*vossemecê*" at some point in time, just as there is now variation between "*você*," "*ocê*," and "*cê*," since they now coexist during the same time period. If the use of "*você*" eventually disappears and gives way to either one of the other forms, we will witness another instance of language change over time.

With the Internet, we predictably see instances of language variation and change, in English as well as in other languages. The most visible of these changes have occurred in terms of vocabulary, both with the creation of new words and with changes in word meaning. This type of alteration is to be expected, since the words in a language can generally change and adapt quite easily and quickly without much effort on the part of the language users, whereas changes in grammar and sounds are usually much slower and may take decades, if not centuries. In addition, we must consider that the transformation of the world in itself, as has been the case with the creation of the Web and the emergence of cyberspace, necessarily brings the need for new words and meanings that can convey this new reality.

Take the example of the creation of **neologisms** (i.e., newly created words or expressions) in English for computer-associated terms, such as *Internet, wifi, weblog, cyberspace, cyberculture, cyberbully, hashtag,* and *selfie* (the latter was *Oxford English Dictionary*'s 2013 word of the year), all of which are words that were coined to name things that only came into existence after the advent of the Web. Most of these new words (perhaps all of them) were created through regular processes of word formation, such as **compounding**, whereby two or more words are combined to form a new term (as is the case with *weblog, web + log*); **blending** (when words are joined, but parts of them are deleted, e.g., *email, electronic + mail*); **derivation** (in which a word is changed without the addition of other words, but possibly with the addition of affixes, sometimes changing the part of speech, e.g., *selfie, self + ie*); and **clipping** (when long words are reduced into shorter ones, e.g., *blog,* from *weblog*); and many of them indeed refer to things that did not exist before the Web.

Similar processes of language change have occurred in languages other than English. In several of these cases, the influence of English **loanwords** (terms borrowed from one language, in this case English, into another) related to the Web and cyberspace are used for the creation of new vocabulary, as we saw at the end of chapter 1. Since the invention of the computer is closely associated with English-speaking environments (as described earlier), it is not surprising that English contributes terms in this **domain of use**.

The neologisms and loanwords that are borrowed from English into other languages we have shown so far are all examples of what we can call **computer lingo**, or language forms that are specifically used in the realm of electronic communication. In fact, perhaps this term needs to be revised, since this type of language is now also present in technologies other than the computer itself, such as smartphones, tablets, smart watches, and so on. In addition, there are many terms that are used for *actual tools* involved in electronic communication, such as *modem* and *CPU* (Central Processing Unit); *technical terms related to the functionality and memory* involved in such communication (e.g., *icon, application, links, byte, RAM*); and terms used for *actions* that are generally required from computer users, like *rebooting, saving,* and *clicking,* etc.

However, with the Internet came new genres and new communication modes; and these new genres and modes have brought with them new ways of using language itself, including a large number of Internet **slang terms**, and ways of writing that were not common before. In terms of slang, for instance, there are words like *noob* (short for newbie), *hacktivism* (activism via hacking), *crapware* (for bad, unwanted software), and *rehi* (for "hi again"), all of which were either created in or are highly associated with the realm of cyberspace and cyberculture. Even when not exclusive to Internet phenomena, certain terms spread fast through cyberspace and come to be used by a large number of people in a short while. Such has been the case with the expressions *on point* and *on fleek* (meaning "perfect"), which have proliferated in a very short period of time (granted they might have already fallen out of fashion by the time this book goes to print). Variation within one language does not tell the whole story, though. In fact, the influence of English over other languages is also present in Internet slang. In Brazilian Portuguese, for example, teenagers and young adults use terms such as "*nerdear*" (or "to nerd," meaning to spend too much time online), and "*hackear*" (or "to hack") – for more, see Diniz de Figueiredo (2010). Thus, the process of borrowing in the case of slang does not differ from that of non-slang terms; what may differ, in this case, is whether the word is actually used simply as slang or is also common in more standard varieties of the language, such as in the case of *mouse,* for example.

As for writing, as we have previously stated, in electronic environments, especially informal ones like chat rooms and some blogs, it is very common that a variety of abbreviations be used, such as *BRB* for "be right back," *BTW* for "by the way," and *lol* for "laughing out loud." Likewise, the use of emoticons and **onomatopoeia** (when words imitate a particular sound as in "hahahaha") denotes the lesser focus on the use of standard, well-accepted writing in favor of faster writing with fewer characters, which may be limited depending on the technology one is using (as in the case of the rule of least effort described earlier). As we will see in the next section, these are all aspects that have caused concern among language purists, who argue that there has been a deterioration of writing, and perhaps of language itself, through these processes – processes that, in the end, were not invented by the digital age but have more obviously documented manifestations in digital spaces.

To sum up, we can say that the Internet has brought many new developments to language use, in English as well as in other languages, for which we many times borrow Internet-related terms in English. Many of these changes have had to do with vocabulary, since this is perhaps the most flexible aspect of any language, and thus examples of actual change are mainly related to neologisms, such as *mouse*, *Internet*, *cyberspace*, and *cyberculture*, all of which are used to name things that did not exist before. At the same time, a process of language variation takes place, as is the case with some of this new vocabulary, which has not exactly replaced old words or been used to denote something that did not exist, but has instead been used concomitantly with older terms that already existed – for example, some people in Brazil still use the Portuguese word *sítio* for website, while others use the English term *site* – oftentimes also displacing them. In addition, variation occurs when new ways of writing begin to emerge, with new forms of language use being created for those purposes. In the next section, we will deal more closely with the political implications of these and other transformations in the Internet era.

The politics of virtual communications

We stated in chapter 1 that language is closely related to political issues, especially when we understand politics not only in relation to the everyday meaning of the term (e.g., elections, political parties, and so on), but rather as having to do with power relations among individuals in any sociocultural sphere (at home, school, work, on the streets, etc.), and the value that is assigned to different objects, events, people, places, and a range of other things in different societies (Gee, 2011). Therefore, any comprehensive explanation of the impact that digital communication has had over language as a whole and English more specifically needs to take into account the political issues mediating social interaction. In this section, we will address three such issues: a) the power of digital communications; b) the challenges that Internet language use has posed to traditional views of written communication and its association with standard varieties; and c) the challenges digital communication has brought to the exclusivity that many think native speakers feel they have in terms of language ownership.

Power and the Web

In his introduction to critical applied linguistics, Alastair Pennycook (2001:28) states that we need to understand "how power operates in and through language" in any politically informed account of linguistics. In order to fully grasp what Pennycook means by that statement, we have to first consider what we mean by **power**. French philosopher Michel Foucault often has been associated with a particular view of power and an understanding of its repercussions. For Foucault (1977), and for many after him, including Pennycook, the term "power" does not only refer to the generally accepted notion of institutional power, including the power of the government or the power of the state; nor should power be considered simply in terms of "an oppressive system bearing down on individuals from above" (Bess, 1988:2). Instead, power must be seen as a set of relations whereby an individual (or a group of individuals) influences (or at least tries to influence) another's thinking or behavior, not by physical force, but rather by using one's age, social status, knowledge, and so forth to do so. In that sense, power relations take place continually, in our homes, at work, at school, at church, in sports events, etc.

In terms of language, therefore, one of the ways in which power functions is through who can say what, when, how, where, and why – and who will be influenced by what is said. Until very recently, those who had this kind of power (or as linguists say, who had a voice in many discussions, in descriptions of the world, and ultimately in the construction of knowledge itself) were very few people, and included especially those coming from the higher socioeconomic classes and who had received formal education (that is, in a broader sense, language power was associated with socioeconomic and institutional power). Such possibility of having a voice usually meant that it was these people's versions of history, of truth, and of value that counted. As explained by Nigerian literary author Chimamanda Adichie in a well-known speech she gave on *TED Talks* (entitled *The Danger of a Single Story*), stories matter, and those who can construct a narrative about themselves and about others generally have the power to shape reality and influence decisions that take place in people's lives. A process of "gate keeping" usually helps delineate who gets to partake in the telling of stories. For example, if you want be on TV, you will be put through an intensive screening process that will select only a very small number of candidates. If you want to publish a book (through more traditional channels), the same will happen.

However, with the Internet, this scenario changes, at least in some ways. Now, many common, ordinary people can see the possibility of having a lot more power and their own voice. For instance, whereas in the past reporting on news required association with a newspaper or magazine, blogs have allowed news enthusiasts to publish information independently from such channels. Furthermore, as we have previously explained, individuals can now portray reality as they see it, by posting their opinions for hundreds, or thousands, or millions of others to see, by publishing their own novels on blogs and other websites, by releasing their own songs and videos, and by recreating stories of their favorite characters through fan fiction, among other things. In other words, the Web has redefined the scope of *who* can say something, as well as the *what* is said, *where*, and *why*, all of which are crucial when we think about the politics of language.

Glenn Reynolds' book *An Army of Davids* (2006) offers a discussion in which Reynolds makes the case that ordinary people (the Davids) now have the necessary tools (digital technology) to stand up to the many Goliaths of our time – for example, big companies, large media conglomerates, and so on. In fact, such power of ordinary people has become so strong that many Goliaths have started to turn to blogs and other social media in order to sell their products or pass their messages along to more people. A recent online article published on the American Express Forum tried to show how bloggers can make a brand or company visible; in fact, the piece even goes as far as to instruct companies on how to get help from bloggers.[6]

The role of English in digital technology has been very significant since the conception of the Internet, and therefore knowing it has been a key factor in determining people's access to content on the Web, their reach towards others online, and ultimately their success in virtual interactions – at least when we think on a global, rather than local, scale. However, the breadth and depth of this role, as well as its implications, have diminished considerably over time. Since a number of other languages have become more and more prominent on the Internet, many websites are now created or translated into them. In fact, advances in digital translation have been extremely fast in past years, with major Internet companies investing a lot of money on it to make their content more accessible. Still, knowledge of English will probably continue, at least for another few decades, to be of great importance in virtual environments, especially when we consider the fact that many major companies operating online are based in English-speaking countries, and that many people use the ever-expanding possibilities enabled by the Web (especially its shrinking of space-time relations) to actually learn this language online. In other words, if the power of individuals online will not necessarily depend on English, it will still benefit from it, at least for a while longer. Because power, in our postmodern understanding of the world, is multi-directional, as other cultures and countries exit and enter the scenario of global influence, we are also likely to see other languages take more predominant roles online.

Challenges to traditional views of written communication

The linguistic **prestige** of **standard varieties** (those associated with high levels of education and economic and political power), coupled with their common connection to formal and official institutions, has led many (especially purists) to believe that language use, particularly writing, must only (or most of the time) follow standard, prescribed rules of language use. Nevertheless, the Web and the technologies associated with it have brought with them an increased usage of public written language that does not necessarily follow those prescriptive rules.

As explained by Crystal (2008), texting (associated with telephones but also with other forms of digital technology) has been met with much antagonism by several people (mostly adults), including many members of the media. The belief behind the criticism is often that texting, supposedly mainly used by young people who do not care about standard language, is implicated in the decline in literacy and in the damaging of language itself. Crystal goes on to show how such beliefs are unfounded and could in reality even bring improvements to **literacy skills** in school-aged children. According to Crystal, one must know language rules to break them in such media as texting (you can watch his entertaining and principled defense of texting in the British television show *It's Only a Theory*[7]). We can hypothesize that the dynamics observed for texting are present in other spheres of digital language use, and that decisions are made on the basis of limitations of space and time, the seriousness and perceived lifespan of a message (even if nothing ever disappears from the Internet, a message's importance and use might fade away quickly), the participants in the conversation, the message's relationship to oral modes, etc.

The fact is that texting and Internet language use in general have brought challenges to purist views on language, especially in the case of written varieties and loanwords. Since many believe that there is an intrinsic association between the standard variety and written language, and between language and nation, it was shocking for those with more purist leanings to see writing modified in texting, capital letters disappearing in certain contexts, and prescribed punctuation ignored. Some also wonder about the loss of important information that these features of writing bring to messages.

However, in practice, despite the fears, what happens is a rearrangement of genres, with adaptations to purpose, message, and audience. The acts of tweeting or SMSing (or text messaging, where SMS means Short Message Service), for example, have a language of their own – one that does not necessarily obviate the need for other, existing genres and/or for formal texts (an academic paper, for instance) to also have a language of their own. In other words, just because a teenager (or an adult, for that matter) writes one way while texting or sending an email to his friends, that person will not necessarily write a formal letter or respond to an exam in the same way. If we work on awareness of purpose and audience, that language user can understand that these different contexts call for different uses of language too (many of us have that intuitive knowledge anyway).

Written communication, in that sense, is not the same as standard language use; in fact, writing has several different forms (some standard and some non-standard), and the appropriate choices on which form to use (including whether or not loanwords are appropriate) will generally be decided on contextually. We already did that analysis of **context of situation** (see page 86) before these digital genres were created. We also do it for oral communication all the time, as explained in chapter 1, and we did it for different forms of writing long before the Internet arrived. When we do not make appropriate choices, both on the Web (also in texting) or outside of it, we are usually faced with situations of miscommunication or linguistic clash.

Students who are taught the distinctions between different varieties, styles, and registers of language (including the standard variety) have an opportunity to add different linguistic forms to their **linguistic repertoire**, learning in the process to use purpose and audience to make the best choice of language possible.

Language ownership

Can language be owned? If so, who owns a language? And what does owning a language mean? These are questions that may seem trivial and perhaps unimportant, but they have shaped the lives of many people around the world. This is especially the case for those who are immigrants and/or who have learned a second, third, or fourth language, and who need to use these languages for communication. Think, for instance, of a newcomer Korean student who has arrived at an American high school, and who learns English and begins to use it on an everyday basis in her academic work and in conversations with her new friends. Does English belong to this student? Does she have to sound like an American to own it?

These are important questions, because a lot is at stake depending on what one believes the answer to be. For example, if the Korean student decides to become a teacher of English after high school, is that possible? Will she be discriminated against at a future workplace because of the fact that she has learned English as a second language? Will her students respect her as a legitimate speaker of the language? How will these factors impact her possibilities of fulfilling her dream and of becoming a valued professional? What if this student were from India, where English is one of the official languages (and not the only one) and is used among bilinguals? Would the same questions apply?

For years now, the matter of language ownership has been one to receive significant attention from linguists, especially in regards to the ownership of English, given its linguistic landscape. This question often has related old labels you saw in chapter 1, such as the ones that divide users of language into such categories as **native speakers** (those who acquired a language as a first language from their childhood) and **nonnative speakers** (those who learned the language as a second or foreign language), and generally involves issues of legitimacy in using the language for general purposes and in teaching it. Such discussions have become even more crucial with the increased flow of people shaping contemporary society, and many individuals being able to move around the planet (intentionally or because they are displaced, as in the case of refugees) at a faster rate than ever before.

The ownership of a language does not depend on one's native status. Rather, a legitimate user of a language is anyone who *takes ownership* of it and uses it for his/ her own purposes in society – whether to communicate with friends, go to college, work, or teach the language to others. The problem is that while this view is shared by many in academia, societal views still do not necessarily reflect this position. It is often the case that people are discriminated against because of their nonnative accents, leading some to be mocked, bullied, and at times lose work opportunities because of their nonnative status as speakers of a certain language or variety of language. In fact, linguists and applied linguists have documented the existence of what is called the "**native speaker fallacy**"[8] and also of "**native-speakerism**,"[9] which are strong ideologies in language teaching that maintain that the ideal teachers of English are native speakers of the language.

A layer of complexity has been added to this issue by the Internet. In online communication, native and nonnative statuses are not always distinguishable at first. Many times, it is even irrelevant (and impossible) to tell whether one is a native or nonnative speaker, even if prolonged contact can give away features associated with these labels. Moreover, we can pinpoint a growing number of instances in which bi/multilingual speakers **code-switch** and **code-mix** (see chapter 3) in online communication in ways that challenge traditional notions of what a language is, how it should be tied to a particular country, and how it should follow particular rules.

In other words, the claim that a language such as English belongs to those who use it has gained more support. After all, in a world where we increasingly see these types of interactions between speakers of different languages, and where we witness a growing number of online users taking ownership of languages for their own purposes, the distinctions between native and nonnative, first or second language user, and so on have become more and more blurred – even if it is true that these distinctions still exist and that it is arguable they serve useful purposes in terms of language description and pedagogy.

The case of English is one that deserves particular attention in this regard, given the language's important worldwide scope. There are very many non-native English speaking users and teachers of the language around the world, all of whom are better assessed by their bi/multilingual skills and teaching quali-fications (in terms of teachers) than by their nonnative status. Moreover, as explained by Crystal (2001), we now have so much contact between different speakers of the language (native and nonnative), both online and in real life, that we can see nonnative English users influencing the way the language is shaping – a phenomenon that is not only normal but that could have been expected. The example Crystal himself provides is the pluralization of the word *information* into *informations*, which is a morphosyntactic change that has become more and more common in Inner Circle environments.

The Internet and Englishes

In this chapter, we have discussed the ways the Internet has changed commu-nication as a whole, and the role that English, more specifically, has played in such transformations, either by influencing other languages or by being trans-formed itself. We gave a lot of emphasis to the status of English as a lingua franca, highlighting that this particular aspect of the language has been crucial in how it has taken shape in the digital world. As we end the chapter, we hope that you have realized that cyberspace contributed to English's status as malleable and plural. The language has been modified in several different ways, ranging from vocabulary changes to adaptations in terms of writing, to influences from other languages, with nonnative speakers having an impact on how the language evolves; and while it is true that similar processes have taken place in some other languages, it is arguable that none of them have experienced as many changes at once, or been transformed in as much depth, as has been the case with English. The digital expansion of English, therefore, has strengthened the need for us to understand the language not as a single entity, but as a myriad of variations that highlight the use of the term "Englishes." The awareness of this linguistic reality can be reapplied to other spheres of life in society at large.

Questions for discussion

1 What linguistic networks are you a part of? Which of them are online and which are not? How do they differ from one another in terms of language use?

2 Have you ever been involved in intercultural communication? If so, when? Describe who the people involved were, what you talked about, and how you negotiated meaning.

3 List a number of neologisms in English (or in another language) that are mainly used online. Which ones do you use most often? Do you know any loanwords in other languages that have come from digital uses of English?

4 If you have ever studied another language, or learned English as a second or foreign language, what were some of the features that made your instructor a good teacher?

5 What are some terms that you have added to your vocabulary because of the influence of Internet communications?

6 Have you ever witnessed or heard of instances of native-speakerism? Describe what happened.

Notes

1 See Kubota and McKay (2009) for an interesting example in rural Japan.

2 Consider our further use of "real life" and "real world" to be in quotations to show contrast with "virtual world."

3 See Wells (2007:80), originally published in 1922.

4 Note that the term *language displacement* (see Phillipson, 1992:27, also for replacement) is generally used for the process of having one system (e.g., a language) or subsystem (e.g., a variety of a language) replace another, making it (practically) extinct. This may (still) not be the case with many of the online genres we are discussing, but it is possible that we are in the beginning of such process, at least in some cases.

5 As sociolinguist Peter Trudgill (2000) has reminded us, it is important not to associate the word "above" with higher social classes and the term "below" with lower social classes, although there seem to be some discrepancies in how the terms are used by some sociolinguists.

6 Accessed July 2015 from: https://www.americanexpress.com/us/small-business/openforum/articles/the-power-of-online-reviews-how-bloggers-can-help-you-get-your-brand-noticed/

7 *Texting Is Good for the English Language*. BBC4, Season 1, Episode 2, originally broadcast on October 13, 2009.

8 See Phillipson (1992).

9 See Holliday (2006).

References and suggested further reading

Bakhtin, M. M. (1986). *Speech genres and other late essays*. Austin: University of Texas Press.

Bernal-Merino, M. A. (2015). *Translation and localization in video games: Making entertainment software global*. New York: Routledge.

Bess, M. (1988). Power, moral values, and the intellectual: An interview with Michel Foucault. *History of the Present* 4, Spring 1988, 1–2, 11–13.

Coiro, J. (2003). Exploring literacy on the internet: Reading comprehension on the internet: expanding our understanding of reading comprehension to encompass new literacies. *The Reading Teacher, 56*(5), 458–464.

Crystal, D. (2001). *Language and the Internet.* Cambridge: Cambridge University Press.

Crystal, D. (2008). *Txtng: The gr8 db8.* Oxford: Oxford University Press.

Diniz de Figueiredo, E. H. (2010). To borrow or not to borrow: The use of English loanwords as slang on websites in Brazilian Portuguese. *English Today, 26*(4), 5–12.

Ferrero, G. (1894). L'inertie mentale et la loi du moindre effort. *Revue Philosophique de la France et de l'Étranger, 37,* 169–182.

Foucault, M. (1977). *Power/knowledge: Selected interviews and other writings, 1972–1977.* New York: Vintage Books.

Fromkin, V., Rodman, R., & Hyams, N. (2013). *An introduction to language.* New York: Wadsworth.

Gee, J. (2011). *An introduction to discourse analysis: Theory and method.* New York: Routledge.

Giles, H., Taylor, D. M., & Bourhis, R. (1973). Towards a theory of interpersonal accommodation through language: Some Canadian data. *Language in Society, 2*(2), 177–192.

Hassouneh, D., & Bregman, M. (2014). A motivation-based typology of social virtual world users. *Computers in Human Behavior, 33,* 330–338.

Holliday, A. (2006). Native-speakerism. *ELT Journal, 60*(4), 385–387.

House, J. (2003). English as a lingua franca: A threat to multilingualism? *Journal of Sociolinguistics, 7*(4), 556–578.

Kubota, R., & McKay, S. (2009). Globalization and language learning in rural Japan: The role of English in the local linguistic ecology. *TESOL Quarterly, 43*(4), 593–619.

Labov, W. (1966). *The social stratification of English in New York City.* Cambridge: Cambridge University Press.

Milroy, J., & Milroy, L. (1985). Linguistic change, social network and speaker innovation. *Journal of Linguistics, 21,* 339–384.

Pennycook, A. (2001). *Critical applied linguistics: A critical introduction.* Mahwah, NJ: Erlbaum.

Phillipson, R. (1992). *Linguistic imperialism.* Oxford: Oxford University Press.

Reynolds, G. (2006). *An army of Davids: How markets and technology empower ordinary people to beat big media, big government and other Goliaths.* Nashville, TN: Thomas Nelson.

Risager, K. (2006). *Language and culture pedagogy: From a national to a transnational paradigm.* Tonawanda: Multilingual Matters.

Romaine, S. (2000). *Language in society: An introduction to sociolinguistics.* Oxford: Oxford University Press.

Thorne, S., Black, R. W., & Skyes, J. M. (2009). Second language use, socialization, and learning in internet interest communities and online gaming. *The Modern Language Journal, 93*(4), 802–821.

Trudgill, P. (2000). *Sociolinguistics: An introduction to language and society.* New York: Penguin Books.

Wells, H. G. (2007). *A short history of the world.* New York: Cosimo.

Chapter 3

Code-switching, code-mixing, and virtual Englishes

This chapter will help you understand that:

1 Human beings live in a state of heteroglossia.
2 Code-mixing and code-switching serve communicative and symbolic functions in "real" and virtual life.
3 Code-switching and linguistic borrowing are different processes even if they both involve combining linguistic codes.
4 Individuals have different emotional relationships with different languages, and that plays out in language choice and mixing.
5 The Internet leads us to explore different ways in which code-mixing and code-switching happen in electronic environments.
6 English(es) contribute(s) to code-mixing and code-switching both in the "real" world and online.
7 Pidgins and creoles are also affected by virtual communications.
8 The Internet poses both challenges and new hope for minority languages and their users.
9 In the process of hybridization that we experience on the Internet, it is not only languages and varieties that work together; pictographs contribute to communication as well.

Diversity everywhere

If the Internet has taught us anything about diversity, it is that diversity is everywhere: it is in the multiple activities we engage in virtually, in the different profiles of Internet users, in the multiple languages that we use in those activities, and in the variety of purposes – work, entertainment, connection, information – that these new media serve. We already knew that diversity brings change, including, but not exclusively, of the linguistic kind. Languages that come in contact with other languages change, people who use multiple languages code-mix and code-switch, and different languages or dialects serving the same society tend to specialize for the sake of economy. Human beings live in this dynamic and diverse linguistic universe where heteroglossia is the rule.

Heteroglossia, code-mixing, and code-switching

Within a single text or linguistic event, there can be many voices, styles, cultural representations, and dialects. Mikhail Bakhtin (1981) was already pointing that out in the 1930s in his essay "Discourse in the Novel." In its etymology, the term heteroglossia itself means something akin to "diverse language." In sociolinguistics, the concept of **heteroglossia** helps us remember that when we use language, we are actually engaging in a selection of interweaved linguistic elements that relate in complex ways to our gender, age, social environment, geography, and occupation, among so many other variables. Discourse, therefore, is never uniform, and as Bakhtin (1986:89) would put it, "the unique speech experience of each individual is shaped and developed in continuous and constant interaction with others' individual utterances." When we interact linguistically, we and our language vary and change too.

Many of us might not realize that the existence of heteroglossia results in our mixing, alternating, and **code-switching** in our daily lives. These alternations happen both in the real world and in the virtual world, even in monolingual communications, given that we are often switching between different varieties, styles, and registers depending on the situation of communication, the participants, the environment, etc. Think of this simple circumstance, for instance: you are a young professional having lunch with three other people – a small child (e.g., a nephew), a friend your age who shares your expertise in computers, and a person senior to you, perhaps a grandparent. You are all sitting around a small table having the meal. The following dialogue fragments might exemplify what could go on:

You to friend:	"So did you detect the cause of the hard-drive failure? Was there evidence of bad sectors? Was the failure mechanical?"
You to small child:	"Peter, no more lemonade, OK? You need to eat your food first. Is it yummy?"
You to grandparent:	"Yes, sir. I'm studying a lot. My favorite class is on computer programming. How's your food?"
You to all the members of the group:	"Do you want to go for a walk after we eat?"

You may not be aware, but each of these fragments has characteristics of different codes, picked from a variety of available options, given the purpose and the interlocutors in the conversation. The first fragment contains a number of technical terms, and the second somewhat simplified language choices, were probably accompanied by a very specific tone of voice and pitch pattern. The third one is more formal, probably a way to show deference to a more senior person. Finally, the last, given that it is supposed to address the needs of a larger audience (e.g., all the people having a meal with you) is less marked, arguably the more neutral, common-denominator-driven utterance. The speaker of these utterances is code-switching, going from one variety and style to another, depending on the particulars of the exchange. In this example, rather than languages (as broadly defined), it is varieties that change depending on the interlocutors in question.

Switching often occurs between a regional or social dialect and an approximation of the standard one. It can also happen between formal and informal varieties (although not everyone would call it by that name). It also occurs between different languages (as languages have traditionally been construed, e.g., English, Spanish, Japanese). In our example, different levels of formality and complexity are represented as the speaker switches from more informal to more formal constructions, but you will also notice different syntax patterns. Being able to make these switches is a sign of responsiveness to the demands of particular interactions and usually leads to a better communicative outcome. We could hypothesize that asking the small child, "Would you care to provide feedback on the quality and taste of your food?" (instead of "Is it yummy?") would indicate a lack of awareness of audience and sociolinguistic patterns. Nevertheless, as formal and seemingly artificial as that one utterance might be, all we have to do is find the right purpose and audience, and it will transform itself from far-fetched to quite reasonable. For example, should an employee from the restaurant be conducting a survey of the opinion of customers, that question would appear much more appropriate.

In addition, we often make choices about the use or avoidance of technical language. It makes more sense not to use **jargon** (i.e., specialized language oftentimes associated with a profession or community of practice) with a small child, or to not speak English to a person who does not share that linguistic code with you. It makes sense not to use the language of a specialized linguistic community (e.g., online gamers, computer programmers) with people who do not share that knowledge and those interests. However, if people working in the food industry, English speakers, and gamers, respectively, were involved in conversation, the code would change; we switch to better serve the needs of the purpose, genre, and audience at hand.

Code-switching, therefore, means alternating between two or more languages or language varieties (codes). The previous examples mostly refer to language varieties and their respective levels of formality. The following example refers to languages themselves:

"I was like, 'no puedes decir eso!' and he was like, 'claro que puedo!'" (I was like, "you can't say that!" and he was like, "of course I can.")

We can deduct that the participants of this interaction are bilingual and that the other interaction, the one being reported, occurred in Spanish, while the main current interaction, previous to this fragment, was happening in English.

Two common situations triggering code-switching include, according to Reyes (2004:84), "imitation quotation" and "representation of speech"; in the first case, the interlocutor is playing a character, and in the second case, the interlocutor is trying to represent the perceived or supposed speech of others. It is easy to see the possibility of these two scenarios in the bilingual interaction example. Nevertheless, we don't believe that participants in a conversation have to always be (symmetrically) bilingual to engage in these processes. Especially in the Internet age, and given increasing **translanguaging**, it becomes ever more necessary to question the boundaries between language and dialect/language variety.

In our example, to give the dialogue being reported further authenticity, the speaker chose to keep the language in which the interaction happened. We can even hypothesize that other elements, such as tone of voice, would change to further signal the switch. Clearly, the speaker could have chosen a different path, and would have likely done so if his/her interlocutor did not speak Spanish. For example, the speaker could have chosen reported speech as in, "I told him he couldn't say that, and he answered that he certainly could," but something that the speaker considered important might have been lost (remember purpose).

When the insertion of codes occurs below the clause level, we can call it **code-mixing** instead of code-switching (e.g., I bought some *parfum français*). Some linguists prefer to use the term code-switching more universally to refer to both aspects of the interweaving of languages/varieties, but here we will make that distinction[1] for the sake of specificity. Take the following example:

"Eu escrevi um comentário que teve uns 100 *likes*. Foi *cool!*[2]" (I wrote a post that received about 100 "likes." It was cool!)

You will notice that in this case, we don't have alternating full clauses in different languages; rather, we have a Portuguese base with words of English inserted, thus mixing. The words *post* and *like* will probably be known to social media users even if they are not completely fluent in English, which enables the mixing by those who are not functional bilinguals.

Code-mixing is, however, different from **lexical borrowing**. Borrowing usually fills a perceived or real gap in the language and eventually, if stabilized, becomes a part of the receiving language. For example, when a new piece of technology is created and a particular language does not yet have a name for it, it is not unusual to borrow a term from another language, oftentimes the language that named the technology in the first place. Many languages adopted the term *mouse* to refer to the electronic device that controls the cursor of a computer once that invention became part of daily life. Borrowing, within the receiving language, usually occurs systematically and can be observed at the societal level, rather than only at the individual level. Oftentimes, **loanwords** (the result of lexical borrowing) can undergo further changes to conform to the rules of the receiving languages (e.g., ping-pong, in Brazilian Portuguese, is written as *pingue-pongue* and pronounced as /pĩ.gɨ.ˈpõ.gɨ/).

In due course, if fully incorporated into the language, a borrowed term (or loanword) can stop being perceived as such. The words *shampoo* (Hindi), *banana* (Portuguese), *salsa* (Spanish), *cinema* (French), *pizza* (Italian), and *kindergarten* (German) were all brought into English as loanwords. When the use of these terms becomes systematic, the pronunciation (and sometimes spelling) might change, and eventually users of the language, unless they study etymology or speak the languages where the terms originated, have little insight into the borrowed status of the term. Other terms might still be in the process of full incorporation and, in these cases, we are more likely aware of their origin and oftentimes less secure about stress, intonation, and pronunciation of the lexical item. Ask a few friends to pronounce the word *croissant* and you will know what we mean.

Some English terms are also incorporated because users have a positive attitude toward them and have detected ways to expand their application to related items. Users of Japanese, for example, have adopted the term *miruku*, a phonetic adaptation of the word *milk*, into the language. While the original term *gyûnyû* already fulfilled its purpose, the new term (besides having positive associations with Westernization) also encompasses such derivative products as coffee creamer, thus filling a perceived lexical gap in the language.

As you can see, code-switching and code-mixing are a different phenomenon from borrowing. In the first two cases, decisions about the alternation and insertion of languages and/or varieties are usually made "on the spot," and there does not need to be consistency across users or from the same user in different instances of communication. In sum, in this chapter, we adopt the term code-switching for the alternation of codes at the clause level or above, code-mixing for the insertion of a different code below the clause level (including single words), and lexical borrowing as the systematic/stable adoption and incorporation of a term from another language due to sustained contact. We also acknowledge that the dynamics of mixing and switching exist between different varieties of the same language, even if it is less common to treat those as part and parcel of the same linguistic phenomenon.

Functions of code-switching and code-mixing

Myers-Scotton and Ury (1977:5) hypothesize that "code-switching occurs because at least one speaker wishes to redefine the interaction by moving it to a different social arena." The following examples we provide all appear to fall within this broad proposition. This move can at times be triggered by reference to a different person, a different aspect of life, a different level of formality (which the interlocutors associate with different languages), or yet a different level of attachment. As for the case we provided previously, the switch falls under what Gumperz (1982:75–76) has referred to as the common instance of providing a quotation or reported speech in the language it originally occurred. As with all of our linguistic choices, code-mixing and code-switching play important roles in communication and in the signaling of beliefs and intentions. They include the following:

A.   Highlighting a particular piece of written or oral text

In this case, the dialect associated with a particular geography or speech community will become more evident when juxtaposed with the more standard one. For example:

> "When we visited grandma, she told us she was *fixin to visit us* up North *real soon.*"

With the appropriate pronunciation and emphasis, the speaker of this sentence would be able to convey that their grandmother is from the South of the US, where the expression "fixing to" can signal intent to do something in a short while and where "real soon" is a vernacular variation of "really soon." This example can also fall into the "person specification" category described in the speech or code-switching children in Reyes's (2004:85) investigation.

B.   Highlighting in-group and out-group relationships

A teenager might use the utterance below to signal membership in a speech community where those who are past their teenage years probably don't belong:

> "Yo, dat game's got swag. Can you come over to play it?"

Notice that the second clause is pretty neutral and could be decoded by most users of English, independently of their age. However, by the time the latter is uttered, the former will have already established the boundaries of the speech community (because of the fleeting nature of slang, that is, slang is only cool if it is fresh, we are fully aware of the fact that by the time this book goes to print, that utterance might sound outdated and the opposite of cool).

Under this broad categorization, we can also add what Gumperz (1982:77) refers to as "addressee specification," which is the attempt to focus on the needs of specific people, for example, a bystander to a group interacting in a given language.

C.   Finding a shortcut to a term

Instead of thinking of exact terms in only one language or code, when participants are members of similar speech communities, they can rely simply on the first language in which an expression comes to mind or on the one that has the most precise term to convey their meaning. For example:

"Ele ficou triste. Achou que eu estava *taking him for granted*."
(He became sad. He thought I was taking him for granted.)

or

"I haven't been back to Brazil for several years. Muita saudade!"
(The Portuguese here roughly translates as "I miss it a lot!")

It is hard to find a word or expression in Portuguese that fully captures "to take for granted." Likewise, *saudade*, a word for a feeling that is not quite longing and not really melancholia, is hard to translate to non-Portuguese speakers. If participants in the conversation are users of both Portuguese and English, using that particular expression allows for a quick and exact way to express an idea with no loss in time, fluency, or meaning.

D. Expanding our creative possibilities by adding dialects or languages to the set of choices available to us

This is very common in advertising, for example. Advertisers have explained that having access to more than one code gives them such options as using shorter words, "better" words, more pleasant-sounding ones, etc. Of course, what constitutes a cute or a pleasant-sounding word is a subjective judgment, but because advertisers often tap into attitudes, this is an important consideration. Having more languages available means more possibilities of puns, more reliance on sounds, and just more creative opportunities altogether. You will read more about advertising in chapter 4.

E. Conveying a certain attitude or mood[3]

Language is not only used to communicate information. It is often employed to create an impression too. Mixing words from another language can be an attempt at conveying messages such as "I'm knowledgeable," "I'm sophisticated," or "I'm cool."
For example, someone might say, "We went to this great hotel and had our *petit dejeuner* there. *C'est magnifique!*" (where the French expressions mean "breakfast" and "it's marvelous," respectively) to convey refinement.

F. Showing solidarity or common ground, or implying/requesting loyalty

Imagine the following situation: an American who has travelled to Italy and enjoyed the stay very much meets an Italian traveler back in the United States. The Italian is bilingual. The American has picked up a few words in Italian during the trip. Upon being introduced, the American says:

"*Ciao*! I had a great time in Florence last summer. *Bellisima*!

For strictly informational purposes, the American person did not need to resort to Italian. However, they might have found that using a few terms in that language could bring the speaker and listener together by calling attention to the cohesion of their experience, in this case exposure to the Italian language and to Italy.

In another case, described by Myers-Scotton (1993) and discussed in Paolillo (2011:8), a bank customer in Kenya approaches the teller in what would be perceived as the appropriate public use of Swahili. When the teller explains the request being made is against bank rules, the customer switches to a minority language shared by both, thus appealing "to the teller's sense of ethnic loyalty, and obligation toward kin." Again, without saying so in as many words, the customer seems to be implying that their kinship should mean extra help in solving the problem.

G.   Showing objectivity or subjectivity (or speaking from the heart or from the mind)

Keysar et al. (2012) write of a phenomenon called "the foreign language effect," according to which, given a certain emotional distance that exists between a speaker and a language other than his/her mother tongue, it is possible to be more objective while using (and thinking) in it. Pavlenko (2005) problematizes this dichotomy a bit more, explaining that affect (i.e., a noun meaning emotional reaction or feeling, not to be confused with *effect*) will be represented differently in different languages depending on the individual's experiences in those languages. For those reasons, it is not uncommon for bilinguals to switch from their primary to their secondary language if the topic changes. For example:

> "Vamos fazer uma festa bonita para o seu aniversário. By the way, we have to sit down and figure out our finances." (Here, the Portuguese text means, "Let's plan a beautiful party to celebrate your birthday.")

The first part of the exchange above refers to a topic that might be closer to the heart of the speaker, who chose to discuss it in (mother tongue) Portuguese. The second is a matter-of-fact, potentially more business-like matter, in this case symbolically related to the perceived less-emotional language for this individual, English. Gumperz (1982:80) writes related commentary under the terms "[p]ersonalization versus objectivization," explaining that this category of code-switching refers to such aspects as the difference between "talk about action and talk as action, the degree of speaker involvement in, or distance from, a message, whether a statement reflects personal opinion or knowledge," among other things.

You can probably attest to those different relationships by imagining deeply personal speech acts (such as praying, exclaiming, or cursing) and examining the ways in which realizing such acts in one language or another might change the emotional charge of the act itself. Usually there is one language in which such acts seem more heartfelt or emotionally meaningful, even if in terms of frequency, the language that you use more often is another. This means you might code-switch from one language to another to fulfill the emotional requisites of each subtopic addressed. This would, of course, mean all participants in the interaction are communicatively competent in those codes and/or have access to the symbolic meaning of switching to another language. However, very crucially, as Myers-Scotton and Ury (1977:11) explain,

> No linguistic variety has any single or fixed meaning for all interactions in a society. [. . .] Societal norms provide information about which attributes are salient in which interactions.

This lack of fixed meaning, to which we call your attention through this book, should be taken in conjunction with purpose and audience when you analyze your own language use and the language use of those around you.

Regular code-switching and code-mixing at the societal level can eventually lead to the development of new linguistic varieties and even languages. Some recognizable recent varieties come from systematic code-mixing and code-switching, for example, *Spanglish*. A construction in this hybrid variety could be:

> "Andale. Estas ready? Vamos al parking del shopping sacar el ticket rapido. Estoy trabajando a full." ("Let's go. Are you ready? Let's go to the parking lot of the mall to get the ticket quickly. I am working at full capacity.")

While *Spanglish* is not (yet) a nativized and institutionalized variety of English or Spanish (i.e., it does not yet have human institutions, such as a fully developed literature of its own, use in education and governmental settings, etc., attached to it), it does point at the kind of linguistic creativity that users of multiple languages and varieties engage in. It also tells us something about the nature of bilingualism (this will be discussed later in the chapter under *Translanguaging*).

Pidgins and **creoles** (examples of a somewhat different but related phenomenon from the *Spanglish* case described above[4]) are also a result of languages coming into contact and mixing. In fact, while there is no agreement on the status of English as having originated from pidginization *per se*, if we go back in time in the history of English, we will see that this is a language heavily formed on the bases of the interaction between such languages as those spoken by the Angles, the Saxons, the Frisians (also the Jutes), and later on, waves of influence by Old Norse, French, and Latin. More on pidgins and creoles will also come later in this chapter. Here, the really important consideration is that languages mix, languages adjust, cultures blend, and these are common processes that do not signal linguistic decay but rather the complexity and richness of human linguistic experience. Nevertheless, prescriptive linguists and language purists tend to see high degrees of language mixing (some will see any mixing whatsoever) as a sign of linguistic crumbling. Yet, all you have to do is study the history of languages to see that this process is natural and intuitive; where there is language contact, there will be language mixing. And where societies change, there will be linguistic change to match.

Language mixing and variety mixing online

Online code-mixing and code-switching can fulfill similar functions to those we see in the real world; but we have to remember that online, we tend to have a confluence of features of oral and written language, given the unique modalities represented in those contexts. That is, while code-switching is less common in formal modes of writing, it appears in informal chats, posts, and other written exchanges, because they share with several oral modes a certain impermanence, informality, and synchronic nature (i.e., response can be immediate). Yet, we write online to potentially large audiences (a social media post might be seen by hundreds of friends, for instance), further requiring that we consider how code-switching fits the purpose of communicating with them better and how intelligibility can be enhanced or hindered by such mixing.

Researchers often make distinctions between **synchronous** and **asynchronous** communication online, where the first refers to such instances where a reply is almost instantaneous, and the second refers to those with a likely delayed response. The rationale is that the more synchronous forms resemble oral communication more closely and therefore would more likely present an oral-like pattern of code-switching. Here, however, we do not mark that division too forcefully, especially because we find it hard to assume that one particular form of communication online will never generate immediate responses. Who hasn't experienced exchanging a chain of emails so fast that it felt more like a chatroom? Or engaging in a social media conversation that generated so many quick notifications that you could not possibly read them all? At the same time, a social media inbox message can either be answered on the spot, making the medium much like a chatroom, or take days or weeks to be answered if people do not log in often.

Among friends who share more than one code, online code-switching can signal membership in more than one speech community simultaneously and comparable cultural associations. For example, two friends who are immigrants to the same country and come from the same original linguistic background might use code-mixing and switching to acknowledge such commonalities. For instance, two Brazilians who live in the US could post, "Onde você vai passar o Thanksgiving?" (Where are you going to spend Thanksgiving?). Although "Thanksgiving day" is easily translated into Portuguese as "dia de Ação de Graças," the use of the English version signals that participants share the code and the culture in which Thanksgiving is celebrated. The use of the Portuguese base can be a nod to their common background and heritage.

On the other hand, friends who are members of distinct speech communities might make accommodations to their varied audience by code-switching, for example, within the same social media post, thus acknowledging that not all in their communities share the same code. For example, a bilingual user of English and French might write, "To my friends, I want to wish a Happy New Year. *Bonne année, mes amis!*" Repeating the expression in both languages can have the goal of making monolingual friends of both backgrounds feel included and encouraged to reply.

As online communities become more global, language users have more choices available, but also more decisions to make. These decisions have implications that reach beyond just the information-exchanging outcomes. The choice of one language over another, a variety over another, or code-switching/mixing over single-language use will provoke different reactions from the interlocutors, who can question the linguistic loyalty of their counterparts and/or feel excluded/included in a conversation depending on language choices.

It is also possible that friends who are still developing communicative competence in different languages could meet somewhere in the middle by combining (and simplifying) the codes they share. Notice, for instance, these chat communications that combine English and Japanese:

1 "II tenki desu ne. Will go out with friends." (Where the Japanese expression is a conversation starter meaning something like, "Nice weather, isn't it?")
2 A: Will send you the information.
   B: Matteru yo.
   (Where the Japanese expression means something like, "I'll wait for it.")
   A: I will find it soon.
   B: I look forward.
   A: *Oyasumi*. See you later.

A few comments are in order here. First of all, awareness of audience is part of the choice of the first Japanese expression, as it is a more formal, textbook way of expressing that particular idea. That is, the tone is appropriate for an audience of acquaintances (perhaps people who are only online friends), and it would also be the default form to talk to nonnative users of Japanese. This is particularly clear in the use of *desu*.

In the second example, we see not only a simple form of Japanese, likely to be decoded by a language student, but also a simplification of the English expressions as well. *I look forward* is much simpler than a less telegraphic expression such as, "I'll be looking forward to it," which therefore fits the needs of the medium (brevity online is desirable) and of the language user who might still be acquiring English.

In the final example in this section, we have "*Oyasumi*. See you later." This chat text provides a sort of useful repetition. While the first expression is a shorthand form of "good night," it works just like "see you later" as a conversation-ending remark. This reiteration (Gumperz, 1982:78) benefits language learners, because even if they don't understand one of the expressions, they can rely on the other.

But the extent of hybridity online does not end there. We now turn to a different but related issue – that of the transfer of metaphorical expressions naming Internet phenomena to languages other than English, either through loanwords or somewhat literal translations.

The fleeting nature of some linguistic innovation and borrowing: Our metaphors

Linguistically speaking, there is much to gain from the study of metaphorical language and how such language plays a part in linguistic innovation and change. Perhaps the most obvious and exemplary case of this is the expression "to go viral" itself, a term that suggests the pattern of linguistic and social spread of Internet phenomena is analogous to that of the spread of pathogens. Indeed, that kind of growth by geometric progression can be observed in many linguistic phenomena relating to language spread. Alexander Tokar (2007) calls our attention to other great examples: "to bookmark" even though no physical books are involved, and even "domain" (which is also fruitful in World Englishes and in sociolinguistics in the expression *domains of use*). Other examples reveal our attachment to technologies of the past, such as those of a mechanical nature. An example of this is the expression "to break the Internet," which is used to refer to news or ideas that go viral so quickly that they would metaphorically make the Internet stop working, as if it were an overwhelmed machine. On the Internet, we do *virtually* that which we many times do *physically* in the real world. That is the case of "tagging," "browsing," and the aforementioned "bookmarking." Finally, "trending" shows the fleeting nature of some linguistic innovation (in this case, a noun made into a verb to express a new type of high-frequency occurrence). When we started writing this book, "trending" was at the top of its game, used in social media, spreading to television, and uttered by people on the streets. Its use seems to have declined since.

In an analysis of metaphorical Internet language, Denis L. Jamet (2010) calls our attention to such terms as the *Web*, *surfing*, *information highway* (which arguably has fallen into disuse), and even *cyberspace*. Many of these terms, he explains, have also made it into other languages, either as loanwords or as translations from English, given the close association between the cultures of English and the creation of the Internet itself. However, Jamet also calls our attention to the fact that these terms are not "real" metaphors. He offers this as a reason:

> . . . the underlying implicit analogy which was the reason for their creation was not perceived by common Internet users. Indeed, when someone utters an expression such as the information highway, they do not visualize a real highway; when someone utters surf the web, they do not imagine themselves on a surfboard. . . The referents of the source domain are bypassed, which is generally the case when metaphors lexicalize quickly.
>
> (Jamet, 2010:11–12; ellipsis in the original)

Table 3.1 Metaphor equivalents and borrowings in other languages (in many cases, these terms exist alongside English loanwords)

	Language 1	*Language 2*	*Language 3*
the Web	a rede (net)/a web Portuguese	red (net)/la web Spanish	rete (net) Italian
surf	netto sa:fin (net surfing) Japanese	navegare Italian (literally to sail)	naviguer French (literally to sail)
information highway	autoroute de l'information French	autopista de la información Spanish (literal)	rede internet Italian
cyberspace	saiba: supe:su Japanese (literal)	Ciberspacio Spanish (literal)	Ciberespaço, espaço cibernético, Portuguese (literal)

Table 3.1 lists a few closely connected versions of these terms in other languages.

In another section, Jamet offers a suitable reason as to why English metaphors in a way predominate in Internet discourse:

> . . . the English metaphors were quite clear, and were no impediment to the understanding of speakers of other languages if those expressions were literally translated, as they were based on more or less universal conceptual metaphors . . .
>
> (Jamet, 2010:10)

These include conceptions of speed, things linked together, virtual reality, etc.

We also like to keep close at hand metaphorical references or icons that remind us of some functions of real life. Notice how pages online can resemble actual pages that can turn, or that a pen and pad tend to represent writing (of new mes-sages), or that many times the delete/trash button looks like a little garbage bin. These metaphorical images help keep us grounded in the everyday life, in things we do in the real world, and therefore may work like an anchor in a world that is otherwise characterized by great speed and constant change.

Translanguaging

Because the alternation of languages can also have a somewhat pedagogical ele-ment, it seems appropriate to introduce the concept of **translanguaging** here – not only because of the way the Internet can be used to further communicative competence in new languages, but also because these concepts speak of the world of bilingualism and multilingualism in ways that make the experience of multi-linguals much more "default" than previous theories have.

The term translanguaging was first coined in Welsh by Cen Williams in the 1990s to refer to the classroom practice of alternating between two languages to better acquire language skills, such as reading and listening. In recent years, it has received a new boost in the work of such scholars as Ofelia Garcia and Camila Leiva (2013:199), who explain it as "the act of bilingual performance, as well as a bilingual pedagogy for teaching and learning."

Garcia further contends that in many circles of post-structuralist sociological thought, the concept of distinct languages has been challenged, given the diversity that exists within and between languages. This may seem a radical view at first, but it only takes looking at the beginning of this chapter and seeing how the same dynamics apply to varieties within a "language" and between "languages" themselves to realize that the concept is not that far-fetched (we have also already explained how the view of the world as a place of fragmentation has become common in the late twentieth and early twenty-first centuries). Furthermore, if we look at how sometimes linguistically related manifestations are considered different languages (e.g., linguistically similar languages of Papua New Guinea as shown by Romaine, 2001) while linguistically unintelligible codes are referred to as one (e.g., Cantonese and Mandarin are both often referred to as dialects of Chinese), it becomes hard to make a purely linguistic case for the separation in languages to which we often subscribe. While Garcia and Leiva (2013:203), as well as other scholars, acknowledge that the social construction that we call language has to be used by us socially to justify our membership in certain networks, the experience of *trans-* means that in the process of switching, mixing, choosing between, using, and changing these languages, "a *new* discourse is being produced by a new *trans-subject.*"

Some of the reasons why we do not rely too forcefully here on a separation between intralanguage (between varieties of a language) and interlanguage (between languages) phenomena are evidenced by the study of translanguaging, because the experience of different linguistic codes is not one where each language or language variety has its own boundaries very firmly defined. Code-switching, mixing, and borrowing themselves show how porous these linguistic boundaries really are.

Again, the Internet might evidence that, despite our more formalistic beliefs to the contrary, we already engage in this process online often enough. Are the hybrid discourses we see in chats the manifestation of two separate languages, or are they a new language and a new linguistic experience themselves? Can we say that the discourse resulting in the manifestation we call *Spanglish* is a mere sum of the languages (English and Spanish) or is it a new entity, more than the sum of its parts? Can the experience of multilingualism be broken down as the individual experience of more than one language, or is the experience of multilingualism itself a new linguistic experience altogether? Your answers to these questions might hint at the complex and socially constructed nature of these linguistic categories in the first place.

Pidgins, creoles, minority languages, and English

In situations of prolonged language contact and hybridity, where there is a strong need for communication among members of different speech communities, it is not uncommon for new languages to develop. At first, such languages might have a limited vocabulary, simplified grammar, and only basic structure. They will be used in specific domains of use (e.g., in trade) and will have no native speakers. These languages are called **pidgins**.

Many pidgins developed under situations of colonization and hegemony, and as a result, many such languages bore witness to instances of linguistic (and social) injustice and domination. At the same time, their very development evidences that linguistic change is the norm, and that even in instances of linguistic imposition, languages continue to change to fulfill the needs of the communities they serve. Just like second-language users make their new language their own, users of these emerging languages have all the right to claim membership in a community of language users.

Notice these examples from tok pisin (talk pidgin), a language (expanded pidgin or creole) that developed in Papua New Guinea from a hybrid of local languages and such European languages as English and Portuguese: "Husat nem bilong yu?" (What's your name?) and "mi sori"("I'm sorry"). While we can recognize the lexical items behind some of these words, the syntax and likely the pronunciation (represented by the different spelling) point to local norms and local uses.

The term "pidgin" was first used in the late nineteenth century to describe a hybrid combination of Chinese and English. Later the term was expanded to include any hybrid combination of the same kind as the original one. **Creoles** are a further stage of the language development of pidgins. Once the vocabulary of a pidgin expands, new uses develop, structure and syntax become more complex, and children are born into the new language, the pidgin has moved into the realm of a creole. English has served as the **lexifier** (i.e., the language that provides the basis for most of the vocabulary) in many creoles, for example, those spoken in Grenada, Guyana, and Jamaica (Jamaican Patois), with local languages contributing pronunciation patterns, elements of grammar and syntax, and other linguistic features. We can see that juxtaposition is common in everyday words such as *man* (/mon/ often in Jamaican creole), or the article *the* (often spelled as *dah* to approximate pronunciation), or yet the verb *have* as *av*, the latter showing a variation that is also common in some vernacular varieties (social varieties) of British English. The phrase "mi a go" for "I am going" shows the grammatical/syntactic variation influenced by local languages.

In practice, creoles work much like any other language. Yet the term reflects both an attitude and also a still-existing memory of the language having once been a pidgin. However, creoles are functional, linguistically rich, and rule-governed just like any other language. By rule-governed, we mean they have internal consistency and rules the language user can abstract (regardless of purists' beliefs about standard language and extrinsic rules). They can also further expand to fulfill the needs of the societies where they are used, and as such, they can be involved in borrowing, mixing, switching, and all the other processes that languages go through.

There are three levels at which we can talk about the role of digital technologies in relation to pidgins and creoles. The first is that Internet communications have allowed for further documentation of the form and change of these languages, as well as their utilization by people who might be geographically dispersed. For example, a piece of text in a creole can potentially be readily found online in both written and audio format, which makes knowledge of it and of its linguistic features much easier. Physical (and temporal) distance, which in the past might have been a barrier to the maintenance of a pidgin or a creole, is less significant if we can bridge such distance electronically. Likewise, the localized and sometimes oral nature of a pidgin/creole can make knowledge of it outside its geographical borders restricted and restricting. With digital communications, that is not necessarily the case anymore, and related cultural expressions in the language, such as music, literature, and poetry, can travel faster and to more distant areas.

The second level is that of maintenance of the pidgin/creole itself. New technologies have meant that at the functional realm, a person can have access to texts, oral and written, in the languages of their communities, even if they are geographically removed from them. They can gain additional fluency, connect to other users, and learn more about these linguistic networks online. At the attitudinal realm, this means that young people, who are drawn to technological developments, might feel more inclined to learn the language of their grandparents if it is available in a medium with which they identify. We know that language death is often associated with the move of young people to big cities, where they gradually lose all contact with the language of their ancestors. We also know that it is with the second generation that heritage languages are often lost. Online exposure can help reestablish these connections. Some creoles and smaller languages (in terms of numbers of users) can also, for the first time, develop a written system so that they can be represented online.

The third level involves the fact that the Internet itself has been a vehicle for new pidginization as people who originally use different languages strive to communicate with one another. It is not unusual to see communications that combine features of different languages, in addition to the use of translation technologies, to generate intelligible or partially intelligible texts. Of course, there are challenges as well; for example, not always is the script of a particular language (if it is a written one) fully available in keyboards and software (if the language is small, developers might not be willing to invest the money), and if the language is primarily oral, users would have to come up with a script, as previously mentioned. Additionally, further communication with the digital world might generate opportunities for the members of a small community to move and engage less with the language by becoming further competent in languages of wider communication, such as English, Spanish, or Swahili.

But despite the challenges, it is not only pidgins and creoles that might have found through the Internet the necessary pull forward to continue developing and thriving. **Minority languages**, many of which are endangered and overpowered by "bigger" regional languages and international lingua francas such as English, may have found on the Internet a space to grow, be documented, and survive.

Mark Warschauer (2000:161) provides a wonderfully illustrative example of the revitalization of Hawaiian online. He explains that the Hawaiian Revitalization Movement has used the Internet to propagate the language(s) and culture(s) of the Hawaiian people, thus offering a chance for language users to interact. With regards to university students who started studying Hawaiian through online technologies, Warschauer explains that he observed that "interacting in cyberspace in the Hawaiian language provided students with an opportunity to explore and strengthen their sense of individual and collective Hawaiian identity." He further explains that between the two governing forces in the perpetuation of languages – that is, *transmission* (the passing of linguistic forms from person to person) and *will* (the desire to engage or not with a particular linguistic code and its users) – the Internet, which points to the future rather than the past, more strongly affects *will*; after all, young people (major players in language change and perpetuation) tend to be motivated by innovation and forward thinking. In sum, the technological mediation of languages causes users of these minority languages to *want* to use them (i.e., engaging with them online is cool, modern, and *avant garde*).

This is particularly clear in the presence of multiple online sites for minority/ creole language users, including children. Through them, it is possible to practice skills, listen to stories, and learn vocabulary in such varieties as Jamaican Creole and Gullah, for example, among many others. The availability of this kind of pedagogical tool online speaks of both the impact of access as well of the value of motivation. Just like Warschauer explained, positive associations with online media can be an important, even decisive element in language maintenance.

While issues of access were at first a consideration in Internet use, as the process of electronization of society continues, more and more people gain access to online communications, a fact that makes it an increasingly democratic space. The English language started ahead; at first, the Internet was completely dominated by English. As time goes by, however, growing numbers of languages are represented, making the Internet a place for linguistic documentation, change, research, and maintenance. Besides giving languages a space to live, the Internet also makes documents about endangered and extinct languages readily available for use, study, and preservation.

However, it is not just other languages that are facing the challenges and the advantages of virtual spaces. Englishes, too, are affected by the elements of new media and by new modes of mixing, some of which involve more than words. While English, as an international lingua franca, spreads and influences languages around the world with its presence, it is also impacted by a process of hybridization, and the extent of such hybridization will be a matter retrospectively evaluated in the future.

Pictographs and language: Another kind of mixing

It seems fitting and interesting to be discussing pictographs in the context of Internet communications and mixing, especially if we remember that they might be the first form of human "written" communication and documentation. After all, the images we find in caverns and rocks (petroglyphs) can be dated as being up to 12,000 years old, yet to this day they are communicating ideas and cultures to us.

The relationship between images and writing is a close one in historical terms, with many "symbols" developing as abstractions of concepts and images. For example, the Arabic numeric system, which forms the basis of the Western numeric representation (i.e., 0, 1, 2, 3. . .), is a direct depiction of angles (where zero is the absence of any angle, one contains one angle, and so on). The idea here is that while we have been employing pictographic representations all along, and that pictographic representations are the basis of writing, new media have caused us to rely increasingly on the mixing of words and images to convey messages and to ascertain our intent, in part to make up for extra-linguistic features present in face-to-face interactions (e.g., tone of voice, facial expressions, body language, interactions with the immediate environment) now that written modes have taken over some of those functions.

In more traditional forms of written communication, writers could rely on the following elements to try and ensure that their tone and intent were not mistaken: greater formality and distance from oral modes of communication, successive revision, and a delay in sharing until appropriate tone and voice had been achieved. However, when writing takes increasingly oral-like functions in written form, the chance for misunderstanding – given the absence of facial expression and tone of voice, and the desire for brevity and speed – and the challenges of little distance from the written material become highlighted. It is in this context that the inclusion of pictographs can occur. Some of the most common such images include emoticons, gifs, and memes.

Consider these examples:

"I can't believe this!" ☺
"I can't believe this!" ☹
"I can't believe this!" <3

If we were to think up contexts for these posts, they would likely be quite different and dependent on the addition the pictograph makes. The first could, for example, occur if a student found out they had been accepted into their university of choice. The second could be used if the outcome of that application had been the opposite. The third could be the response of a friend upon learning of the good news of an engagement. Of course, verbal forms of communicating these feelings exist. "I'm so happy that. . . ." or "It is a pity that. . ." or yet "I love that you. . ." would all convey in written form what tone of voice would express in oral communication exchanges. However, such longer forms do not always fulfill the need (and wish) for brevity that often accompany these posts; therefore, the use of emoticons facilitates and accelerates the message.

Conclusion

So if code-mixing, code-switching, borrowing, pidginization, and other processes involving languages fulfill so many functional roles in the real and in the virtual world, why are some of us so afraid of them? What could be undesirable about engaging more people, in more conversation, more often? It seems that the answer would have to consider fear of that which is new and that which is unknown. Linguistic innovation, just like innovation in other realms of human experience, is often accompanied by the fear that things will deteriorate: with the television came the fear that people would not read anymore; with the advent of VHS tapes and later DVDs, people worried that no one would go to the movies; and currently, we see warnings that no one will talk face-to-face anymore because everyone is constantly looking at a screen. While these advancements do indeed mean a certain displacement of older forms of interaction, they do not necessarily mean the end of the latter. Usually, the initial enthusiasm is replaced by a sense that while it is convenient to watch movies at home, for example, it is also nice to be able to dress up and meet friends at the movie theater. In sum, while some ways of reframing our social existence in time reshape the ways we live, interact, and talk, it is not all bad news.

Questions for discussion

1   What are some of the contexts in which you have used code-mixing and code-switching? What purpose was behind your choices?
2   Make a list of loanwords that are common in a language you speak (English included). What do you think were the initial motivations for borrowing?
3   Look back at your online communications. What kinds of patterns of borrowing, code-switching, and code-mixing are you able to identify, if any?
4   Compare your use of language mixing in the "real" world and online. What do you find?
5   Look for instructional sites on creole languages. What features call your attention? Share your observations with your peers.
6   What are some of the emoticons that you use the most? What kinds of messages do you try and convey through them? Are there ever misunderstandings?
7   Do you think the Internet will ultimately accelerate or curb the issue of language loss? Explain your reasons for thinking that way.

Notes

1 Many different authors use the terms code-switching and code-mixing, and not always do their definitions match. The same applies to the scope of the terms, with some using them to include several related phenomena. In this text, we have tried to offer a definition that is both simple and principled, but we by no means consider it definitive. The same goes for the term borrowing.
2 Since the term "cool" is increasingly being used in Brazilian Portuguese, it may eventually become a part of the language, introduced as a lexical borrowing. For now, it still seems appropriate to think of its use as "on-the-spot," spontaneous mixing.
3 Mood has a specific linguistic meaning too, but here we are using the word in its everyday sense.
4 One difference here is that while a variety such as Spanglish often results from bilingualism, a pidgin usually starts as an improvised variety, given the contact between people who don't share any language, and thus have to design a rudimentary linguistic form to try and communicate with one another.

References and suggested further reading

Bailey, B. (2000). Social and interactional functions of code switching among Dominican Americans. *IPrA Pragmatics, 10*(2), 165–193.

Bakhtin, M. (1981). Discourse in the novel. In M. Holquist and C. Emerson (Trans.), *The dialogic imagination: Four essays* (pp. 259–422). Austin: University of Texas Press.

Bakhtin, M. (1986). *Speech genres and other late essays.* Translated by V. W. McGee. Austin, TX: University of Texas Press.

Garcia, O., & Leiva, C. (2013). Theorizing and enacting translanguaging for social justice. In A. Creese and A. Blackledge (Eds.), *Heteroglossia as practice and pedagogy* (pp. 199–216). New York: Springer.

Gumperz, J. (1982). *Discourse strategies.* New York: Cambridge University Press.

Jamet, D. L. (2010). What do Internet metaphors reveal about the perception of the Internet? *Metaphorik.de, 18*, 7–32.

Keysar, B., Hayakawa, S., & Sun Gyu, A. (2012). The foreign language effect: Thinking in a foreign tongue reduces decision biases. *Psychological Science, 23*, 661–668.

Myers-Scotton, C. (1993). *Social motivations for codeswitching.* Oxford: Oxford University Press.

Myers-Scotton, C., & Ury, W. (1977). Bilingual strategies: The social functions of code-switching. *International Journal of the Sociology of Language, 13*, 5–20.

Paolillo, J. (2011). *"Conversational" codeswitching on Usenet and Internet Relay Chat.* Language@Internet. Retrieved August 15, 2015, from http://www.languageatinternet.org/articles/2011/Paolillo

Pavlenko, A. (2005). *Emotions and multilingualism.* New York: Cambridge University Press.

Pavlenko, A. (2014). *The bilingual mind: And what it tells us about language and thought.* New York: Cambridge University Press.

Reyes, I. (2004). Functions of code switching in schoolchildren's conversations. *Bilingual Research Journal, 28*(1), 77–98.

Romaine, S. (2001). *Language in society.* Oxford: Oxford University Press.

Tokar, A. (2007). Internet metaphors: A cross-linguistic perspective. *Cultura, Lenguaje y Representación, 5*, 209–220.

Warschauer, M. (2000). Language, identity, and the Internet. In B. Kolko, L. Nakamura, and G. Rodman (Eds.), *Race in cyberspace* (pp. 151–170). New York: Routledge.

Chapter 4

English knowledge, power, and Internet competence

This chapter will help you understand that:

1 Power operates through language in many different ways.
2 Power is present in every one of our interactions with others, and not only in instances involving institutions of power.
3 Power, in the Internet age, is fragmented.
4 English knowledge and digital literacy (also separately, but especially when combined) are strong symbols of mobility and empowerment, both in the "real" world and online.
5 Like power, ideologies (our theories about how the world is and how it should be) are strongly related to language and are present everywhere, all of the time.
6 The construction of nativeness has been challenged by the online sphere.
7 Some key agents in online English teaching worldwide have brought back old ideologies regarding English speaking and teaching.
8 The dominance of English internationally has led many to question whether the language is being imposed upon people around the world through different methods – including the Internet.
9 Academic and (online) media discourses are influenced by English in different ways.

Power as it operates through language

Alastair Pennycook (2001:28) has, as we mentioned before, called our attention to the need of understanding how power operates in and through language in any politically informed account of linguistics. This kind of understanding has been the focus of many scholars in linguistics and applied linguistics, especially after Fairclough's account on language use and unequal power relations (Fairclough, 1989), and the establishment of critical discourse analysis as a field of inquiry – both in its broader (see Gee, 2011) and narrower sense (for more, see Fairclough, 1995; van Dijk, 2008; van Leeuwen, 2008; Wodak and Chilton, 2005). The relation between language and power is particularly important in sociolinguistics, because our subject area is predominantly interested in how language, society, and culture relate to one another. In fact, when you think about it, power relations and value assignment are always involved in how we communicate and interact with others, both at the macro and micro levels.

When you invite a friend to a party, for instance, you are showing this friend that you value him/her and that his/her presence is important. Similarly, when a child asks their mother or father to let them go somewhere, the child is recognizing the existence of power relations within the family and trying to work through these relations in ways that will favor their ability to attend the event. And even in more everyday, supposedly meaningless situations, like asking someone to pass the salt at a table, sociopolitical issues (such as who the other people at the table are, their relationship to you, how long you have known each other, and whether you are trying to impress them, among others) will influence your linguistic choices – for example, how polite you will be, what tone of voice will you use, and so on. Imagine how different an utterance would be, for instance, if one were asking one's young brother to pass the salt as opposed to one's boss, who was invited to dinner, or one's mother. Here is a possible scenario:

To younger brother: "Yo, gimme the salt." (constant, unmarked volume, very informal language)

To boss: "I'm sorry, but do you think you could pass me the salt?" (voice starting at lower volume and increasing in volume towards the end; more formal as a way to acknowledge hierarchical distance)

To mother: "Hey mom, can you pass the salt?" (starting with rising intonation, possibly the most unmarked version)

At the macro level, power relations influence what language is used, what variety enjoys the most prestige, and what gets taught and spread. Pierre Bourdieu, in his 1991 book *Language and Symbolic Power*, states that the study of language "must take as its object *the relationship between the structured systems of sociologically pertinent linguistic differences and the equally structured systems of social differences*" (p. 54, emphasis in the original). In other words, Bourdieu argued for a study of language that looks at how external factors, such as socioeconomic status, determine who is a legitimate speaker, who has authority to speak, and ultimately whose voice counts. Language, in this sense, is strictly linked to **power**, and one's linguistic use symbolizes his/her socioeconomic and cultural backgrounds, often contributing to the establishment of the world order. To cite Bourdieu once again,

> The competence adequate to produce sentences that are likely to be understood may be quite inadequate to produce sentences that are likely to be *listened to*, likely to be recognized as *acceptable* in all the situations in which there is occasion to speak.
>
> (Bourdieu, 1991:55; emphasis in the original)

Thus, according to Bourdieu, we must look at the **linguistic habitus** (i.e., one's propensity and capacity to speak) in relation to a **linguistic market**, which is a system of sanctions and censorships that imposes itself on our language use, mainly through prescriptivism and correction. Such prescriptivism and the resulting rules are often attributed to institutions, such as language academies and schools, and certain individuals, such as purist grammarians and teachers. In this sense, the value of what one says in any interaction (notice that the word value is itself related to the notion of a market, in economic terms) is determined by the power relations that exist among the speakers involved, which are, in their turn, related to the social structure as a whole, including issues of gender, ethnicity, socioeconomic status, age, etc. (remember our description of prescriptivism in chapter 1).

One's knowledge of the languages or language varieties that are considered more prestigious in any given society, that is, one's **linguistic capital** to use another market-related term, is thus directly related to one's economic and cultural capital (the latter refers to the cultural background a person has that enables him/her to become successful in society). That is, language use reflects and at the same time symbolizes power. This includes a perception of what language is utilized in a certain interaction, which variety of that language is being spoken/written, and who has the authority to say what. Think of how someone who speaks English with Received Pronunciation (RP) in the UK may generally be perceived as more knowledgeable, competent, or important than a person with a northern British accent, based on pronunciation criteria alone – and how it is often the case that a person who speaks RP is seen by others as likely coming from wealthier backgrounds with more educational opportunities, even if, in more linguistic terms, nothing commends one variety over the other. Of course, there is nothing intrinsic in these varieties that makes one "better" than the other; there is instead a social perception of the power associated with them and their users, and consequently a social judgment. Yet, this judgment has impacting consequences for the language users, even if we should find it unwarranted and unfair. In fact, the less linguistic-aware a person is, the more likely they will be to resort to such rushed and stereotypical judgments about another person's variety.

Bourdieu's ideas that linguistic power reflects sociocultural and economic capital, and the fact that certain institutions and people serve as gatekeepers to that kind of power, are very important here. In chapter 2, for example, we explained that one way through which power operates in language is in the establishment of who has a voice in discussions, descriptions, and understandings of the world. If we take into consideration Bourdieu's theory, we will come to the conclusion that those with such voice, those who are likely to be listened to and accepted when they speak, are generally those who come from dominant sociocultural and economic backgrounds – which is, in fact, true, even though we may be witnessing some changes in that respect with the Internet and other hierarchy-flattening, democratizing social forces.

However, Bourdieu's notion of language and power may not be enough for us here, since it may imply that an understanding of the concept depends on the employment of a top-down approach, one that connects its very notion to the power of the State and of sociological institutions, such as education and the mainstream media, as well as to the idea of oppression from one group over another. In that respect, French philosopher Michel Foucault (1977) has proposed a more nuanced idea of power. As we brought up in chapter 2, Foucault not only sees power as a force of the State or formal institutions, but also as operating through a set of relations whereby individuals influence each other based on factors such as age, knowledge, and social status. Power, therefore, must be considered in its capacity to cause human beings to influence one another's thinking or behavior, not (necessarily) by physical force, but rather by using one's age, social status, knowledge, and so forth to do so.

In that sense, power is discursive, which means it is expressed through our practices and language use (our **discourses**), and power relations take place *all of the time*, and exist everywhere, in our homes, at work, at school, at church, in sports events, etc. – an idea that is closer to our assumption that power relations and value assignment are always involved in communication. Power, including linguistic power, is dynamic and contextual, established or re-established practically every time we engage in communication.

Foucault also established that power should not be seen necessarily as a negative thing, as other thinkers before him had believed. What this means is that power is not only used as a form of oppression, or as a means of coercion of a person or group by another, but that it is also a way to construct things and advance ideas. When you use your knowledge to solve a problem or achieve a goal, for example, it may well be the case that you are using power in a positive rather than negative way, and in the course of your action help other people. When a leader uses their power to advocate for better social conditions – for the bringing of clear water to a remote region, for the building of a school, or for a new piece of legislation that will help students – they, too, are using power in positive ways. Even in more mundane ways, for example, when you take the leadership of a school project to help the group finish the task (maybe your authority comes from advanced knowledge of the subject matter), power can be used to move the work forward.

Nevertheless, Bourdieu's and Foucault's views of power do not have to be mutually exclusive. We are not saying that Bourdieu is wrong and Foucault is right, or that we should consider the latter and not the former, or even that the two notions of power presented by these authors are necessarily in contradiction. In fact, we believe that the two ideas may be better seen as somewhat complementary rather than opposites. That is, while we believe that power is present in every relation – whether or not some sociocultural/economic form of oppression or inequality is present – we are also aware that privilege does exist (in terms of gender, class, ethnicity, and so on), and that it still has a lot of influence over whose voices count; and we are also aware that many times, such privilege is mediated by certain institutions, including the State itself (although, as we will see later, the power of the State has been challenged in some respects in the current era of globalization). As Foucault (1980:122) himself has stated:

> I don't want to say that the State isn't important; what I want to say is that relations of power, and hence the analysis that must be made of them, necessarily extend beyond the limits of the State. In two senses: first of all because the State, for all the omnipotence of its apparatuses, is far from being able to occupy the whole field of actual power, and further because the State can only operate on the basis of other, already existing power relations.

So power can be seen *both* (rather than *either*) as something that is exerted by the State, by institutions, and by those members of society who are privileged, *and* (rather than *or*) as something that is decentralized, diffuse, more local, and specific, which is present in every single interaction that takes place. Similarly, it can be seen as something negative or positive (or somewhere in between) depending on how it is exercised and its results. And, more importantly for us here, it is closely related to language use in our everyday lives.

The Internet may be the epitome of the fragmentation of centers of power proposed by postmodernists and post-structuralists like Foucault. How to harness power, as well as what power means, results in a variety of new shapes for the foci of influence in virtual environments. Taking all of these notions into consideration, in this chapter we look at how power operates in and through Englishes, especially digital Englishes, and Internet competence. For instance, what does it mean to know English in the digital era? What **symbolic meanings** does the language have on the Web? Is **native-speakerism** still present in virtual worlds, and if so, what kinds of power does it have over people online? Do States and other institutions have any kind of power over Englishes in the virtual sphere? By the end of this chapter, we hope to have addressed these and some of the other power-related issues that have become crucial for sociolinguistics and world Englishes in the digital age, and for the lives of language and Internet users everywhere.

What it means to know English in the Internet age

In chapters 1 and 2, we talked about how the status of English as a major worldwide **lingua franca**, as well as its close connection to technology and to the birth of computers and the Internet, have made it the **dominant language** of cyberspace. We also wrote about how the competence to use a computer and other similar technology – like smartphones, smart watches, and tablets – and to access and utilize the Web (a competence which is usually referred to as **digital literacy**) is not universal, since many people in less-developed places and/or from lower socioeconomic classes still lack such skills and such access. When we translate these two facts into the terms used by Bourdieu to talk about power, we may say that knowing English is a form of **linguistic capital** in cyberspace (and also outside of cyberspace, in fact), and that digital literacy is a form of **cultural capital**. And when we see that such cultural capital of being digitally literate is generally acquired by those in more developed countries and higher socioeconomic classes, and that the same is true for the linguistic capital of learning English (in many of the places where it is not a native language, that is), we see that Bourdieu has a point in associating these types of capital to economic power.

It is true that the Internet has become more and more multilingual with time, boasting an increase in many languages other than English in online environments. It is also the case that the Internet has provided a fertile terrain for **linguistic hybridity** and **linguistic innovation** as evidenced by our examples of code-mixing and borrowing. However, **multilingualism**, as well as hybridity, does not in and by itself mean that all languages and varieties in virtual space will have the same social value or the same power, or will be perceived in the same way. Nor, perhaps more importantly, does it mean that the speakers of all of these languages will have similar access and the same types of opportunities online. Rather, in multilingual societies (and we can consider the online community as a whole as a multilingual society), the linguistic capital of some people (e.g., knowing English) will give them more and oftentimes better opportunities than the linguistic capital of other people (e.g., knowing German or Latin; see Blackledge, 2005); and in cyberspace, a form of linguistic capital that has been very powerful, even with other languages gaining more and more space, has been English knowledge.

Think, for example, that in 2012, out of the top ten most popular websites online, eight were originally developed in English (interestingly, the other two were in Chinese)[1]; or that many of the websites that have been translated over the years were translated from English into another language, rather than vice versa. Or that many computer and Internet-related terms worldwide have been borrowed from English. What is perhaps more interesting than those numbers, however, is the fact that although other languages have gained, and will continue to gain, space and more importance in terms of numbers on the Web, English is still perceived as the language of the Internet – that is, it has a symbolic meaning, perceived to be associated to the Web itself.

In making those observations, we want to make sure the reader understands that we are not engaging in **triumphalism**, that is, we are not celebrating or postulating that English *should* be a language of power. Rather, we are describing the phenomenon as we perceive it. This is important to say, because oftentimes when researchers present evidence of the current power of English, they are met in certain circles with criticism and the charge that they are "happy" that English is so dominant. While we believe in a multilingual world full of variety (variety that includes the diversity within Englishes themselves), ignoring the current role of English does little to guarantee more access and more human rights to populations around the globe, especially those whose languages are, in numbers of users and in terms of power, less evident.

Major **symbolic meanings** of both English knowledge and digital literacy involve the concept of **mobility**. In today's world, where physical boundaries have, in practical terms, started to disappear, and time and space have begun to shrink, many people are able to see the possibility of moving – not because one has to, but because one *can* and/or *wants to* – as an important value (Bauman, 1998). And the more such possibility becomes real, the more powerful that possibility is considered. Note that by **mobility** we do not mean the actual, physical moving of a person (although it may also mean that) or at least the possibility of doing that. An individual's capability of navigating the world and establishing relationships with people around the globe, without having to physically move from his/her own single space, has been enhanced by digital technology. English and digital literacy are key symbols of this capability, whether they are realized or not.

We need to make it clear, however, that in reality, the power that is associated with knowing English and with having access to the online world is not the same for all English speakers or Internet users. Many times a number of other factors, such as a person's **communicative competence** (see page 137) in the language or the ability to speak other languages as well, for instance, will affect what this person can actually do and achieve with English knowledge and/or digital literacy. For example, for a monolingual speaker of English who is digitally literate, access to online information may be broad and the possibilities of reaching others online may be many, but these opportunities will likely be more limited than those of a bilingual or multilingual speaker of English plus another language(s) who is also digitally literate – and who will, for this reason, be able to visit websites not only in English but also in other languages, and to communicate with a larger number of people online. In this case, the linguistic capital of bi/multilingualism will be of more value than simply knowing English, especially as a monolingual speaker. Thus, we can say that while many may see power as something absolute and intrinsic to a condition (for example, knowing English means better possibilities of accessing knowledge, as explained in chapter 1), clout, access, and influence are actually oftentimes more situated and fragmented (i.e., power will vary a lot based on a number of issues).

In sum, then, we may say that the perception that English is the language of the Web, and that this language is a strong linguistic capital online, is not unfounded. After all, knowledge of the language, mainly when combined with digital literacy, may be an empowering factor for many individuals around the world, especially with the shrinking of time and space, and the higher possibilities of cross-cultural contact and communication that have become so strong in the digital era. It is no wonder that the number of people who study English and who associate the need to do so with its symbolic status (both online and in the "real world") has grown so much in many countries, especially in the Expanding Circle. Nevertheless, when we look at such perceived power from a more micro and also more fragmented perspective, we see that there is variation in how potential power materializes itself into actual occurrences.

Virtual worlds and the construction of nativeness

Complementary to the idea of power is the concept of **ideology**. In brief, an ideology is a theory of the world, which generally includes notions of what and who is and/or needs to be valued, how people are supposed to act and behave, what counts as normal, and so on – in other words, an ideology is about how, in our own "best case scenario," people and the world should function (Gee, 2008). Like power, ideologies exist everywhere and are present all of the time. They are embedded in our practices, a fact which many times makes it hard for us to see them, despite the fact that they are indeed there.

Here is an example. A controversy took place in the United States around a commercial that was broadcast during the Super Bowl (the last game of the American Football season) in February 2014 advertising a very famous drink and its brand. The commercial showed different people in different parts of the US singing a national song entitled "America the Beautiful" (by Katharine Lee Bates, 1913).

For those who are unfamiliar with the song and its context, we will explain that the song has been considered a symbol of US pride and patriotism, and for many it represents the American spirit itself. What was so polemic about the commercial was that the song was sung in languages other than English. Upon watching the commercial, some people took its multilingual version as an offense to the very idea of being an American, and openly manifested such view on social media websites and online discussions. Others hailed the version as an appropriate nod to the diverse nature of the US itself. A few days after the airing of the commercial, manifestations both of condemnation and support for the ad were "trending" in many social media outlets, blogs, and online news media sites.

We can surely see a number of ideologies at play in this case. One of them (manifested in the commercial) is that the United States is a country of many immigrants and languages, all of whom and all of which are part of the nation, and thus American. A very different idea was expressed online by those who opposed this representation. Critiques included ad hominem attacks directed at the advertisers and expressions of anger at the variety of languages being used in the song.[2]

According to this latter view, English is what represents and what symbolizes "Americanness," and therefore no other language should be used in the song. In other words, these two ideas denote beliefs of what the US is, what language(s) is (are) spoken in the country, and who is valued there. In addition, and more importantly, these views express what the US *should be*, what language(s) *should be* spoken there, who *should be* valued, and why they *should be* valued according to the ideologies of various stakeholders. They also represent different types of ideology, such as the belief that languages are tied to nations; that monolingualism (in the view of some) or multilingualism (in the view of others) makes us stronger; and that certain groups are the (only) ones that can be considered legitimate members of a given culture.

As we hope this example illustrates, ideologies can play a big role in power relations because they guide our actions and because different ideologies are, at times, in conflict with one another. The people who manifested their opinion for or against the aforementioned commercial were influenced by their theories of the world, and in this case more specifically, of the United States. Similarly, disputes between what we call the Left and the Right are based on different ways of seeing how society and the economy – including the role of the State, work relations, workers' rights, social benefits, gender roles, and even languages – should function.

The connection between ideologies and languages is a very strong one for at least two reasons. First, ideologies are constructed and passed on through language. That is, language is of key importance in helping us build, express, and teach our ideas about the world and about people. And second, because there are ideologies *of* language (or **language ideologies**), which are the notions we form about what languages are and how they should be viewed and used – including, but not limited to, who is a good speaker, what good vocabulary is, how a particular word should be pronounced, and what forms are better accepted.

Language ideologies generally reflect our ideas about the world, about society, and about ourselves (Blommaert, 2010; Ricento, 2000; Woolard & Shieffelin, 1994). When we say (or think) that a particular linguistic variety is better or more prestigious than another, we are also making a statement regarding the people who use these varieties, whether we are conscious of it or not (like we said, ideologies are many times difficult to see). When someone says that a language should or should not be used or accepted in a particular context (as is the case with the English Only Movement in the US, which has tried to ban languages other than English from official discourses in that country, and which we can relate to the example of the Super Bowl commercial), they are making a statement also about those who speak these other languages, even if that may not seem the case. To put it shortly, ideologies of language are about much more than just language.

As we said in chapter 2, a strong ideology that has perpetuated the field of English language teaching, and actually in the very idea of speaking English, is **native-speakerism**, according to which an ideal speaker (and teacher) of English is a native one, or someone who acquired the language in its "naturally occurring" environment at a very early age. Generally, such *nativeness* is constructed and perceived around discreet skills related to speaking, like one's pronunciation of specific words and sounds, intonation, and usage of idiomatic expressions. There are actually many dictionaries and guidebooks worldwide that try to teach nonnative speakers common idioms, as well as accent-reduction courses aimed at helping students sound like native speakers of English. These courses have even become popular among some native speakers of English, who at times feel that their regional or social accents have prevented or could prevent them from getting certain jobs (the best example perhaps being that presented by Jan Blommaert (2010) about online American accent courses aimed at nationals from

India who work or wish to work in outsourced services, such as telemarketing and customer service). In other words, in some cases the perception (fueled by a particular kind of language ideology) is that it is not enough to be a native speaker; it is necessary to become a specific type of native speaker.

Many are the well-documented issues involving the ideology of native-speakerism. One that we wish to highlight here is that such ideology generally also implies a view of culture as a monolithic construct, in very simplistic terms. The complexities of any culture and of the concept of culture itself are simplified into a single view of what a culture is (as we will see in more detail in chapter 8). The basic premise behind native-speakerism in this case is that only native speakers of a language truly know *the* culture of that language and the language itself; they are the only ones, according to this view, who can actually speak of that culture legitimately. Not only that: in the specific case of English, such culture is generally thought of as the habits of specific groups (many times based on race and region of origin) from a very limited number of countries, especially the UK and US. In native-speakerism, the polycentric nature of culture(s) is relegated to a secondary position, if at all acknowledged.

The new context of globalization we live in challenges these assumptions, and the Web has been a major factor in such problematization. First of all, virtual culture(s) of their own have developed (cyberculture), with several other embedded cultures being part of the picture (online gamers, bloggers and their followers, fan fiction writers, etc.). Being a so-called insider to this cyberculture and to these other cultural forms within it is less a matter of territory, nationality, or speaking a language as a native speaker, and more a question of affinity, similar interests, linguistic repertoire, and actual participation and interaction in the specific speech community. The English language manifests itself in several different ways within these different cultures, in ways that are negotiated by native and nonnative speakers alike without a specific territory, and all of these speakers are true insiders to these cultures. This is particularly visible in the language of social media websites and other online spaces, of which certain groups of people based on age or affinity (e.g., teenagers who like Japanese anime) are the legitimate members.

Second of all, the almost infinite amount of information available on the Web and the growing contact between people from different backgrounds online have allowed for an increase in intercultural exchanges, in ways that will help shape users' **identities** and views of the world in an increasingly hybrid manner. Furthermore, such contact and information have made it easier for us to see culture as multifaceted – to realize, for instance, that English goes beyond the borders of the US and UK, and exists in many other spaces around the world (within Inner, Outer, and Expanding Circle countries) in different forms; and that our understandings of British and American cultures themselves have many times been monolithic and *essentialized*. And finally, this vast amount of information and growing contact among individuals has started to make us reshape our understanding of culture and languages themselves, as we will see in more detail in chapter 8.

Another problem of native-speakerism is that it generally fails to account for the fact that language is more than speaking and pronunciation; it actually involves other skills, such as reading and writing, and the level of competence in a given skill does not have to be proportional to any other (i.e., you may be "better" at speaking in one language and at writing in another, given, for example, your degree of practice and experience). Basing one's judgment of language proficiency and ownership solely (or mainly) on those abilities means having a narrow understanding of these concepts. To put it more directly: being a native speaker of a language does not mean being multiliterate in it, or having a good command of it in all contexts and genres. Similarly, being a nonnative speaker does not mean having lower proficiency in these skills. And when we look at many interactions on the Web, mainly written ones, the lines that supposedly separate native and nonnative speakers (especially of English, given its strong global spread) become blurred and in several occasions irrelevant, especially because many times the speakers do not know one another's origins and backgrounds.

In fact, as we briefly explained in chapter 2, it has sometimes been the case that nonnative speakers' uses of English (mainly on the Internet, due to the large number of encounters between native and nonnative speakers that take place online) have led to changes in how the language is used by native speakers. According to David Crystal, this is now particularly visible in terms of countable and non-countable nouns (like *furniture* vs. *furnitures*, *information* vs. *informations*, or *research* vs. *researches*), where the non-count forms are being made countable. For Crystal, these types of influence are inevitable, especially because of the large statistical weight of usage by nonnative speakers in relation to native speakers of the language.[3] Examples show that the actual axis of influence of English is gradually shifting away from those who have usually been associated with it, namely British and American native speakers.

In summary, then, we can say that the virtual worlds that have come into existence with the Internet have posed challenges to the actual construction of nativeness, especially in regards to the major worldwide lingua franca. Nevertheless, in spite of the factors we have presented here and of many other claims made by several scholars against native-speakerism, this ideology has remained strong, especially in English language teaching. As a matter of fact, many have actually used the online space and its array of possibilities in ways that perpetuate native-speakerism, as we will see in the following section. Such strengthening of native-speakerism should actually not be surprising. After all, ideologies are usually very hard to change, even when considered against strong evidence and new media.

English and online education

Another area influenced by digital communications is education. Since the popularization of the Internet, new possibilities of research and learning have grown exponentially and become much faster, with easy access to encyclopedias, videos, apps, and dictionaries; we have also seen online platforms be developed in order to facilitate the storage and sharing of information, and to improve communication between teachers and students. People actually participate in the construction and dissemination of knowledge and information to a much greater degree than before; in addition, the development of online classes has allowed students to participate from remote locations. Finally, top universities around the world now offer classes for free, and instruct students from around the world on an ever-expanding number of topics. These are, to be sure, just a few of the elements of virtual learning at present. It is hard to think of a time when knowledge was so accessible and learning so democratic, at least from a technological standpoint.

English has been at the forefront of the development of online education for a number of reasons. One of them is the fact that the United States and United Kingdom adopted electronic learning (or **e-learning**) very early when compared to other countries, and have played a leading role in the ways the online education industry has advanced. Another reason is that many of the leading corporations involved in e-learning are based either in the US or Europe (although now many are in Asia, too), and several of them have used English as their main language. According to *Elearning Magazine*, the US and Europe account for over 70% of the global e-learning industry, and Asia has had the largest growth in the sector.[4] In fact, in 2011 over 75% of American corporations were using some form of online training or education. In the UK, that number was 53%, and in Europe as a whole, it was over 50% as well.

The same is true in the case of colleges and universities. Many of the leading institutions of higher education that offer online learning are based in the US and UK (with a few others in other English-speaking countries, and many others in continental Europe and Asia – with English as their main language). Furthermore, in recent years there has been development of *massive open online courses* (MOOCs) through technology companies that are either run by, owned by, or associated with several universities worldwide – most of which are from the United States. One of the major companies in this sector (which was founded in the US) had 108 affiliated universities in 2014 – over 40% of which were American – and has been a partner of the US State Department since 2013. According to the Detroit chapter of Black Data Processing Associates (BDPA), the top ten sites for free education within elite universities are based in the US.[5] And as it turns out, the idea of MOOCs has gained so much strength globally that the *New York Times* declared 2012 as "The Year of the MOOC," when at least two million students were enrolled in these types of courses (a number that has grown considerably since then).[6]

Therefore, it would not be an overstatement to say that there are new digital borders and configurations for education and training, and that the influence of mainly British and American corporations and universities over online education has had an impact on the spread of English in recent years. In fact, based on recent numbers, one could even go so far as to speculate that online education has further catalyzed the spread of the language. For instance, as of January 2014, over 22 million people from around 190 countries had enrolled in at least one course from one of the major technology companies that offers MOOCs; and over 88% of the courses offered in that platform were offered in English, which highlights the need for the language in the domain of education.[7] Online teaching and learning, in other words, enhance the status of English as cultural and linguistic capital.

The virtual world has also created new possibilities for **English language teaching** itself (i.e., in the teaching of English as an additional language to those who do not speak it). It is now the case that many individuals look for online options to learn the language, guided mainly by the Internet's ubiquitous presence and time/space constraints. English language schools that offer these types of services have multiplied in recent years in many parts of the world, and they have come in a number of different formats. Some of them are the online versions of traditional institutions that already existed before the Internet, while others were actually born on the Web; some are completely free, and others charge much money for their services; some are affiliated with colleges and universities or funded by governmental initiatives, while others are totally independent. In any case, they usually market themselves to fill the niche created by students' time and space limitations. In addition to these new schools, a growing number of independent instructors post online videos and create their own channels for English teaching, many of which are free of charge.

Needless to say, MOOCs, online English language teaching, and other forms of virtual teaching and learning have received criticism from different angles. Perhaps the most important one for us here is the fact that they are a good source of information, but not necessarily of education. In the 1970s, Brazilian educator Paulo Freire, who remains one of the most celebrated and influential scholars in the field (even after his death in the 1990s), began to question what he called a *banking model* of teaching and learning. The basic premise of this model, according to Freire (1970), is that teachers "deposit" knowledge (in the form of information) into the students' minds through their lectures and notes, and later expect to simply withdraw such information from students in tests and other forms of evaluation. Therefore, the model sees students as a *tabula rasa* that must be filled with information, and disregards their contexts, relationships, background experiences, wishes, expectations, personalities, and so on. This model also implies that reality is static, resulting in an overly simplistic concept, which hides other possibilities of truth that may be in conflict with those established by people in power. True education for Freire, on the other hand, must be *problem-posing* and *transformative*, meaning that it should take critical factors into account and be able to give students an opportunity to grow and change while ultimately transforming the world itself in positive, significant ways.

In the case of MOOCs, while the information provided in different courses is valuable and may ultimately be essential for many of the people who take them, anxiety exists over the possibility that these courses might not guarantee true learning in ways that the students will be able to develop critical thinking, engage with hands-on experiences, and question realities. Instead, they might simply make sure that a certain type of information about a specific topic will be made available to a large number of people. Because there can be so much unaddressed diversity in the student population (i.e., the larger an audience, the harder it is to anticipate and address everyone's needs), there is fear of a new process of hierarchization of education, with those able to pay large sums having access to more individualized instruction and others being taught information as described in Freire's banking model. A 2013 article[8] published in the *MIT Technology Review* explains that Web-based courses generally have a dramatic decline in student participation (with some universities reporting completion rates as low as 4%) and finalization of the course. In the particular case of online English language teaching, there have been similar problems. For one, as we explained in a study presented at the International Congress of Linguists in 2013, in Geneva, Switzerland (Friedrich and Diniz de Figueiredo, 2013), many online English courses do not necessarily use the innovations of technology in creative ways, but rather utilize them simply to create online versions of common (and several times old-fashioned) activities, such as fill-in-the-blanks, matching pictures and words, translation and unscrambling exercises, and answering grammar-based questions. That is not to say that innovation does not exist in the online platform. As it turns out, some services use new, interesting tools, such as instant progress reports, voice recognition instruments, questions that increase in difficulty depending on performance, and fluency calculators. The development of new apps and services for language learning is bound to bring new, creative ideas and to change the ways we teach and learn languages. However, thus far many online activities have served more as a way of putting old activities on a new, fancier platform, rather than provide true innovations in terms of language education.

As explained by Warschauer (1997), computer-mediated activities can sometimes be used to reinforce traditional methods and theories of language teaching and learning. Furthermore, the high number of dropouts that exist in MOOCs may also be a reality for online English teaching programs, since that seems to be a trend among online courses in general. One advantage that online English language courses do have, however, is their possibility for interactivity and collaborative activities. The advancement of technologies that enable online chats, face-to-face conversations, and so forth is promising if used in a principled way.

All of that notwithstanding, in the same study we conducted (Friedrich and Diniz de Figueiredo, 2013), we found that the interaction alternatives enabled by the Internet – such as the option of connecting with people from different parts of the world, learning about different places, and embracing a pluralistic approach to language education and to English itself – are often overcast by a strong discourse emphasizing native-speakerism. That is, several of the online English language schools we investigated took advantage of the globalization of communication online to highlight the fact that students can now be taught by teachers who are native speakers of the language, without having to leave their homes and workplaces in the Expanding Circle, for example (and/or the supposed "nonnative" environments in which they operate), instead of calling attention to the other, much more innovative and inclusion-fostering possibilities that we previously mentioned. In this case, we see the use of new technologies not necessarily fostering new ideas and exploring novel potentials, but simply bringing back old myths and practices that have been questioned by years of research in applied linguistics and sociolinguistics, such as the myth of the native speaker we discussed at the beginning of the chapter, and the choosing of one linguistic variety as a model regardless of the goals and objectives of the students.

This may sound pessimistic, but that is not our intention. In fact, we are sure new technologies have significantly helped the advancement of education in general, and language teaching and learning more specifically, and we think this is only the beginning. However, we must be critical of instances when such powerful tools are being used to promote exclusionary ideologies and to simply bring fancier versions of old-fashioned activities. Moreover, we must be aware that many times, new technologies are being used for informative or entertainment purposes only rather than educational ones, as claimed; in the end, we should not confuse exposure to information with the acquisition of knowledge and development of critical thinking. One can be a conduit to the next, but not always is that relationship so straightforward.

English, academic discourse, and virtual libraries

In chapters 1 and 2, we discussed English's status as the main international language of science and technology. We also pointed out how knowledge of English is of great importance if one wants to access content and expand the possibilities of virtual interaction and reach, especially when we think about a global scale. Given that about 75% of scientific articles are written in English (Hamel, 2007), the very construction of knowledge and truth in today's world is mediated by that language – and controlling what understanding of the world gets reproduced, as well as what counts as knowledge, is an influential way to channel power.

Given that our values, our actions, our interests, our ideologies, and our perceptions of reality are mediated by different levels of subjectivity, and since these values, interests, and perceptions play an important role in determining what we consider to be true and right, we rely and create *discourses* that evidence the ways we think and what we value. An important agent in the construction of knowledge is **academic discourse**, which is the language and its underlying assumptions of the scholarly community. Such community is comprised of universities, colleges, schools, libraries, think tanks, museums, research institutions, and so forth.

This language often follows a type of pattern we can call a specific **genre** (with some variations). Such language works as an instrument but also as a symbol of rigor and compliance in the presentation of the results of research. Through it, we come to understand how the world (including its societies, nature, and constructions) functions. The findings of such research are generally transmitted to others through educational institutions – from elementary schools to Ph.D. programs. In fact, this book itself is inserted within a certain type of subgenre within academic discourse.

Academic discourse is thus a very important tool of power. Together with other forms of discourse, such as **legal discourse** (language of law), **media discourse**, **historical discourse**, **political discourse**, and **military discourse**, it guides people's understandings of the world, what they consider to be true, and how they construct their realities. Ultimately, discourse influences their actions. As explained by Foucault (1980:131)

> . . . truth isn't outside power, or lacking in power [. . .] Each society has its régime of truth, its 'general politics' of truth: that is, the general types of discourse which it accepts and makes function as true; the mechanisms and instances which enable one to distinguish true and false statements, the means by which each is sanctioned, the techniques and procedures accorded value in the acquisition of truth; the status of those who are charged with saying what counts as true.

When we think of a worldwide society, therefore, which has been using a common lingua franca for most of its affairs on a global scale, we come to the conclusion that a lot of what counts as truth and knowledge, on an international level, is expressed in English.

The power of English in terms of academic discourse is thus very widespread. The **dominance of English** globally has been seen by several scholars as a form of **linguistic imperialism** (see Phillipson, 1992). In other words, fear exists that the knowledge and truths of the centers of English spread have been forced upon other societies through different forms of power (many times subtle ones), one of which is the English language itself.

While we can say that a number of truths and knowledge from more economically and politically powerful societies end up being imposed upon less-powerful countries and groups (however we define those) through English, it is also the case that in many Outer and Expanding Circle contexts, the language is **nativized** (through a process that enables it to develop local rules) and learned for the purpose of **empowerment** and resistance against imposed values – mostly outside of academia, but also within academic circles as well (see Canagarajah, 1999). That is, wherever there is language contact, there will be change, even if the rate, spread, and proportion of change might not be bidirectionally even. Once nativized, a language fulfills the needs and purposes of local populations (communicative and political/economical) without asking original contexts for permission; that is, language ownership in practical terms is in the hands of those who use and modify such languages, even if challenges, obstacles, and contrary attitudes to such ownership exist. With nativization, local values, beliefs, and practices are also inserted in the language. One example currently in evidence is that of Singlish, the English vernacular variety often spoken in Singapore. In a recent article for the BBC,[9] Tessa Wong explained that "Singapore is known for its efficiency and Singlish is no different – it's colourful and snappy" (where "snappy," we can conclude, refers to the secondary dictionary meaning of "cleverly concise"), thus evidencing that the values of Singapore's people have found a way into the Singlish language. Examples of that include the fact that Singaporeans often use prepositions as verbs (e.g., "to off the television," or "to on the lights"), thus making sentences more succinct.

What this means in terms of academic discourse is that, although the use of English may in one way impose the knowledge and truths of Inner Circle contexts upon other societies and contexts, it is also the case that scholars from these other contexts can – through English – share their own knowledge and perspectives on a broader, international scale, therefore helping to shape that discourse, too. In addition, the idea that English in itself has such vast power over academia (and consequently over academics) is counterbalanced by the agency and power that scholars worldwide have in their disciplines, which they are able to share in English or the other languages they speak, despite the barriers for entry in academic dialogue (through limited acceptance into journals, for example).

English and online advertising

One last issue we wish to discuss in relation to Englishes, the Internet, and power has to do with another type of discourse, namely, online advertising. As it happens with academic discourse, advertising shapes our understandings of the world and of reality. The difference in this case is that whereas academic discourses progressively help build our understandings of truth and knowledge (however subjectively), advertising has a much larger immediate relation to our behaviors. That is, many of our daily actions and attitudes, including what we eat, how we dress, what we buy, where we go, and so on, are influenced by the media and by what it offers to us in the form of commercial messages.

Note that when we use the terms "advertising" and "commercial," we are not referring simply to the traditional understandings of these terms, where a product, event, activity, or anything else is publicized directly. As we know, several forms of indirect advertising exist, as it happens many times in movies, music, TV, and so on – where products, beliefs, and behaviors are promoted subtly rather than straightforwardly. A lifestyle, a valuing of some aspect of consumer society, and beliefs about what is fashionable or in vogue can all be both directly and indirectly featured to us. Take, for instance, the case of how movies and music shape the way we dress, talk, and even call each other, ultimately having an influence on our personal identities. Joseph Tobin (2000) writes about the influence of the media over children; because they are developing identities and ideas about the world, children can be particularly susceptible to powerful messages, even if such power is felt by people in all age groups.

The Internet itself and the development and continuous growth of a **cyberculture** have served to advertise the English language. When we consider the commonplace association between English and cyberculture, and the perceived link between cyberculture and such concepts as coolness, youth, and modernization, we also begin to see a connection between English and those characteristics, which in turn facilitates a global *desire* for English. Conducting research with participants from Mainland China on local social media, Wei Zhang (2012:45) has concluded that:

> As the participants practice the art of 'mixing' together through sharing their 'mixed-code' posts, their 'mixing' strategies, and their experiences and opinions about 'mixing' practices, they are slowly evolving into an online community of practice with a common goal of enjoying the 'highend *feel*' of English 'mixing', a state of living for the bilingual urbanites. [emphasis in the original]

Notice several features that might remind you of what we mentioned earlier in relation to attitudes about English: it is urban (associated with modernity), and it provides a feeling of high-end membership in a community; and from there we can deduct it is desirable and status-generating.

Because of these associations, English has fulfilled a symbolic function in many online commercials, especially in combination with other languages. As explained by many sociolinguists, a language can be demarcated according to its **functional range**. According to Braj Kachru (1992), in the particular case of English in contexts where it is not used as a primary language, these functions are: a) instrumental, where English is used for teaching and learning; b) interpersonal, when it is used for communicative purposes between speakers of different languages or when it symbolizes modernity and elitism; c) imaginative, when it is used for creative purposes; and d) regulative, where English is used as a code to control conduct. In the case of English being used in online commercials, we can extend Kachru's theory and say that the language performs a symbolic function, which involves its representation of modernity, cosmopolitanism, and of the Web itself, as well as the creativity of users. Notice that the effects of a symbolic function can be experienced even by those who do not "know" a particular language. That is, a teenager who sees a tee shirt that displays a phrase in English might think it is "cool" even if he/she cannot decode the words written. If English to him/her is a symbol of modernity, youth culture, and popularity, the results of English use will be felt regardless, provided that the code can be identified as English.

This particular use of English in the advertising world is, of course, understandable and even expected. After all, the advertising industry is one that deals with creativity all of the time, and with the play on words and languages in general – especially with words and languages that have a highly symbolic meaning. In fact, relying on symbolic meaning is only one of the many strategies that those working in this industry use on a regular basis to convey their messages and sell their products. It is actually quite common to see a lot of multimodality in this type of discourse, where images, sounds, and words (sometimes in more than one language) are combined to create highly complex, sophisticated, inventive messages.

So what does power have to do with all of this? For some (especially purists), as explained in chapter 2, the use of borrowings as a whole is considered to result in the degeneration of the receiving language and should be avoided, if not completely prohibited. One of the main arguments put forth by those who defend this type of thinking is that many individuals who do not speak English, for example, will not be able to understand the messages that are being conveyed, and may thus be misled by them. They also believe that the use of English will harm the languages that are borrowing from it. But even when such propositions are taken seriously and result in regulations, as happens in some contexts, in the case of the online world, the regulation of loanwords would seem almost impossible given the scale and **polycentricity** of Web discourses. This is especially the case in terms of advertising, where creativity and playfulness are the norm.

On the other hand, the **borrowing** of English vocabulary for users' own purposes actually shows that it is people themselves who have the power to choose how to use language, and to do so in their own terms, in creative ways. Taking ownership of particular elements of English (mainly vocabulary) and playing with them in symbolic ways is thus a way to show active participation in a growing global community, even from the most remote locations – and the Internet is an ideal space to do that.

In any case, the symbolic power of English in the realm of online advertising is strong. That is because, as we have stated previously, English is highly associated with notions of modernization, coolness, and mobility (see Friedrich, 2002) – all of which are key components in the current reality of advertising, especially online. In general, whether English is used as an oppressive force that is imposed upon individuals, or re-appropriated in ways that actually oppose claims defending the existence of such imperialism, has been a matter of debate for a few decades among linguists. The case of online advertising in particular, however, seems to clearly favor the argument that such a phenomenon is a matter of linguistic choice in the face of mitigating pressures.

The power of English

In summary, then, we can see that the understanding of English as a symbol of empowerment and mobility, as well as its importance in the academic and scientific worlds, have grown with the Web. Such growth can also be seen in at least two different ways: a) as part of an imperialistic threat to local realities and languages; or b) as a possibility of also increasing a global sense of belonging, an integration of individuals who can communicate with one another from distant places through a worldwide lingua franca. Both of these options have their complexities, and so do any in-between interpretations. In the first case, any deterministic notion of linguistic imperialism needs to better take into account the claim that individuals can make a language their own by using and modifying it. On the Internet, these individuals resisted imperialism by using English creatively, by critically accessing knowledge through it, by mixing it with other languages, and by influencing the use by native-speakers themselves. As for the second case, despite enthusiasm, one needs to continue to consider the actual differences that already exist among individuals, and how these differences affect their true possibilities of empowerment, mobility, and cultural or linguistic integration.

When we look at some practical illustrations of how online Englishes have been grasped and used by different people and institutions, we also see a multitude of different notions. People's inclination and ability to use English have grown over the years. It is now possible to imagine individuals learning a language exclusively online. At the same time, however, some institutions, particularly online English schools, have come to emphasize old endorsements and restrictions regarding who is a good speaker of English, and who can actually teach it. In other words, old prescriptive and restrictive notions related to native-speakerism, which seemed to have disappeared, have proved to be alive, and are being incorporated back into the linguistic market of English speaking and teaching.

Considering that power can operate at different stages of interaction, it is even possible that such ideologies are also present at smaller levels, such as in individual exchanges between native and nonnative speakers. Nevertheless, when we consider the growing power of individuals that has been evident on the Web, the polycentricity of Englishes in the online sphere, the emergence of a cyberculture that has been more pluralistic than restrictive, and the intense fluidity of Englishes on the Internet, we can at least hypothesize that such a scenario is losing space. It would not hurt to investigate it further, though.

Questions for discussion

1   What are some power-related language issues that exist in your own country, state, city, neighborhood, school, etc.? (For example, questions regarding making a language official, standardization, language-based discrimination, and so forth.)

2   Have you ever experienced unequal power relations when speaking to other English users because of your native or nonnative status? (In other words, have you ever been in a situation where your status as a native or nonnative speaker influenced how much power you had in that particular interaction?)

3   Have you ever taken a massive open online course (MOOC) or an online English course? Please share your experience, including the positive and negative issues you encountered.

4   Have you taken any other online course? What features of it enhanced or made your learning more challenging?

5   In this chapter, we mentioned that some students have stated that they learned English completely online, through video games and other electronic tools. Do you think that is possible? Have you ever met someone who has done the same?

6   Find examples of advertisements where English has been borrowed into another language. Has the borrowed term kept its standard-English form and meaning? If not, how have they changed?

7   What are your predictions for the future dynamics of power on the Internet?

Notes

1 Information based on numbers provided by Alexa, a web information company.
2 For more, see http://time.com/3773/coca-colas-its-beautiful-super-bowl-ad-brings-out-some-ugly-americans/ (accessed July 2015).
3 From Global English, an interview with David Crystal, conducted by MacMillan English. Accessed in March 2014 from https://www.youtube.com/watch?v=YJ29zDW9gLI
4 Taken from *Elearning Magazine*, April 2013. Accessed in March 2014 from http://elmezine.epubxp.com/title/55545/28
5 Data taken from http://www.bdpa-detroit.org/portal/index.php/comittees/high-school-computer-competition-hscc/29-education/57-moocs-top-10-sites-for-free-education-with-elite-universities.html. Accessed in March 2014.
6 Of course, it remains to be seen whether the enthusiasm over these courses will last, and at this writing it seems it has already started to diminish, especially because while enrollment is high, dropout rates are very significant too.
7 Data from Coursera. Accessed in March 2014 from www.coursera.com
8 Article accessed in March 2014 from http://www.technologyreview.com/view/522816/data-mining-exposes-embarrassing-problems-for-massive-open-online-courses/
9 *The Rise of Singlish*, published August 6, 2015, and retrieved August 8, 2015, from http://www.bbc.com/news/magazine-33809914

References and suggested further reading

Bauman, Z. (1998). *Globalization: The human consequences*. New York: Columbia University Press.
Blackledge, A. (2005). *Discourse and power in a multilingual world*. Philadelphia: John Benjamins.
Blommaert, J. (2010). *The sociolinguistics of globalization*. Cambridge: Cambridge University Press.
Bourdieu, P. (1991). *Language and symbolic power*. Cambridge, MA: Harvard University Press.
Canagarajah, A. S. (1999). *Resisting linguistic imperialism in English teaching*. Oxford: Oxford University Press.
Fairclough, N. (1989). *Language and power*. New York: Longman.
Fairclough, N. (1995). *Critical discourse analysis: The critical study of language*. Harlow: Pearson Education.
Foucault, M. (1977). *Power/knowledge: Selected interviews and other writings 1972–1977*. New York: Vintage Books.
Foucault, M. (1980). *Power/knowledge: Selected interviews and other writings 1972–1977*. Edited by C. Gordon. New York: Vintage Books.
Freire, P. (1970). *Pedagogy of the oppressed*. New York: Continuum.
Freire, P. (1992). *Pedagogy of hope*. New York: Continuum.
Freire, P. (1998). *Pedagogy of freedom: Ethics, democracy, and civic courage*. Lanham, MD: Rowman & Littlefield Publishers.
Friedrich, P. (2002). English in advertising and brand naming: Sociolinguistic considerations and the case of Brazil. *English Today*, 18(3), 21–28.
Friedrich, P., & Diniz de Figueiredo, E. H. (2013). *New technologies, old myths: A study of language ideologies in the discourses of online English schools in Brazil and their implication for the sociolinguistics of globalization*. International Congress of Linguists, Geneva, presented July 23, 2013.

Gee, J. P. (2008). *Social linguistics and literacies: Ideology in discourses*. New York: Routledge.

Gee, J. (2011). *An introduction to discourse analysis: Theory and method*. New York: Routledge.

Gee, J. P., & Hayes, E. R. (2011). *Language and learning in the digital age*. New York: Routledge.

Hamel, R. E. (2007). The dominance of English in the international scientific periodical literature and the future of language use in science. *AILA Review, 20*, 53–71.

Kachru, B. (1992). Models for non-native Englishes. In B. Kachru (Ed.), *The other tongue: English across cultures* (pp. 48–74). Chicago: University of Illinois Press.

Mufwene, S. S. (2010). Globalization, global English, and world English(es): Myths and facts. In N. Coupland (Ed.), *The handbook of language and globalization* (pp. 31–55). Malden: Wiley-Blackwell.

Pennycook, A. (2001). *Critical applied linguistics: A critical introduction*. Mahwah, NJ: Erlbaum.

Phillipson, R. (1992). *Linguistic imperialism*. Oxford: Oxford University Press.

Ricento, T. (2000). *Ideology, politics and language policies: Focus on English*. Philadelphia: John Benjamins.

Tobin, J. (2000). *Good guys don't wear hats: Children's talk about the media*. New York: Teachers College Press.

van Dijk, T. (2008). *Discourse and power*. New York: Palgrave Macmillan.

van Leeuwen, T. (2008). *Discourse and practice: New tools for critical discourse analysis*. Oxford: Oxford University Press.

Warschauer, M. (1997). Computer-mediated collaborative learning: Theory and practice. *The Modern Language Journal, 81*(4), 470–481.

Wodak, R., & Chilton, P. (Eds.). (2005). *A new agenda in (critical) discourse analysis*. Amsterdam: John Benjamins.

Woolard, K. A., & Schieffelin, B. B. (1994). Language ideology. *Annual Review of Anthropology, 23*, 55–82.

Zhang, W. (2012). Chinese-English code-mixing among China's netizens. *English Today, 28*(3), 40–52.

Chapter 5

Changing varieties, discourse practices, and identity

This chapter will help you understand that:

1   Identity may be seen as built on the basis of specific categories (such as race, gender, sexuality, and nationality), but it is very useful to understand it as a concept that is constructed discursively (rather than as based on fixed traits).
2   Language may serve for individuals to cross and/or share certain identity barriers, and to construct hybrid identities.
3   Digital technologies have enabled different text, discourse, and social practices, including the birth of online, informal dictionaries, but these new practices have not and will not endanger standard English.
4   The concept of identity is also closely related to language learning, and the Internet may have a large impact upon the way in which language learners position themselves.

Who am I, and who are you?

In the past few decades, **identity** has received much attention in the field of applied linguistics – and actually in the humanities and social sciences as a whole. With such interest, new possibilities and different perspectives on its meaning, scope, and definition also appeared. For instance, while some see identity as an absolute and constitutive part of one's distinctiveness and base its formation on such traits as ethnicity, geographical origin, and accent, others understand it as a more subjective notion, one that can easily change and fluctuate depending on context. In this latter case, identity is constructed and fluid, rather than fixed.

In this book, we take both of these views seriously, although it is evident that we favor the latter. While personal traits relating to origin and geography are important for perceptions of identity, in the end we believe identity is mutable, never constant, and always constructed in discourse. Thus, even characteristics such as ethnicity, religion, gender, occupation, accent, marital status, and nationality are subject to one's agency. These particular traits, in and by themselves, are not enough to account for the complexities that exist in the construction of a person or a group's identity even when we acknowledge that their meaning and scope is dependent on social consensus and scrutiny too.

We should begin with some basic definitions. If we use Gee's (2011) definition, **identity** can be understood as the different ways of being something or someone in the world at different moments for distinct purposes. In other words, identity refers to the ways in which a person can be identified as a blogger, an activist, a surfer, a "good kid," an "A student," Latino, a supporter of this or that political party, and so on. There are two main paths to this process of identification. The first (Edwards, 2009) refers to a person's or a group's self-definition, that is, how an individual or a collective of individuals perceives him/herself (or themselves). The second (Gee, 2001:99) relates to what others imagine a person or group to be. When we bring these two understandings together, we can better appreciate not only how one's self-perception affects their place in the world, but also how one's image(s), observed and defined by others, influence(s) their sense of belonging.

This process of identity creation is not without tension. A person's perception of himself or herself can greatly differ from the way this same person is perceived by others. Just because we may think of ourselves as, for example, hard-working or artistically talented, it does not necessarily follow that this same perception is shared by others (even if our understandings of the concepts behind the words *talented* or *hard-working* are similar). The second consideration is that the words *hard-working* and *talented* (or any other identity-related terms) can vary a lot from one person (or culture, or society) to another. These factors actually support the claim that identities are constructed in discourse, since they depend on the people who are enacting them, their interlocutors, and the contexts of culture and situation at hand.

As explained by Halliday and Hasan (1989), **context of culture** refers to the shared cultural knowledge among interlocutors in a communicative interaction. **Context of situation** (which is within a context of culture), in its turn, reflects the contextual factors that are immediate to a particular interaction, including what is taking place, who is interacting, and what role language plays in that particular instance (if it is written, spoken, etc., and the purpose of its use). Therefore, in our example, within one group, "hard-working" might be primarily a function of how many hours a person works, or how much effort is put in, or how many different tasks they attempt at the same time; while for another group, the term might be directly related to the results a person obtains or how much money they make or even how much they advertise their working habits to others. The discourse around work will help establish what counts, and from then on, the construct will be talked about in those terms.

The following fictitious examples, inspired by ideas and interviews we found in open online sites, illustrate the point, this time focusing on concepts related to fame, such as being an icon or an artist.

> *Celebrity 1: I won't rest until I am thought of as an icon. Being just famous is not such a big deal anymore. In this virtual world we live in, anyone can be a celebrity*

or claim to be famous. "Pop Star" has even become just another word for 'great.' You do something nice for someone and they say, "You're a pop star!" Being an icon, now that's another story. People paint icons and hang their portraits in museums. Those are the people history remembers. Even the word has a nice ring to it. The adjective iconic is very nice too, as in "The year he released his iconic record." I really like that.

Celebrity 2: I don't like the word "celebrity." "Pop star" is also a little behind the times, and "diva" means that you are difficult. It's nice to be celebrated sometimes, but I think of myself more as an artist than a celebrity. Where I come from, that's what counts – how artistic you are. Celebrity passes really fast. In years to come, people only remember the true artists. They might say "one of the most important artists of the 20th century." They would never say "one of the most important celebrities of the 20th century."

Suppose that these statements were actually made by two celebrities (our fictitious interlocutors). These two quotes express somewhat different opinions about being a pop star. However, there is more in play than just mere opinion. If we look at the statements closely, we will see that both interlocutors want to be respected and strive for a place in history. They are also distancing themselves from the terms that they believe carry negative connotations (e.g., diva, celebrity, and even pop star). Where they differ is in the identity marker they want to pursue, with one preferring *icon* and the other *artist*. A sense of identity, then, will be pursued in relation to this construction, and success will be relative to the distance the person imagines there exists between them and the desired concept.

In these examples, language – even just a few words and statements – is generally used to enact identities. That is, people use words to make claims about who they are, who they wish to be, what they think matters, how they would like to be seen by others, and even how others actually see them. When you choose to speak to your teacher or professor in a certain way, and to your friends in a different way, and to your employer in yet another way, you are not only showing you know that certain manners of speaking (more formally or informally, for instance) and certain words are more appropriate in particular contexts, but also that you are a particular type of person in each of those situations (a close friend, a good employee or student, or – in the case of the examples cited above – an artist or an icon). Furthermore, you are showing that you wish to be seen in that light by your interlocutors (i.e., those communicating with you).

You make use of the resources in your **linguistic repertoire,** that is, your linguistic tool kit, to show different aspects of your identity, both actual and projected, to different people in different situations. In addition, in each one of these interactions, the language you use and the identities you enact will be closely related to other factors, including what types of relationships you have with your interlocutors, and how each one of you asserts, questions, and ultimately negotiates **linguistic power.**

By the same token, language is used to construct social links (such as relationships), and to establish boundaries, not only between concepts – like "artist" versus "pop star" – but also between people, countries, places, and many more. All of these notions (especially the more subjective ones, like what it means to be "good" or "bad," "hard-working," or "talented") and how they are used by people to enact their identities are built through language use in each individual interaction and context, which is what we mean when we say that identities are constructed **discursively**.

Discourse and identity are therefore closely linked. We will expand our notion of the latter by saying that discourse includes not only the use of verbal language, but also nonverbal language. As a result, how people dress, the tools and symbols they use, how they act, and how such elements affect the identities they enact are all part of discourse. This broader understanding of discourse is closely related to what Gee (2011) calls Big "D" Discourse (as opposed to little "d" discourse). Although we do not use that particular distinction in this book, you can refer to Gee (2011) for more details.

The concept of discourse thus presupposes the idea that language is a social phenomenon (Bakhtin, 1981:259). It also presumes that form and content in discourse "are one, once we understand that verbal discourse is a social phenomenon – social throughout its entire range and in each and every of its factors, from the sound image to the furthest reaches of abstract meaning," and therefore the study of it "must overcome the divorce between an abstract 'formal' approach and an equally abstract 'ideological' approach."

By the same token, therefore, the study of the construction of identities in virtual spaces necessitates an understanding of **online discourses**, including their forms and meanings, and their cultural and situational contexts, as well as an analysis of how people actually use technological tools and the online world as a whole to construct images of self and of different groups, to establish relationships with one another, and to accomplish different tasks in the world. Much like it happens with other domains of use, in the digital world, people select what aspects of their geographical, cultural, ethnic, racial, gender, and linguistic universe they display to others.

Complex understandings of identity: Nationality, class, ethnicity, race, gender, and sexual orientation in the virtual world

Factors generally considered fixed in one's life, such as one's ethnicity, nationality, gender, race, sexual orientation, and so forth (what Gee, 2001, calls **core identity**) play a significant part in the identity(ies) we enact and the relationships we build every day. As shown by John Edwards (2009:34–39), even things we may generally take for granted – such as an individual's or group's name – play a significant part in the identity that is built by such person or group. In fact, such presumably static factors as the ones mentioned earlier (nationality, gender, and so forth) are so strong that we often form our relationships solely based on them, and are judged based mainly on the labels that accompany them. Think, for instance, of how southerners and northerners in the US are perceived and portrayed in many circles, including mainstream media; of how some complex tensions are built on perceptions of "gender wars" (whether that is the case or not) or bring with them a strong tie to ethnicity and cultural heritage. These are just a few examples that illustrate how much the relationships we form, the groups we join, the manner we portray ourselves, and the ways we are seen by others are influenced by our looks, speech, the name we have, and our sociocultural backgrounds as a whole.

However, identity goes far beyond these factors. In fact, for the most part, it is in our discourses that we have the possibility (and some would actually say power) to construct our identities as we wish without being bound by identifiable characteristics over which (many times) we have no or little control. Several examples from different scholars in the humanities and social sciences illustrate what we mean. One example is **language crossing**, proposed by Ben Rampton (1995:485), whereby people who do not think of themselves (or who are not accepted) as members of a particular group (e.g., an ethnic group) **code-switch** into linguistic varieties that are not often associated with them. This process "involves a distinct sense of movement across social or ethnic boundaries and [. . .] raises issues of legitimacy which, in one way or another, participants need to negotiate in the course of their encounter" (Rampton, 1995:485).

Rampton (1995:489) looks specifically at "The ways that youngsters [in Britain] of Asian and Anglo descent used Caribbean-based Creole, the ways Anglos and Caribbeans used Panjabi, and the way stylized Indian English ('stylised Asian English - 'SAE') was used by all three." His investigation shows that this type of practice brings with it the possibility of negotiating ethnic and social identities through language. Language crossing helps young people both create common spaces with peers from different ethnicities, and also to denaturalize ethnic boundaries and identities in ways through which they can invoke and explore "momentarily inhabited ethnicities other than their own" (Rampton, 1995:508).

Language crossing also happens in online spaces. For instance, in a work investigating linguistic diversity on websites maintained for and by diaspora group members in Germany, Androutsopoulos (2006) shows that users of such websites often relied on various codes, as well as code-switching from their home languages to German and to English, in order to negotiate their diaspora-related identities. In another example (Thorne and Black, 2011:259), online language and literacy practices, such as Internet-mediated intercultural communication, blogging, and fan fiction, enable second language learners "to develop language skills as they participate in socially meaningful practices and develop situated identities." In one section of their text, Thorne and Black (2011:261–268) look at two different classroom-related contexts in which the use of Internet communication technologies allowed students to evoke new selves through a new language. In one of these contexts (where American high school students were enrolled in an advanced Spanish class), the authors observed that students considered Spanish to be a viable code for identity construction. Language crossing enabled them to develop ritualized greeting such as "Hola Señora."

According to Stuart Hall (1997:226), identity "is not an essence but a positioning." If this is the case for traits that seem to be so embedded into one's identity (such as language use, nationality, and ethnicity), it is even more true for other types of identities we may have – such as being a good student, a surfer, a video gamer, and so on. In fact, Judith Butler (1990) has claimed that our identities are usually performed to fit socially and culturally accepted prototypes of what it means to be a particular type of person. Many times our discourses are used to fit certain patterns and expectations, and to enact our identities in particular ways that may – at times, at least – differ from our true selves and feelings (in which case we would be forging our identities). Conversely, it also means that we can use our discourses to counter predetermined conventions on what it means to be this or that kind of person.[1]

Still, as pointed out by Django Paris (2009:431), it is important to be careful not to overstate what such phenomena as language crossing can do in unequal societies like many of the ones we have in the contemporary world. As Paris (2009:431) explains, though it is true that these and other practices are powerful, it is also the case that "other major markers of race, like skin color, play heavily into systems of discrimination, racism, and privilege." As a result, it is essential that we "recognize the importance of interethnic practices without falsely implying that they surmount systemic barriers." To bridge those barriers, we need equally systematic changes in institutional practices and discourse as well as in Culture, with the Big "C" (to speak of a parallel concept to Gee's Big "D" Discourse).

Global Englishes, linguistic networks, and identity

So, what exactly do the discussions we have advanced so far have to do with the online world and digital Englishes? First, let us take the importance of naming for one's identity. While we generally do not have any say in what we are called for the first few years of our lives (and in some places there are some restrictions on how you can name a child and what you can change your name to), in the online world such constraints do not exist. People (from any age group, ethnicity, nationality, etc.) choose different nicknames and take on different **pseudonyms**, **pen names**, and **avatars** based on their interests and on whatever else they see fit, reflecting their personalities and/or the identities they wish to enact and portray. Furthermore, one can have a number of different names in different realms of cyberspace, each reflecting a different persona or facet of identity. In fact, it is not unusual to hear of people who pretend to be someone different from who they are in "real life" when they go online, or people who actually become a different person when they play games or go on chat websites on the Internet (for more on the electronic personality, see Aboujaoude, 2011).

Still, on the subject of naming, it is quite common to find that many of the "new names" people give themselves (or their new selves) sometimes use elements (i.e., words or affixes) from other languages, including English, depending on the references they want to make (e.g., to manga or video game characters). However, it is not just personal names that are influenced by their online environments. A number of new businesses and startups created online also highlight aspects of their commercial identities, at times choosing English or some element from it (notice the predominance of affixes such as *tech*, *inter*, or *tel*) due to reasons such as its association with modernity, globalization, and technology, or its wide appeal to larger groups on a worldwide level (Friedrich, 2002).

The discursive construction of an individual's, a group's, or a company's online identities thus starts from the act of naming themselves. Such construction can then take on different routes. For instance, in social network websites, we have the choice of uploading avatars, pictures, and videos; entering certain discussion groups; "liking" specific people and things; showing where we have been; commenting on others' posts and pictures; and so on. All of these choices reflect an identity (or a number of identities) we want to build for ourselves – how we want to think of ourselves and how we wish to be seen by others. In blogs and websites, in the forums where we participate, and even in the sites we just simply visit, we are not only constructing and publishing (or viewing) the information we find interesting and/or important, but we are also (and at times most of all) constructing our identities as cool people, nerds, popular teens, jocks, intellectuals, feminists, wine connoisseurs, fashionistas, environmentalists, etc. Moreover, with the high flexibility of the Internet, its chaotic nature, and the innumerous influences we get online from different locations, cultures, and so on, we have the chance of being more than one thing at the same time, and multiple things at different times. That is, the Internet has given us more elasticity in terms of building and rebuilding different (and many times hybrid) identities (see Clothier, 2005).

English has played some interesting roles in such discursive constructions of online identities, roles that go beyond naming the possibilities it affords. For instance, in a study of English words used by Brazilian speakers of English online (Diniz de Figueiredo, 2010), it became clear that some groups (e.g., skateboarders, gamers, bloggers, surfers) use English loanwords both to mark exclusive group identity within Brazil, and to create intergroup associations with people of similar interests and hobbies on an international level. In another, Wei Zhang (2012:51) discusses mixing languages in China:

> For the young generation in mainland China, mixing is neither shame nor showing off, it is simply part of their everyday communication practices through which they build their multicultural identities, transform traditional social relationships and practice their social responsibilities (often coated with irony) in an increasingly open China, using new communication technologies as well as their linguistic and cultural repertoires.

The concept of identity (and of global or international identifications) is thus very closely tied to the notion of **social networks** we presented in chapter 2, and to the expansion of those networks that has been caused by digital communications. In terms of online interactions, we have the possibility of engaging with different people around the world, and of positioning ourselves as global individuals who belong to spaces that go beyond our territorial, ethnic, socioeconomic, and cultural barriers and borders – at times engaging in acts of **code-switching**, **language crossing**, and/or **language sharing** (see more in Paris, 2009).[2] And as shown by Diniz de Figueiredo (2010), in the case of English loanword use online, the bonds and ties established by certain groups are based on more than notions of territory, ethnicity, gender, or class; they are many times based on affinity and similar interests. It is through these affinities and interests that we develop our linguistic networks, not only on a local level but also on a global one, through the mediation of, among other things, the Internet and English.

Googlish, textish, Facebookean, and life in 140 characters

In his conceptualization of critical discourse analysis (or CDA), Norman Fairclough (1995) explains that there are three types of practice that must be taken into account in the study of discourses: a) the **text practice**, which refers to the textual features of a particular discourse (i.e., its grammar, vocabulary, and so on); b) the **discourse practice**, which has to do with the production, distribution, and consumption of a text; and c) the **social practice**, which consists of the sociocultural context of which the text or communicative event is part.

If we take this framework proposed by Fairclough into consideration in order to better appreciate language practices in virtual space, then much can be said (although it must be made clear that we will not strictly follow Fairclough's CDA here) in regards to virtual communications. For one, text practices in the digital sphere have shown interesting changes in terms of spelling (as seen in the language of texting), grammar (with much approximation of written language to spoken conventions and uses), punctuation (many times omitted or ignored), and vocabulary (with the coining of new words to account for new trends and technologies, and the use of English loanwords in many other languages to reflect such changes as well). For another, discourse practices have their own peculiarities, given the emergence of new (many times hybrid) genres in online spaces, and the new roles that individuals and groups can now have as co-constructors of knowledge and information. Moreover, in terms of such discourse practices, we can say that there exists much faster production, distribution, and consumption of texts. Such speed has led to a certain banalization of news and information (both in terms of *what* is news and how easy it is for us to forget and/or replace information) and to a constant need for everything (or at least almost everything) to be new, fast, and more easily digestible.

Finally, we see that the current textual and discursive practices just described both reflect our current social practices (which have to do with the emergence of the digital era itself) and influence them at the same time – since new discursive and textual habits bring new necessities, trends, and inventions with them (e.g., new genres like the "social media website" have increased our necessity to feel always connected with one another, in turn influencing the ways we have incorporated smartphones into our daily realities).

If we look at different media (websites, apps, etc.) more specifically, we can better illustrate the changes we are discussing. For instance, in terms of discourse practices, the creation of search engines, which may be considered new genres or new versions of older genres such as "the encyclopedia," have led to a change in how we conceptualize, search for, and even store information, making it easier and faster for us to do so.

In fact, the same can be said of many other types of discourse practices. The way and speed at which we produce, distribute, and consume news, personal opinion, personal data (including images and videos), professional products such as music, e-books, and websites have changed dramatically since the arrival of personal computers and of the Internet. This is especially the case with media such as social network websites and apps, blogs, video- and music-sharing platforms, and online forums. With certain devices and platforms limiting the number of characters and/or words that can be written in a message, chances are the ways we write in other platforms have been modified too. These limitations have also taught us new skills: if you have to ensure that a message is effective in 140 characters, you need special linguistic abilities to accomplish that goal. Even more interestingly, those new genres and formats reflect back into "real world" practices.

What matters in communication is also a feature of the times in which texts are produced. For example, in the past, many people (especially when using type-writers) had to pay more attention to such linguistic elements as spelling and punctuation while writing than we do today, given the now widespread availability of spell check and grammar check tools. Other changes include the language of texting itself (with its own spelling and other conventions) and the more informal manner in which certain texts (sometimes even more serious ones) are written. While these changes might make it seem that the very dynamics of language have changed, we do not believe that is the case. It is the very respect for the dynamics of language that lead to these changes. If it is matters of purpose and audience that define how we use language in the real world and in the virtual world, should the purpose change (e.g., communicate succinctly, not for the purpose of documentation but for immediate response, at an informal level, with peers), then language will also change to conform to these expectations.

As for social practices, a direct relationship exists between them and the changes we have just mentioned. Discourse and text practices have been influenced by a sociocultural world that has become faster and has welcomed the creation and development of new technologies (especially the Internet) and spaces (mainly cyberspace). For that reason, we can also make the claim that our new ways of using language have influenced society and culture as a whole. Consider, for instance, the way certain words and expressions that were originally used exclusively online (or in texting language) have now extrapolated into the "real" world, not only in writing but also in speaking. Examples include OMG, lol, lawlz, IDK, BFF, etc. Consider as well how the practice of writing with a limited number of characters (140 usually, if we try to be more exact) may have influenced the way we write in other spheres. Consider, for example, the possibility of a professor asking a student to be as succinct in stating her thesis as she would be in writing a post on Twitter (an event that actually did take place and was witnessed by one of the present authors more than once in academia).

Thus, it is not an overstatement to say that certain digital media (such as specific blog platforms or social media websites) have developed their own types of language in terms of text and discourse practices. Perhaps more interestingly, it is also not an exaggeration to claim that such practices have not only reflected social changes, but have themselves sometimes been the cause of such transformations. Whether we can call some of these discourses new varieties, and come up with new names for them (like *textish* or *googlish*), as some already do, may be an entirely different question; in any case, the influence that these new types of language use have had in our sociocultural realities seems unquestionable.

Cross-wiring spaces and identities

In this latest reality of text, discourse, and social practices (as defined by Fairclough, 1995), new virtual spaces and networks emerge and are navigated by different people, thus becoming important for the enactment of their identities. An illustration of this statement in terms of text practices is the use of texting in digital language, which we have discussed in previous chapters. The fact that texting language was (and most likely still is) mainly associated with teenagers and young adults has meant that that particular type of language use is considered an identity marker associated with these groups. When individuals who are not members of such groups use texting, it may seem that they are either trying to convey new identities for themselves, or that they are engaging in acts of **language crossing** or **language sharing** for one reason or another.

The recent higher rate of usage and acceptability of texting has led more and more people from different kinds of backgrounds and social networks to engage with it more often. Nevertheless, this fact alone does not signal socially ratified acceptance of the use of texting by anyone at any given moment. For instance, although the term *lol* seems to have entered into the mainstream usage of English speakers – with people from various different social groups using it, especially online – it has gained new meanings for different groups, especially for those who most likely coined or popularized the expression: teenagers. In that manner, many adolescents simply stopped using *lol* once the term became prevalent among adults, which is a clear sign that they felt the expression no longer served to identify their distinctiveness in comparison to other groups. This, again, is part of dynamics that have been in operation in the real world in the case of slang, for example. One of the reasons for the transitory nature of slang is that once it becomes mainstream, many of the groups that originated the trend disengage from the use, as it is not an identifier of their uniqueness anymore. In time, the term can also lose currency among those who originally engaged in language crossing because the motivation (to share the identity of a group they found cool, modern, or influential) is not there anymore.

However, what is perhaps more interesting (and even fascinating) is that some of these teens now claim the term back, but with a different meaning: that of mocking the adults who use it.[3] The very term *lawlz* (which reproduces the way the acronym *lol* would sound if read as a word) points to that reclaiming. In other words, when many teens now use the expressions *lol* and *lawlz*, they are mainly doing it to show irony and/or sarcasm towards those who had **appropriated** the term, perhaps due to its supposed coolness or practicality in informal messages and conversations (most of which happens online).

Thus, we may say that the text practices of different groups and/or individuals are generally in conflict with those of others, mainly because of identity issues; that is, the spaces certain groups navigate and the identities they wish to enact for themselves many times cross-wire with those of other people and groups, a fact that is clearly reflected in how they construct (or not) their texts.

The same is true for discourse practices, especially in regards to the spaces in which different types of individuals seem to enter to encounter and dissemi-nate information. The most popular and widely used social media website we know today, Facebook, was once closed only to students of specific elite universi-ties, first in the US and then worldwide. This factor alone ensured users a sense of exclusivity, of belonging to a group that only pertained to those similar to them (in terms of academic – and usually socioeconomic – background, at least). Being part of such a network thus provided a sense of coolness and distinctive-ness among those who had access to that social networking website – as if they belonged (and actually they did) to a restricted club or society.

Later, that particular website became open to the general public and started to become more and more popular among adolescents. Until 2013, it was actually the most popular social network for this particular group. This demographic only began to change from 2013 to 2014, after the site started to grow in popularity among adults also. As put by Victor Luckerson in an article published in *Time* in March 2013,[4] the site had lost its "cool" for teenagers, since it increasingly included not only their friends but also their parents, aunts, uncles, grandparents, and so on. As reported by Aaron Pressman of *Yahoo Finance*, as of January 2014, over three million teenage users in the US alone had fled the website.[5] As you can see, the linguistic phenomenon involving acronym and slang mirror the larger social phenomenon of identification, dis-identification, and network formation.

Even though this may seem to be simply a case of saving face and not exposing oneself to authority figures, like parents and older people in general, it is clearly also one of identity. *Coolness* is generally not only linked to but also sought after by teens; and thus, once a product begins to "lose its cool," it no longer serves to distinguish teens from adults (who are generally believed by adolescents to be uncool). That is, it can no longer be used by them to assert a particular trait that they think belongs exclusively to them, and not to their parents and other older relatives.

Overall, these examples of cross-wiring spaces and identities, reflected in the text and discourse practices of individuals and groups, reveal the symbolic strength that language has in how people define themselves and are defined by others. As explained by John Edwards (2009:5), "it is the symbolic charge that language carries that makes it such an important component in individual and group identity." Although such a statement may be understood by some simply in terms of one's native language (English versus Spanish, for instance) or dominant linguistic variety (e.g., African American Vernacular English or Chicano English), it encompasses all of our text, discourse, and ultimately social practices.

In the online world more specifically, such strength is undeniable and has served to define many boundaries between groups, either through methods and spaces used for finding and disseminating information (discourse practice), or text practices themselves, as exemplified by the case of texting. In fact, some of the most intriguing issues that have taken place in the online sphere (including websites that become more or less popular, or discussions over whether texting is harmful and/or should be banned) are related to identity.

Online reference sources

In this fast-changing world of new language practices being influenced by digital technology and by the power many now have to construct and disseminate knowledge and information, it is not surprising to see a growing number of innovative reference materials being created and published online to encapsulate collective knowledge and understanding. What is probably more curious from a linguistic point of view, however, is the emergence and growth of online informal dictionaries, which exist in different languages; these informal dictionaries have become very popular and widely used over the years, and were created and are updated not by academic experts or so-called knowledge authorities, but by laypeople – many of whom are (not surprisingly) teenagers. Their purely online nature and extensive (in many cases unlimited) number of contributors ensure that they can be (and are) updated at a much faster pace than our traditional dictionaries. In addition, such influence has gone beyond language alone (in its strict sense) and has extended into realms such as politics, pop culture, law, and the media (all of which are closely related to language).

Urban Dictionary (UD), the most widely used and widespread of these online dictionaries in the English language, is a perfect illustration of what we have been discussing. According to linguistic anthropologist Rachel E. Smith, as of 2009 over 2.5 million authors had submitted more than 5.5 million definitions to this particular online source, and in 2010 alone the website had been visited by 146 million people 260 million times.[6] Smith's article (2011:45) shows how UD has subverted traditional lexicography – that in which dictionaries had the ultimate say on what was or was not a real word – and allowed for "an alternative to this prescriptivist tradition as an online democratic dictionary shaped by the masses." She explains that the dictionary has four particular types of definitions: 1) standard words with standard definitions; 2) standard words with non-standard definitions; 3) new words comprising completely new morphemes (the example provided is *meh*, which is a "universal, non-committal answer to every question ever posed"); and 4) new words that combine old morphemes for new meanings (an interesting example of which is *slanguage*). While standard meanings may be respected (at least at times), non-traditional, non-restrictive forms of conceptualizing words and ultimately language itself are also featured. In Smith's (2011:47) own words, UD "provides an alternative to prescriptive norms and practices as well as the way in which an entire generation is thinking about language."

This kind of democratization of language conceptualizing, which relies primarily on a descriptive stance rather than a prescriptive one, significantly shakes the belief that language knowledge is in the hands of specialists rather than with language users everywhere. While some may think that the influence of UD and other similar dictionaries is limited to youth culture (or even to a broader pop culture), evidence has shown that their impact extends far beyond these realms. For instance, as shown by Johnny Davis in a 2011 article for *The Guardian*,[7] UD has been used by the Royal Courts of Justice in the UK to help a judge understand the meaning of *fo shizzle my nizzle* (slang for "for sure, my friend" and other expressions of agreement[8]) and *mish mish man* (a person with a reputation for being the center of intense but superficial social life); and by the Department of Motor Vehicles in the US to decide whether to grant certain requests for license plates. It has also been very important for the media industry, UD having played a part in decisions made by television channels of whether or not to air certain movies and episodes of TV shows.

In fact, as shown by Smith, UD has had major impact even on the **lexicography** of English itself, with many words (such as *bromance* and *chillax*) moving up from informal dictionaries to some more formal and highly regarded ones, such as the *Oxford English Dictionary*. She goes on to claim that:

> This shift in paradigm for traditional lexicography thus indicates an increasing openness to new words, moving from a model historically based on rationality, analogy, logic, and etymology to one based more on usage. By slowly increasing entries to reflect popular and current usage, prescriptivist dictionaries have begun to acknowledge speakers, rather than solely texts, as sources of authority. And much of that authority is now coming from Urban Dictionary.
>
> (Smith, 2011:47)

When we think of identity more specifically, then, we see that *Urban Dictionary* and other similar sources are important in at least two ways. First, they empower young people in such a manner that they are able to contest their historical reduced linguistic capital and authority, and allow a global youth community to reposition themselves "as lexicographers able to make and review linguistic meanings" (Smith, 2011:47). Second, they force authoritative voices themselves to at least question more prescriptivist actions and decisions in relation to language, and to rethink the roles of real language users and the importance they have in how a language is shaped. In other words, the roles and identities of users and authority figures have been reshaped by themselves and in relation to each other.

Has standard English been deleted?

When we think about all of these changes in language as a whole, especially the ones that have to do with text practices, new vocabulary, and even the development of a new, unofficial, parallel lexicography, a new question may also emerge: has standard English been erased or deleted altogether? The answer, of course, is no – despite the fact that many today (especially purist commentators) claim that "real" or "correct" English (or even language as a whole, for that matter) has become or is becoming extinct.

Standard English not only continues to exist, but it also remains quite strong, especially because standard language is a matter of dynamic positioning rather than form. Many of the books we read, mainly the academic ones, are (and will most likely continue to be) written in standard English (even if the *form* that English takes changes). The same holds true for many other academic and non-academic publications, such as magazines, newspapers, journals, and so on. Human institutions such as schools and institutes, grammar books, and individuals in positions of academic and writing authority continue to teach and spread information regarding standard varieties. The same case also applies to official documents, such as contracts, bills, and laws. In fact, we would not have to look for very long to see that even on websites, including those created and updated by regular, ordinary people – and we mean many of them – we will find clear examples of standard English being used.

Standard English is also an important source in spoken language. When you watch the news on most channels in the US and in other English-using environments, when you listen to public radio, or when you hear a public address by the president of that country, for instance, you will likely hear standard American English. When you watch the news on British television, or hear the Prime Minister or the Queen of England speak on television, you are being exposed to standard British English varieties. If you attend a conference in India, or Nigeria, or Jamaica, you will most likely hear many of the attendees using the standard varieties of Indian, Nigerian, and Jamaican English, respectively; and if you watch the news in those countries, the same will also hold true.

In fact, it is very probable that you, the educated reader of this book, also use a particular standard variety of English in certain specific settings and situations (both spoken and written), such as academic conferences, college classes, conversations with your in-laws, or when writing a response to a website article that you found interesting or appalling. In other words, standard English remains real, not only in the mouths and pens and keyboards of those who work for the news, but also in those of many other, regular people. The boundaries of what constitutes standard language as well as the particular forms considered standard at a given time and place are the elements likely to change over a period of time.

What has actually happened, then, to the English language with the emergence of new text practices such as texting, or the development of new words and a completely new lexicography, such as the one we see in online informal dictionaries? One answer we can give to this question when we think about vocabulary more specifically is that new words have always been developed and incorporated into English and other languages alike, in which case nothing really new would be taking place, other than the fact that the new vocabulary we now see being used reflects a new cyber-reality. When we think more in relation to changes in spelling, as it happens in texting, we can also say something similar: spelling reductions and/or abbreviations have always been part of English in its development throughout history (for a more detailed explanation, see Crystal, 2008). Overall, all of these changes reflect the incorporation of new technologies into our world. To confirm this hypothesis, consider how English was modified from the standard of the time to conform to the new demands of the telegraph or telegram (it was expensive to include too many words, so only content words tended to make it), or how shorthand note-taking relied on a really abbreviated system of writing. Is that really so different from the 140-character message?

There is a little more to it than that, though. As we said earlier, the emergence of online dictionaries and the new lexicography that has come with them reveal the power that such new technologies has afforded to people (for more on power, see chapter 4); and this power has made it possible for many – especially youth – to re-conceptualize themselves in relation to institutions that once had total control over what counted in relation to language (such as dictionaries and grammar books). Informally and privately, in their spheres of influence, people had been doing this all along. The new public spaces now allow for further broadcasting of innovation and collaboration among language users. In other words, the Web has allowed people to locate themselves in positions of power, and to enact identities either as creators of new knowledge and rules for several things (including language), or as contesters (or mockers) of the authorities that seemed to hold such power exclusively in the first place.

What some may fear – either consciously or unconsciously – to be at stake, therefore, is not standard English per se, but the exclusivity that some groups once had in terms of what counts or does not count in relation to English language use. In fact, when we think of standard English itself (and not of those who serve to establish it), we may actually say that its power remains intact; after all, standard English is still the prestige variety in several institutions that are associ-ated with power and privilege, such as schools, universities, and the government.

Identity and English language learning in virtual space

A final issue that we must consider here is the close relationship between iden-tity and language learning and the implications that the online sphere may have had upon such relation. As shown by Norton and Toohey (2011), the intersection between language learning and identity issues has been of grow-ing interest to scholars and practitioners in TESOL (Teachers of English to Speakers of Other Languages) and applied linguistics. Although such work was once considered from a **structuralist** perspective, Norton and Toohey have explained that more recently, a more **poststructuralist** understanding of iden-tity has developed, implying that the term has been understood as not fixed or decontextualized, but as discursively constructed, "fluid, context-dependent, and context-producing, in particular historical and cultural circumstances" (Norton and Toohey, 2011:419).

Two very important concepts for the existing relation between identity and language learning are **investment** and **imagined communities/imagined identi-ties**, both of which bring a more sociolinguistic perspective to the area of second-language acquisition. The former (**investment**) was proposed by Norton Peirce (1995:17) as learners' understanding that if they devote time, effort, and energy to learning a second language, "they will acquire a wider range of symbolic and material resources, which will in turn increase the value of their cultural capi-tal."[9] The concept contrasts with the construct of **motivation**, which is framed as a fixed (as opposed to fluid) characteristic of individual learners, who may or may not have enough or appropriate desire to learn for a number of reasons. Invest-ment, on the other hand, sees such desire as a flowing characteristic, one that can change depending on contextual factors, and that is tightly linked to students' changing identities. Thus, for instance, while a student may be highly motivated to learn, he/she may not invest in certain activities in a language classroom for various reasons (feeling of embarrassment, different views on learning from those of the instructor, understanding that he/she has nothing to gain from that activ-ity, etc.).

As for the term **imagined community**, it was first proposed by Benedict Ander-son (1991) to refer to the fact that the nation-state exists as an imagined entity, one in which we feel to be connected to the other members (even those we have never met), thus creating imagined alliances with them. For example, when one thinks of the US, France, Nigeria, etc., as one's nation, that person generally assumes he/she is united with the other members of such community, although that person will never actually see, hear, or directly engage with a large number of those other members in any particular manner. In second-language acquisition, the term **imagined community** was adapted and applied by Norton (2010:355) and gained a new meaning: "A reconstruction of past communities and historically constituted relationships, but also a community of the imagination – a desired community that offers possibilities for an enhanced range of identity options in the future."[10] In practice, this means that students' learning of a second language is many times related to the communities in which they participate – or wish to participate – and to how they imagine their particular involvement in those communities. Such notions may play a very important part in how much they actually invest in learning a particular language, and how they position themselves in relation to other users.

These concepts are very important when we consider the impact of digital technology and especially of the Internet upon English language learning. For instance, considering the shrinkage of time and space barriers that existed before the Web, it is arguable that the possibilities of communities in which students can imagine to participate (and their actual potential to effectively be part of them) has increased. This is true when we think of the growing number of video game communities online, or of the increasing number of people who interact in blogs or in fan-fiction communities.

It is also arguable that there is more room for positions of power to be negotiated (among native and nonnative speakers, for example) in the online sphere, since Internet users can shape their identities in a larger number of ways without any of the time/space constraints that might make such positioning more difficult. Take, for instance, how a student can now portray himself/herself (on the Web) as an expert in video games, a book reviewer, a movie critic, and so on. In fact, some studies have already started to look into these issues, showing how in some cases pupils may provide themselves broader learning opportunities online than those available to them in schools (see Lam, 2006), or improve their social relationships and reputations through instant messaging (Lewis and Fabos, 2005).

The case of English may be particularly interesting when we look at these factors, especially because its large number of speakers may give learners larger possibilities of communities with which to interact, and a higher chance of finding others who may share their interests and/or expertise, anxieties, insecurities, etc. (and with whom they may possibly communicate more comfortably, therefore). Moreover, the global status of the language may give students the possibility of imagining themselves as members of larger global communities, which expand far beyond their territorial boundaries.

Still, as explained by Norton and Toohey (2011), we cannot view digital technology in language learning only in positive terms. At the same time that they can empower students and give them a voice in a context that goes beyond their local realities, technological advances can also cause cultural misunderstandings and even more inequality between those who have access to them and those who do not. To question the extent, tenor, and form of the use of technology in education is paramount to arriving at socially responsible, cultural-understanding fostering, and ultimately, collaborative practices.

The importance of identity

In this chapter, we hope to have shown you the importance of identity in relation to language, and how the two concepts are closely intertwined. It is our belief – and many other scholars in applied linguistics, sociolinguistics, and language education would agree – that one cannot have a complete account of language and society, and language teaching and learning, without a consideration of identity issues. Although we believe we have provided a thorough introduction to the topic in this chapter, we know that the complexities of identity cannot be exhausted in a few pages, especially when we consider the virtual domain. In fact, we can say with much certainty that the online world and all of its nuances have made the construct of identity even more complex and less fixed. It is not an overstatement to say that many new challenges lie ahead for those of us who wish to continue studying the intricacies of identity and its implications, especially after the emergence of new digital communications.

Questions for discussion

1   Do you agree with the statement that identity is better conceived as a discursively constructed entity, rather than a fixed one? Why/why not? Can you think of examples from your own life that illustrate your perspective?

2   We showed different text, discourse, and social practices that have been enabled by digital technologies. Can you think of other examples? Have they impacted your own language use? If so, how?

3   What bits of your identity do you think you have reinforced online? What kind of language have you used to do that?

4   Have you ever used and/or contributed to an online dictionary? Tell us about your experience.

5   Can you come up with terms that could be added to an online dictionary of informal, slang, and emerging words and expressions?

Notes

1 For more on **performativity**, see Butler (1990).
2 See, for instance, Moita Lopes (2008).
3 More data and a systematic analysis would be necessary in order to substantiate these claims more strongly. Still, these anecdotal accounts by, and observations of, the teenagers seem at least worthy of noting and presenting here. We encourage further research to investigate this type of phenomenon.
4 Retrieved in August 2014 from http://business.time.com/2013/03/08/is-facebook-losing-its-cool-some-teens-think-so/

5 For more details, see http://finance.yahoo.com/blogs/the-exchange/about-11-million-fewer-likes-for-facebook-among-the-teenage-set-154852067.html (retrieved in August 2014).
6 Smith (2011). See also Damaso and Cotter (2007).
7 Retrieved in August 2014 from http://www.theguardian.com/books/2011/apr/21/in-praise-urban-dictionaries
8 We are aware that the use of standard language ("for sure, my friend") does not capture the full dimension and connotation of the expression. However, we cannot decide if the expression employs a softener to avoid the original offensive term or is simply a play on words. At any rate, any one of these choices carries cultural meanings and social repercussions that the reader must be wise to.
9 For more on cultural capital, see chapter 4.
10 See also Kanno and Norton (2003).

References and suggested further reading

Aboujaoude, E. (2011). *Virtually you: The dangerous powers of the e-personality*. New York: W. W. Norton & Company.

Anderson, B. (1991). *Imagined communities: Reflections on the origin and spread of nationalism*. New York: Verso.

Androutsopoulos, J. (2006). Multilingualism, diaspora, and the Internet: Codes and identities on German-based diaspora websites. *Journal of Sociolinguistics, 10*(4), 520–547.

Bakhtin, M. M. (1981). *The dialogic imagination: Four essays*. Austin: University of Texas Press.

Bhabha, H. K. (1994). *The location of culture*. London: Routledge.

Butler, J. (1990). *Gender trouble: Feminism and the subversion of identity*. New York: Routledge.

Clothier, I. M. (2005). Created identities: Hybrid cultures and the internet. *Convergence, 11*(4), 44–59.

Crystal, D. (2008). *Txtng: The gr8 db8*. Oxford: Oxford University Press.

Damaso, J., & Cotter, C. (2007). Urbandictionary.com. *English Today, 23*(2), 19–26.

Diniz de Figueiredo, E. H. (2010). To borrow or not to borrow: The use of English loanwords as slang on websites in Brazilian Portuguese. *English Today, 26*(4), 5–12.

Edwards, J. (2009). *Language and identity*. Cambridge: Cambridge University Press.

Fairclough, N. (1995). *Critical discourse analysis: The critical study of language*. Harlow: Pearson.

Friedrich, P. (2002). English in advertising and brand naming: Sociolinguistic considerations and the case of Brazil. *English Today, 18*(3), 21–28.

Gee, J. P. (2001). Identity as an analytic lens for research in education. *Review of Research in Education, 25*, 99–125.

Gee, J. (2011). *An introduction to discourse analysis: Theory and method*. New York: Routledge.

Hall, S. (1997). *Representation: Cultural representations and signifying practices*. London: Sage.

Halliday, M. A. K., & Hasan, R. (1989). *Language, context, and text: Aspects of text in a social-semiotic perspective*. Oxford: Oxford University Press.

Kanno, Y., & Norton, B. (Eds.) (2003). Imagined communities and educational possibilities. *Journal of Language, Identity, and Education, 2*(4), 285–300.

Lam, W. S. E. (2006). Re-envisioning language, literacy and the immigrant subject in new mediascapes. *Pedagogies: An International Journal, 1*(3), 171–195.

Lewis, C., & Fabos, B. (2005). Instant messages, literacies and social identities. *Reading Research Quarterly*, 40(4), 470–501.

Moita Lopes, L. P. (2008). Inglês e globalização em uma epistemologia de fronteira: Ideologia linguística para tempos híbridos [English and globalization in a border epistemology: Linguistic ideology for hybrid times]. *D.E.L.T.A.*, 24(2), 309–340.

Norton, B. (2010). Language and identity. In N. H. Hornberger and S. L. McKay (Eds.), *Sociolinguistics and language education* (pp. 349–369). Tonawanda, NY: Multilingual Matters.

Norton, B., & Toohey, K. (2011). Identity, language learning, and social change. *Language Teaching*, 44(4), 412–446.

Norton Peirce, B. (1995). Social identity, investment, and language learning. *TESOL Quarterly*, 29(1), 9–31.

Paris, D. (2009). They're in my culture, they speak the same way: African American language in multiethnic high schools. *Harvard Education Review*, 79(3), 428–447.

Rampton, B. (1995). Language crossing and the problematisation of ethnicity and socialization. *Pragmatics*, 5(4), 485–513.

Smith, R. E. (2011). Urban dictionary: Youths language and the redefining of definition. *English Today*, 27(4), 43–48.

Thorne, S. L., & Black, R. W. (2011). Identity and interaction in Internet-mediated contexts. In C. Higgins (Ed.), *Identity formation in globalizing contexts: Language learning in the new millennium* (pp. 257–278). New York: Mouton de Gruyter.

Zhang, W. (2012). Chinese-English code-mixing among China's netizens. *English Today*, 28(3), 40–52.

Chapter 6

The sociolinguistics of gender and race construction on the Internet

This chapter will help you understand that:

1   To better figure out the role of gender and race in society, one needs to address the socially constructed aspects of those concepts.
2   The Internet is a new site for the presentation, discussion, and study of gender, race, and ethnicity issues.
3   Cyberspaces offer the opportunity for the reaffirmation and expansion of gender, racial, and ethnic identity.
4   Cyberspaces also present new challenges vis-à-vis the representation and appropriation of gender, race, and ethnicity-related linguistic expressions.
5   Disability must be considered alongside gender and ethnicity when it comes to discussions about diversity in the real world and in the virtual world.
6   The Internet may be the newest and one of the most prolific sites for gender and race activism. In many instances, the two intersect.

Introduction

The Internet era has created new challenges but also new and endless possibilities for communication and for the construction of our digital selves, as you saw in chapter 5 about identity. We say construction because, as we have explained throughout this book, through language (specifically our different discourses), we have the power of enacting our selves in the manners we wish; moreover, in our current times more specifically, the relative anonymity and the mediated nature of communications on the Web allow us to select what to become with fewer boundaries and what to show the world more deliberately. Consequently, these new media have also brought with their innovation new questions about the ways we build our identities, use language, and present ourselves to others.

One only needs to observe their contacts in social media networks, for example, to start forming a taxonomy of the people they interact with; and if they are self-aware of their own linguistic, topic, and subject-area preferences, they will see that individuals tend to utilize online media in ways that soon become a pattern, showing that certain primary purposes predominate, even when others are present. For instance, some people see the networks where they interact as potential loci for activism, for presenting points of view and information regarding subjects and issues they care about, and that they believe need attention and awareness. Others might choose subjects and pieces of information that are more inspirational in nature, seeing in the vast number of Internet sources and contacts a possibility of personal growth and spiritual fulfillment, and, in social media, an opportunity to broadcast such processes. Others might have more everyday but equally important goals, such as keeping in touch with family and friends who live far away, and thus reveal themselves to the world as social beings who engage in social and family activities often, and who care about their personal relationships whether they are near or far. Others still, shy and introverted in the "real" world, might find that their ability to communicate and share ideas is enhanced by a computer-mediated environment, and thus might choose to learn and/or teach through virtual communications.

While the possibilities are endless, and one person is likely to use digital communications for a variety of purposes, it is not unusual for a few of those to prevail, especially at the personal level. Our "avatars" are not ourselves; they are the ways we choose to make ourselves known to the world; and the language choices we make (i.e., which language we pick, level of formality, length, tone) are important aspects of this composition and storytelling.

Even though we generally expect to find great informality and less-formal linguistic styles on the Internet, that is not uniformly the case. Factors such as age and occupation do mediate the language choices of Internet users, and also, as you saw in chapter 5, help us establish who is inside and outside particular networks. We, the writers of this book, see, for example, among our network of language teachers and academics, a much greater attempt to strive for a variety of English closer to a notion of "standard." On the other hand, younger users or those belonging to particular linguistic networks (e.g., gamers) might use other degrees of formality that they might associate with the purpose and audience of their messages. They might further specialize their language, as we mentioned in earlier chapters, to help demarcate who is in and who is out of the group by sometimes even being unintelligible to others, as if they were using a secret language.

The way we present ourselves in virtual environments is therefore that construction, linguistic and otherwise. It does not represent us in our entirety, but is rather a facet of our human experience (remember the fragmented nature of self for poststructuralism) that is somewhat dictated by the aspects of ourselves we want others to know, the demands of the medium, as well as the elements of our experience we care about more at a given point in time. From our choice of media to the topics we focus on, to the people we interact with more often, everything is related to our purposes, our audience, and our constructed identity.

Gender

Given the above introduction, it is reasonable to assume that issues of gender, ethnicity, and race are also mediated, influenced, and modified by our use of new media. As we explained in chapter 5, these elements – which play a significant role in how we are seen by ourselves and by others – are sometimes mistakenly taken as static in one's identity, as if they were always the same and meant the same thing to everyone. However, as we also stated in chapter 5, through our discourses (e.g., in moments of **language crossing** and **language sharing**), we have the chance of shaping our experience and of either approximating or distancing ourselves from easily identifiable characteristics which – many believe – often serve to identify us.

Some more specific questions we can raise in regards to gender, race, and ethnicity in this digital era therefore include whether digital communications have accelerated activism and awareness of issues, if representation has changed, and if linguistic change has followed (or sometimes spearheaded) these other aspects of change. In this chapter, we will write about these issues in general, but also give specific attention to how they have particularly affected those from **minority linguistic groups**. By minority, we (and many other humanities and social sciences scholars) do not necessarily mean those groups with fewer numbers of people, but actually those who have less social and linguistic power within a society, and who are often **othered** (against a mainstream "majority") when it comes to having a strong say in sociopolitical issues. In many Western societies, they generally include, but are not limited to, women, members of the LGBTQA (lesbian, gay, bi-, trans-, queer,[1] and asexual) community, immigrants, people of color, people living with disabilities, and any combination therein.

The first of these elements we will reflect on is gender construction. In some contexts, you may have read "sex" and "gender" being used interchangeably. However, most people engaged in humanities and social sciences scholarship/research distinguish between the biologically driven description of sex and the culturally mediated construction of gender. In this sense, biological sex tends to be a binary (i.e., female vs. male) classification, while gender tends to be increasingly described as fluid and non-binary (refer to our discussion on identity). This is not to say that the binary nature of sex, or its basis on strictly natural factors, cannot and has not been contested. In fact, the work of Judith Butler (1990), mentioned in the previous chapter, has proposed that just like gender, sex too is a cultural construction, especially because the idea of different sexes has a history. These notions are generally constructed under the discourse of science (which is, however "true" and "objective" it claims to be, still a discourse that may be bound to a certain degree of subjectivity). Moreover, some have also argued that the distinction between sex and gender has stayed within academic discussions and thus has not been accepted beyond scholarly environments. We acknowledge and accept these arguments, at least to a certain degree. Still, considering the introductory nature of this book and our purposes here, we will not explore these arguments in detail; instead, we will start from the differentiation between gender and sex, and encourage readers who wish to explore other arguments in more detail to refer to Butler's work and to the work of other scholars in feminism, sexuality studies, and queer theory. You will see that we ourselves use the terms *men* and *women* at times to rely on the often-accepted (even if limiting) classifications.

Therefore, according to this view, sex is a categorization based on anatomical/chromosomal differences and hormonal profile, while gender is a taxonomy based on culturally defined norms, roles, and expectations with which one might or might not identify, against which one might or might not rebel (by refusing to undertake such roles, for example), and which one can stretch and redefine. In this sense, as stated by John Edwards (2009:127), "male or femaleness is seen to exist along a continuum of elaborations, manipulations or, indeed, rejections of sexual inheritance." Because of that fluidity, we can speak of gender diversity, (in) equality, nonconformity, and bias.

These gender roles have been constructed over time, and they are generally so embedded into our cultures and societies that we tend to accept them without questioning. Think, for example, of the widespread practice (at least in the West) of dressing baby boys in blue and baby girls in pink – and consequently of having their rooms and other environments decorated based on this dichotomy. Likewise, store aisles designate spaces separating toys for boys from those for girls.[2] Even more generic, potentially neutral toys such as building blocks are often painted in pastel colors for girls and primary colors for boys. In this way, sex and gender roles start to become almost synonymous if we fail to question these associations, as if every boy and girl needed to abide by predetermined conventions that define what it actually means to be a man or woman.

In fact, much work in sociology has shown that even schools and other educational institutions help propagate these stereotypical notions, in what we can refer to as a **hidden curricula**. In brief, hidden curricula refer to the teachings of schools and colleges (in terms of norms, behavior, practice, and so forth) that are not stated overtly in their written documents.[3] At times, even teachers are unaware of the social beliefs they may be perpetuating, and some of the main values propagated in such institutions are those of gender roles.

However, many times such roles are contested and ultimately changed in society. As explained by critical scholars in several different fields (e.g., applied linguistics, education, sociology, psychology, etc.), the structures of predetermined roles (in relation to gender, race, class, language, and so on) can be (and many times are or have been) resisted and transformed by members of society once they become aware of them and reflect critically on their meanings.

Gender nonconformity, for example, can mean defying social roles and expectations in both concrete and symbolic ways. When women started wearing pants in the early decades of the twentieth century, they were signaling nonconformity with the culturally determined dressing codes of the time (more symbolic) but also pointing to larger issues of gender inequality, such as disparities in opportunity and access (more concrete). There is no biological mandate for men to wear pants and women to wear dresses; it was cultural normativity that established and maintained such practices. Conversely, and as evidence of the agreed-upon nature of many gender roles and rules, we can easily think of historical moments and societies in which men wore dress-like garments, long hair, or ear adornments, which are forms of expressions that in most of the twentieth-century Western world were perceived to belong to women. But it is exactly when a large number of people start disagreeing with such agreements and questioning their validity that change tends to follow. According to the same example, now in the twenty-first century, it is much more common to find fluidity in forms of expression through hair, jewelry, and clothing between men and women, and more people who question and choose not to identify fixedly with either.

That does not mean that gender-motivated change is easy: quite the contrary, more often than not, change is met with great resistance. The entrance of women in the job market, especially in areas previously dominated by men, challenges to dress codes, and the more recent phenomenon of stay-at-home dads were all met with opposition and even suspicion. In fact, we still see many work environments in which male employees earn higher salaries than their female counterparts (who perform the exact same job), work institutions where certain ways of dressing or hairstyles for women are still frowned upon, and people who view men who cook or who stay at home as either powerless or facing a problem. Likewise, individuals whose identity defies the existing assumptions about gender tend to face great challenges to having their human rights upheld. At the moment, the depth and breadth of the discussions involving issues pertaining to the well-being and the rights of transgender persons is evidence of that.

In sum, gender is a construct that encompasses complexities that we have been carrying with us throughout the centuries, and in terms of language, it has provided interesting and enlightening debates. Many of these debates now take place on the Internet.

Gender and language

If sex and gender may be seen as different facets of a phenomenon, pointing to a biological difference and a cultural representation, respectively, another important distinction is to be made between cultural and grammatical gender. Languages differ in the ways they represent grammatical gender. In some, where the system is binary, gender is clearly assigned to every noun, whether the noun names an abstraction, an object, or a living being. For example, in Romance languages such as Portuguese and Spanish, the chair is "a cadeira" and "la silla," correspondingly, with the feminine definite article "a/la" denoting the feminine grammatical gender, while in "o caminho/el camino," or the path in English, the articles and the nouns they accompany are masculine.

The non-equivalence between sex, gender, and grammatical gender is further evidenced by pairs of nouns, in these two closely related languages, in which the grammatical gender of corresponding words is not the same. For example, the terms for *the tree* in Portuguese and Spanish are "a árvore" and "el arbor," where the first is feminine and the second is masculine. Likewise, the pairs "o nariz/ la nariz" (*the nose*) and "a água/el agua" (*the water*) have opposing grammatical genders in Portuguese and Spanish (though the plural "las aguas" in Spanish is also feminine). In addition, when it comes to a noun referring to both female and male entities, grammatical gender at times can also not correspond to biological sex. For example, in Portuguese, both the words "pessoa" and "criança," respectively *person* and *child*, are feminine, even though they apply to people of both sexes (to use the common binary).

In English, grammatical gender works differently. Articles, be they definite (e.g., the) or indefinite (e.g., a, an) do not denote gender, so it is basically through pronouns that we express this difference. Because such pronouns as *she* and *he* align more closely with the biological sex of the referent, it is common for monolingual users of that language to struggle with grammatical gender when they learn a foreign/second language. German, for example, has three: feminine, masculine, and neuter. Again, while some correspondence exists between a referent's gender and the grammatical gender of the noun in the case of animate beings, that correspondence is not universal and it is much less so in the case of other nouns (i.e., not all nouns referring to inanimate referents take the neuter).

That is not to say that representation of grammatical gender is not influenced or subject to change when changes to (cultural) gender dynamics occur. For example, for a long time in centuries past, it was the norm in English that the masculine pronoun "he" (and its corresponding possessive adjectives and pronouns) should stand for both masculine and feminine in generic contexts. The same was true for such nouns as "man," which stood for "human being" in many sentences. In that sense, "Man has the capacity and the need to live in society with his peers," would in the past have stood in for what we now would most likely rephrase as "A human being has the capacity and the need to live in society with their peers"[4] or some equivalent construction. It was activism and awareness-raising by feminists, as well as social change, which came to include women in more realms of human experience and action, that made for the necessity of grammatical adaptation to follow.

Grammatical gender and words associated with it can also be questioned and changed. In the last decade, a wish to have a pronoun that could dis-identify gender when that was wanted, be it to offer transgender persons a linguistic choice or have a neutral, flexible term, has led the Swedish to develop a new pronoun that could do that – *hen* (which comes as an alternative to *hon*, "she," and *han*, "he"). The term is being added to the official Swedish language dictionary. In the past, women in English-speaking environments had already questioned the practice of formal reference to women by marital status (through *Miss* or *Mrs.*), which led to the development of the form Ms., which does not give away such information, just like Mr. did not.

While sometimes people feel that such decisions are out of their hands, being that they are not grammarians or dictionary writers, that is not the case. An interesting example in this regard is given by Paulo Freire in his book *Pedagogy of Hope*. In it, Freire discusses how, back in the 1970s – when the first edition of his famous *Pedagogy of the Oppressed* (cited in chapter 4) came out – he was contacted by many North American women who, in spite of finding his book and his work useful, had thought his language was sexist. The reason was simple: Freire had used the term "men" to refer to both men and women in his world-renowned book, and he had done so because he felt it was natural. However, as pointed out by many of those who wrote to him, such assumption could lead to an understanding of men as superior to women. The incident led Freire to later use the more encompassing phrase "men and women," rather than simply "men." As Freire (1992:54) has explained, this was "not a grammatical problem, but an ideological one" – one that shows "how much ideology resides in language." Still, on the matter of linguistic institutions, it is a known fact that dictionary editors rely on extensive research on what is being used by actual people to decide on new additions to dictionaries, which means the choices we make as language users do have weight.

When we speak in this chapter about issues of gender and the Internet, we will make sure we are clear about what "kind" of gender we are referring to. The general point here is that if one studies issues of gender pertaining to language, they must realize that they could be speaking of several different things. These range from theoretical discussions on grammatical gender, as presented previously (e.g., whether it is acceptable to use a plural "neutral" *they* to refer to a singular entity when we don't know the gender), to perceptions of words referring to both men and women (e.g., the pairs *spinster* and *bachelor*, *witch* and *wizard* are an often-cited example, because one has negative connotations and the other does not – see Romaine, 2001), to differences in the discourse and conversational rituals of men and women (e.g., women have been documented as using more rituals that foster consensus – see Tannen, 1990[5]). They can include reactions to those who speak based on their gender (e.g., is a woman who complains more likely to be called "nagging" as opposed to an "assertive" male?), and a host of other issues. We venture to say that most of them, if not all, are interceded by culture, and can many times be ideological.

Gender and Internet access

Even though many see, in the rise of computer-mediated communication, a great equalizing force, research has shown that this is not universally the case, as inequality starts with access. According to a report by the United Nations' Broadband Commission Working Group, worldwide 200 million more men than women have access to the Internet.[6] That fact alone has far-reaching consequences when it comes to the kind and amount of information one has access to, the networks they interact with, and their say in critical issues.

In addition, access means more than just being able to visit a website or search for information online. As explained by Susan Herring (2003:204), in *The Handbook of Language and Gender*, although it is true that there has been a significant increase in the number of female Internet users (especially in more developed countries),

> ... women and men still do not have equal access to the creation and control of what takes place on the Internet. Roles that require technical expertise, such as network administrator, are disproportionately filled by men, consistent with the traditional association of technology with masculinity.

In other words, logging on the Internet is only part of what it means to have real power in how the online world is being directed and shaped; men, who are still higher in numbers in fields such as computer science, still seem to have most of this power.

Interactive patterns that have been observed in the real world are also at play when it comes to virtual interactions. Herring (2003), reflecting on postings to academic discussion lists online, considers "why men tend to post longer messages and receive more responses to their messages than women do, regardless of context"[7] and, alluding to her original research from 1993, that "computer-mediated discourse was not democratic, because gendered patterns of interaction that favored men over women were carried over from F2F communication." She discovered that men's postings were indeed significantly longer and received more replies than female postings. Subsequent male postings are also more likely to initiate disagreement. Men are also more likely to "flame" (that is, initiate flame wars – see chapter 7) and post "joke" messages, and those seem to receive a lot of attention too.

The same male bias has also been observed in relation to blogs. Herring and colleagues (2004:267) have found that while the number of females and males authoring blogs tends to be balanced, "contemporary discourses about weblogs, such as those propagated through the mainstream media, in scholarly communication, and in weblogs themselves, tend to disproportionately feature adult, male bloggers." Out of curiosity, at this writing, we searched for the names of the top 20 blogs (in popularity) in the UK, and lo and behold, all of those associated with a particular blogger starred a male author (the few that did not were collective efforts with no particular blogger named), though our short search is, of course, only anecdotal.

Several different studies have also indicated the content of blogs tends to differ depending on whether a man or woman is penning the entries. Sarah Pedersen and Caroline Macafee (2007) confirmed for British bloggers what was already established for their American counterparts: that female bloggers tend to write more diary-like posts, while males write opinion-based texts that are oftentimes about politics or technology – topics that, in turn, would give them an edge in terms of popularity. All of these forces combined point to the fact that conditions, access, voice, and linguistic power are still distributed unequally online, too, across gender lines.

Determining gender

The information just relayed is, for the most part, focused on environments where the identity and gender of the interlocutors is known. However, the Internet offers many opportunities for interaction in which gender and identity can be not only hidden but also manipulated. That is, a person can choose to hide their gender or pretend to be another gender. A person can also play with common assumptions and representations of gender. As we stated in chapter 5, identities are generally performed, which means that they are often constructed to fit socially and culturally accepted norms regarding what it means to be a particular type of person. When we think of gender identity, in particular, in the context of the Internet, then we can say that such possibilities for performativity may be greatly increased, especially because many times certain boundaries and/or constraints, such as one's physical characteristics, can be hidden or easily manipulated. That is what it means to say that gender identity (not only on the Internet) is *performative*, the same way that identity in general is performative. Think of a theater and all of the characters one could play.

Herring and Martinson (2004:425) pose an intriguing question: "How can one determine the gender of participants in public Internet communication spaces when language provides the only cues?" In certain cases, it is true that one cannot be absolutely sure of the biological sex of a person communicating online. However, on the other hand, much research exists that demonstrates a tendency for certain linguistic rituals to be more prevalent among men and among women (see Tannen, 1990 and 2001). Therefore, in some cases it might indeed be possible to determine the likely gender of participants given linguistic clues alone (see, for example, our previous discussion on men posting more jokes or starting flame wars more often, and the discussion that follows on English and gender).

English and gender

What language/Englishes have to do with gender

As discussed by Suzanne Romaine (2000), Peter Trudgill (2000) and other sociolinguists, a large number of studies focusing on correlations between gender and language use have shown that women tend to use higher-status (i.e., close to standard) varieties than men. This is generally the case for a number of languages – in fact, Trudgill (2000:73) has made the case that "gender differentiation of this type is the single most consistent finding to emerge from sociolinguistic work around the world" for decades. This means that given a man and a woman of the same socio-educational level, chances are, the woman will more likely aspire to a social dialect above the social expectation of their environment.

Thus, in the case of English in particular, it is not surprising to see that this observation seems to hold true, at least when Inner Circle contexts are considered. As explained by Trudgill, studies in Anglo-Saxon communities in North America, Great Britain, Australia, South Africa, and New Zealand, for example, have shown that women, on average, use forms that are closer to the prestige variety and accent than men (it would be interesting to investigate whether the same pattern holds for Outer and Expanding Circle Englishes). The question that sociolinguists working with Englishes, and also with other languages, have asked, then, is why exactly this happens.

Trudgill offers two main reasons. The first is that working-class speech is generally linked to masculinity in many societies, due to an association between this type of language use and the supposed "toughness" of working-class individuals. In fact, in an earlier study in Ireland, reported by Edwards (2009:1310), judges had to guess if young children were boys or girls based on speech samples, and they were able to do so accurately around 75 – 80% of the time. Interestingly, there were cases when the association of masculinity with working-class speech led girls to be misidentified as boys by middle-class judges.

The second reason given by Trudgill is that many societies expect a higher level of obedience and conformity to social norms from women as opposed to men. This factor shows that there are double standards for people based on sex and/or gender differences, and most of the time (if not always), such standards are more moderate for men than they are for women. In this case, then, the different expectations and standards placed on men and women may reflect the different power relations between them that are still so present in society.

In the case of English specifically, a strong argument has been made by linguist Deborah Tannen in her well-know 1990 bestseller focusing on miscommunication between men and women. In *You Just don't Understand: Women and Men in Conversation*, Tannen explains two aspects that are relevant to our discussion here – namely, that when communicating with others, men often tend to perform competitive rituals, while women more often tend to perform collaborative, agreement-seeking rituals. As Tannen herself stresses, this does *not* mean men are more competitive while women are more collaborative. Rather, the rituals, social and linguistic, that they more often engage in tend to have those characteristics. In a conversation among men, for example, where one is complaining that his car broke down in a remote part of town, another might build rapport by starting, "That's nothing. Once my car died in the middle of the desert!" By the same token, a woman would be more likely to reply, "I know how that feels. Once my car broke down in a remote area too!" We have to remember, however, that, given that these are rituals, a great degree of variance can occur; what Tannen writes about is a *tendency*, with individual preferences and past experiences helping shape discourse in these cases too.

The other consideration is that men and women tend to be more direct or indirect in different areas and aspects of interaction. For example, women tend to make requests more indirectly: "Are you hungry?" for example, standing in for "I'm hungry. Let's stop to eat"; while men tend to be more indirect when apologizing or acknowledging a mistake. In that respect, "I washed your car" could stand in for, "I'm sorry I forgot about our dinner reservation." The disclaimer from the previous paragraph, nonetheless, should be applied here as well, because individuals, given their personalities and histories, will vary in their responses to these situations.

Another take on men and women in communication is offered by Deborah Cameron (2007). For her, miscommunication occurs due to power relations and variations in the power of men and women in society, rather than because of linguistic gender differences. In this sense, when a man asks a question like, "Is there any soy sauce?" from his wife, it is the power relation between them that establishes whether he wants her to go and get it, rather than a purely linguistic understanding that men speak this or that way. Moreover, Cameron goes on to argue, there is much variation and many differences in language use within each gender, and not only across genders, which shows that differences and miscommunication, although impacted by it, involve many more factors than gender alone.

Gender construction on the Internet: Maintenance or challenging of stereotypes?

Much is speculated about the Internet as a place for change and challenge of gender roles, and we agree that, to a large extent, this is a legitimate and worthy consideration. You were probably able to observe that in the previous discussions, several assumptions on the nature of gender had to be drawn for arguments to be made. Digital communications have provided opportunities for innumerous discussions and challenges to those same assumptions. Just how much such change is a result of the medium itself or the changing nature of new generations who populate it is hard to determine. That is, were perceptions of gender and gender roles bound to change because of changing beliefs that would have also changed, even if we lived solely in the "real world?" And just how much have roles really changed?

We do not believe that the answer is unilateral, because neither people nor sites of interaction are uniform. For example, William and colleagues (2009) have explained that in regards to online gaming, although an estimated 40% of players are now women, the activity is still heavily perceived as "masculine" across the gender spectrum. In addition, women are more likely to be introduced to gaming by, and play the game with, a partner, while men are more likely to play for achievement and competition. That seems to indicate that, even when the actual interactions change (after all, women already make for a large number of players), the social perception of who plays, or who an Internet activity's target audience is, has not yet caught up with that fact. It is possible that other features still lag behind, too: we hear anecdotal reports that language in that realm is oftentimes offensive to women, and that representations of female characters are secondary and problematic (very few protagonists are women, too).

On the other hand, the Internet has been a place for linguistic gender-related innovation. For example, the birth of the term "trans*," which is different from "transgender" or "trans," can be directly linked to netspeak. "Trans*" is usually used in a broad sense to represent anyone of a very diverse gender spectrum that does not identify as a cisgender man or woman, where cisgender is a person whose biological sex and reported gender self-identity conform to "traditional" roles. Thus, "trans*" is more far-reaching than "trans," which is usually employed in reference to "transgender" or "transsexual"; but oftentimes its use is avoided with interlocutors who are unfamiliar with gender issues because of potential misrepresentations. The use of the asterisk comes from Internet searches. When using a search engine, a person types a word followed by that symbol, they are asking for the computer to search for those characters *and* any additional characters that might come after the asterisk, hence the symbolic representation of inclusiveness. Again, while this linguistic change was initiated and spread through digital communication, it has not uniformly spread across different populations, and many might still be unaware of this discussion.

Another change whose origin is connected to virtual spaces is the allocation of the personal pronoun "they" (and corresponding possessive adjective and pronoun) as a reference to gender-fluid or non-cisgender persons. We had already seen the use, now endorsed by most dictionaries and grammar books, of the plural non-gender-specific pronoun for singular use when the noun/pronoun it refers to is of unknown/neutral gender. In that sense, we can grammatically say, "No person has arrived to see me, have they?" and "Does anyone know their seat assignment?" and "A student needs to have their materials ready on the first day of class," as we explained above. In addition, through the Internet, persons of non-cisgender identities and activists have advocated for the use of the pronoun "they" whenever the gender preference of the person being spoken of is unknown or when they have voiced a preference for being referred to through a gender-neutral form (in a way performing the same role of *hen* in Swedish) and/or for an opportunity for individuals themselves to state the pronoun of their preference.

Gender activism online

The next locus of feminist activism is likely to be more virtual than academic. After all, outside of academia there is still a wide belief that sex determines gender roles, and we still see a lot of gender-related discrimination taking place. It is not surprising, then, to see a growing number of initiatives devoted to feminist action and the upholding of the rights of gender minorities online, given the Internet's widespread growth and the power it has given to people and groups. Recently a host of online initiatives that promote gender awareness online have become well-known. The number of online zines, blogs, and journals dedicated to discussing issues of gender has increased exponentially too. It is intuitive, then, to accept that a number of linguistic innovations should follow.

Disability and online modes

While the focus of this chapter is on the ethnic, racial, and gender dimensions of identity vis-à-vis Internet and virtual communications, we would be amiss not to mention disability in this context. Currently many calls exist to situate disability alongside race, gender, and ethnicity as constructs that need to be addressed in relation to language and society. This call is compatible with a disability studies perspective, according to which disability is (to varying degrees) a feature of limiting environments. That is, the environment is often designed for the "average" person, which means that people who fall outside of the "norm" may be further disabled by the features of the environment that are not made for their unique abilities and needs. In that way, a building without an automatic door or a ramp disables the user of a wheelchair. An environment made for people who present an "average" mental makeup might disable those individuals who present forms of mental diversity. Written directions or information not provided concomitantly in Braille disables people living with vision impairment.

The digital age has brought opportunities for the environment to be less disabling. Mobility is now at least as virtual as physical, and adaptive technology allows individuals with alternative abilities to thrive. Not only have new modes allowed for the manifestation of these unique skills and contributions, but also these virtual platforms can be used to denounce and change ableist practices and language. Terms such as *neurotypical, neurodiverse, mental difference, mental diversity,* and *mad pride* can be discussed, problematized, advocated for, and included where pertinent in online discussions. Definitions can and have been added to online collaborative dictionaries, and implications can be discussed in large-scale forums. Ableist language (i.e., language that discriminates against people living with disabilities) can then be problematized. Terms that reduce the experience and role of persons living with disabilities can be questioned. While this questioning is not exclusive to the digital age, our virtual involvement has facilitated and multiplied the opportunities for people to organize in new speech communities, embrace disability, discuss recovery (rather than cure), share experiences so as not to feel isolated, seek better understanding, or simply (but importantly) build community on the basis of shared experiences. For more on linguistics and disability, see Friedrich (2015).

Race and ethnicity

In some contexts, especially in the past, the concepts of race and ethnicity were often conflated as if they were one and the same. In that sense, for example, forms in the US collecting demographic information oftentimes had such categories as "Caucasian," "Hispanic," and others as mutually exclusive. However, the more diverse and the more fluid our identities become, but also the more global our community tends to be, the better we understand that these categories can be quite fluid too; and that people who are bi- or multicultural, bi- or multiracial, and bi- or multilingual may prefer to think of themselves as integrating expressions and honoring manifestations that cannot be narrowed down to one racial and/or one ethnic category alone. Besides, linguistically and culturally speaking, global communications, and especially virtual communications, have contributed to the dissemination of expressions that might originate within a certain linguistic/racial/ethnic network, but that then spread in speeds never experienced before. While on the one hand, people can use virtual spaces to reaffirm aspects of their racial and ethnic identities – aspects that are important to them, their families, and their communities, or that they think need advocacy and awareness – they can also use these same spaces to expand their experience and to incorporate other elements of cultural knowledge that they might not have access to otherwise.

Of course, this poses questions about **cultural and linguistic appropriation**. The line between appropriation and legitimate hybridization is one we need to negotiate carefully. We are using the term linguistic appropriation in the sense proposed by Jane H. Hill (2008:158), who explains that "some linguistic borrowing" can be seen "as a kind of theft." She argues that in this kind of phenomenon, rather than words and expressions gradually shifting in meaning by use itself and changes to society, "words are commodified and become property, with their meanings and uses determined by their owners." Hill provides such examples as expressions in "mock Spanish," for instance "No problemo," which are available to a white majority but do not represent knowledge or the incorporation of loanwords. We can see here that such an expression does not fulfill the needs left by a lexical gap, nor does it really represent the impetus of multilinguals to mix and switch between languages that they rely on for communication (if they did, they would say "no problema"). Instead, there is a scornful element to its use, one that makes evident that a word or words were appropriated for purposes of disenfranchising the very linguistic groups where it (they) originated. So, as you can see, not only do class and geography make sociolinguistic realities complex, but issues of race, gender, and ethnicity also add to the important considerations and observations we must make when discussing language use in context.

Other forms of linguistic appropriation include, for example, the claiming of proprietary rights over public linguist forms. David Bollier (2006) has called this phenomenon **lingo-piracy**, an example of which is the appropriation of Brazilian local terms for fruit and culturally influenced food products for the purposes of trademarking. The well-known cases of such common nouns as *açaí* (a local term for a purplish berry fruit) and *rapadura* (a block of brown sugar) that were trademarked abroad exemplify lingo-piracy. Besides all of the symbolic colonialist nature of such practice, the trademarking of these common words made it harder for Brazilians to sell their products abroad, as they faced the threat of trademark infringements of the words that had been appropriated *from* them in the first place. We estimate that online environments can accelerate these processes of appropriation, given the frequency and scope of linguistic interaction as well as access to words that would otherwise remain longer in the communities where they originated.

Race/ethnicity and linguistic prejudice

An important factor to consider in relation to race/ethnicity and language is that **linguistic prejudice** still takes place in many societies. In brief, linguistic prejudice refers to the phenomenon of characterizing people based on the linguistic varieties/languages they speak, and of giving higher status (i.e., prestige) to those who speak varieties closer to the standard and lower status to those who use less standard-like variations. In the case of English, we see linguistic prejudice take place many times based on racial/ethnic associations, as is the case of Chicano English, African American Vernacular, Hillbilly English, Indian English, and so forth.[8] Prejudice can also be directed at those associated with certain localities and geographies.

Here we must emphasize claims we have made in previous chapters that standard varieties are not "better" or "more correct" in themselves. Linguistically speaking, all systematic language varieties are (internally) rule-governed; that is, they have an internal logic that allows them to be acquired by the users of such varieties, and for those users to create sentences, phrases, and utterances that have never been created before by extrapolating those internal rules. It is the **linguistic attitudes** towards cultural and socioeconomic factors that lead one variation of a language to be seen as more acceptable, more "correct," or more prestigious (however unjustly these assignments are made). In that way, it is not surprising that the linguistic varieties that do suffer from prejudice are generally (but not always) the ones associated with minorities (e.g., people of color, immigrants, ethnic minorities, and people of lower socioeconomic standing and/or certain regions) who might have been historically and socially disenfranchised or denied social and linguistic power. If we want to understand and positively impact language relations, that is where we should start our investigations.

Racial/ethnic construction and Englishes

If the Internet is a space for gender activism and gender-related linguistic innovation, the same can be said for race and ethnicity representations that serve to build community, call attention to social injustices, bring members of linguistic networks closer together, and resist forms of marginalization and *othering* (Lacan, 1966). If race and ethnicity in the real world are often performed in the body – after all, manners of dress, physical expressions (e.g., dance), and cultural manifestations are very representative of racial and ethnic identity – online, the role of linguistic representation, in the absence of performance through the body, becomes heightened and even more crucial.[9]

For example, Sarah Florini (2013:2) explains that "Generations of Black Americans have used signifyin' as a space for the expression of Black cultural knowledge, as a vehicle for social critique, and as a means of creating group solidarity." By performing race, members of different linguistic communities resist oppression and marginalization (Florini, 2013; Nakamura, 2008) and create in-group unity and support. Florini goes on to demonstrate how Twitter has become a virtual space where African American Vernacular (AAV) and signifyin' are widely represented; from there, they spread much beyond physical/geographical boundaries in the real world, reaffirming aspects of a cultural representation in places that are public and therefore reachable by a much larger audience.[10]

Signifying involves elements of wordplay and misdirection, repetition, joking, and referencing to cultural elements. Signifying has been a very productive manifestation, one that depends on a level of sociolinguistic membership to be accessed and fully decoded. The collaborative nature of signifying means that not only are social media users invited to read, they are also invited to add their own textual contributions. To do so, one needs to be familiar with the particular language varieties at play. Andre Brock (2009:15–16) explains that

> The Internet offers yet another context in which Black identity is shaped by the in- and out-group. Compared to older forms of media, the Internet adds an interactive, discursive dimension to exterior renditions of Black identity and thus enabling interior perspectives on Black identity to become part of the conversation.

He further contends that through Internet spaces, people can reaffirm their identity but also expand it and even test it; and we posit that language is a big part, crucial really, of this experimentation.

Put in historical perspective, the blueprint of language spread through Twitter mirrors known sociolinguistic dynamics, such as the wavelike pattern known to have been in operation in the real world for many linguistic phenomena that we have studied. Eisenstein and colleagues (2012), for example, have shown how slang from AAV spreads through the Internet from regions to large cities elsewhere, and then to many other parts of the US. This wavelike pattern, minus the virtual element, of course, is hypothesized to have been at play, for example, in the spread of the London variety of English in the period preceding the birth of modern English (and of a standard and standardized variety). Stephan Gramley (2012:105) explains the dynamics of that earlier time:

> As particular speakers and their speech communities gained in power and prestige, the language variants they used were adopted in neighboring areas, spreading like waves around a stone thrown into a pond.

This is also the pattern of spread proposed by Braj Kachru (1983 and after) through the Concentric Circles model to explain the historical spread of English from the Inner Circle (e.g., Britain and the US), to the Outer Circle (e.g., Nigeria and India), to the rest of the world or Expanding Circle (e.g., Brazil and Mexico).

So in the case of Twitter and AAV, if expressions gain currency as "cool" language, or gain currency as symbolic of youth culture and desirable trends, they spread to other areas, that is, larger networks (which, virtually, do not need to be geographical neighbors), and from there are further taken to even broader virtual and non-virtual spaces.

The Internet as a space for gender, ethnicity, and race discussions

As we hope to have showed in this chapter, issues of gender and sex, and of race and ethnicity, and their relation to language, are much more complex than our usual understandings of them. As we have also stated – particularly in the case of gender affirmation, but also true in the case of racial/ethnic issues – it is still the case that, while at certain historical moments these discussions have been paramount to societies going forward (e.g., civil rights movement in the US), many other times punctual discussions have taken place within the walls of academic circles only and have not been exposed and debated by the public at large. With the Internet, we have begun to witness a change in this scenario. Gender and racial/ethnic activism have become quite strong online and have served not only to spread the debates, but also to add new layers to them – such as the complex construction of identities in cyberspace. And again, we must say, English has been quite present in this new picture, mainly because of its lingua franca status and association with technology. It is possible that, just as it happens with the Web itself (in terms of speed, number of users, etc.), the growth in this type of activism can be exponential. Lisa Nakamura (2002: xii) posits that

> In these post-Internet times, it may be true that possessing access to the Internet no longer guarantees one a place at the 'cutting age of history.' However, *lack of access* to the Internet – often found along raced, classed, and still, to a narrowing extent, gendered lines – continues to cut particular bodies *out* of various histories in the making (emphases in the original).

Understanding the ways that gender, ethnicity, disability, class, and race intersect on the Internet can make for advancements in the inclusion of all social groups, despite the challenges we face every day.

Questions for discussion

1   Think of a social media outlet you are familiar with. What linguistic changes have you observed over the years that might impact perceptions of gender? What linguistic networks might have exited and which new ones were formed? Are there any particular linguistic terms referring to gender that might have originated or changed within that network?

2   Many times, Internet communities defy the grammatical and linguistic conventions established by institutions such as schools, but in the process, they might create new rules and new consequences for those who do not follow them (e.g., ridicule, ostracism, etc.). Can you think of a community and describe what some of the rules related to gender construction are, and what consequences of not following the rules might be for users?

3   Some terms are created by members of specific linguistic networks and are originally used to denote membership in the community. Once larger and larger populations and an ever-widening network employ the term, it may be dropped by the original smaller group, only to resurface with a different connotation. Can you think of terms that fit this profile? Explain.

4   Can you think of examples of lingo-piracy and linguistic appropriation involving English?

5   In what ways do you think disability can (or cannot) be thought of as belonging to the same discussions that involve ethnicity, race, and gender?

Notes

1   Sometimes the "Q" in the acronym stands for "questioning."
2   As we write this sentence, stores in the US are beginning to reconsider and review this practice.
3   The term "hidden curriculum" is often cited as having been coined by Philip Jackson in his 1968 book *Life in Classrooms*. For examples of work in this particular topic, see Lynch (1989) and the edited volume by Margolis (2001).
4   We are aware that some people refuse to use "their" with a singular noun and would use avoidance strategies (such as making the subject plural) to prevent the combination of the singular subject form and the "plural" word "their." However, most dictionaries and grammar books, even the most prescriptive, already accept that use as grammatical.
5   Which does not mean that women are more "agreeable," or that men are more confrontational, given that these are rituals – *ways* of doing things.
6   *Doubling Digital Opportunities: Enhancing the Inclusion of Women and Girls in the Information Society*, a report by the Broadband Commission.
7   Online source, no page number. See Herring (2003) in the references.

8 For a wonderful discussion on linguistic prejudice in relation to different varieties, see Rosina Lippi-Green's famous 1997 book *English with an Accent*.
9 See Florini (2013), whose theories about body, race, and signifying inform this section.
10 See also Brock (2009) in the references.

References and suggested further reading

Bangou, F., & Wong, S. (2009). Race and technology in teacher education: Where is the access? In R. Kubota and A. Lin (Eds.), *Race, culture and identities in second language education: Exploring critically engaged practice* (pp. 158–175). New York: Routledge.

Bollier, D. (2006). *Brazil fights lingo-piracy, the privatization of its words*. Retrieved August 31, 2014, from http://bollier.org/brazil-fights-lingo-piracy-privatization-its-words

Broadband Commission (September 21, 2013). *Doubling digital opportunities: Enhancing the inclusion of women and girls in the information society*, a report by the Broadband Commission.

Brock, A. (2009). Who do you think you are?: Race, representation, and cultural rhetorics in online spaces. *Poroi*, 6(1), 15–16.

Butler, J. (1990). *Gender trouble: Feminism and the subversion of identity*. New York: Routledge.

Cameron, D. (2007). *The myth of Mars and Venus: Do men and women really speak different languages?* Oxford: Oxford University Press.

Dill, K. E., & Thill, K. P. (2007). Video game characters and the socialization of gender roles: Young people's perceptions mirror sexist media depictions. *Sex Role, 57*, 851–864.

Eckert, P., & McConnell-Ginet, S. (2003). *Language and gender*. Cambridge: Cambridge University Press.

Edwards, J. (2009). *Language and identity*. Cambridge: Cambridge University Press.

Eisenstein, Jacob, O'Connor, Brendan, Smith, Noah A., & Xing, E. P. (2012). *Mapping the geographical diffusion of new words* (Working paper).

Florini, S. (2013). Tweets, tweeps, and signifyin': Communication and cultural performance on "Black Twitter." *Television and New Media*, March, pp. 1–15.

Freire, P. (1970). *Pedagogy of the oppressed*. New York: Continuum.

Freire, P. (1992). *Pedagogy of hope*. New York: Continuum.

Friedrich, P. (2015). *The literary and linguistic construction of obsessive-compulsive disorder: No ordinary doubt*. Hampshire: Palgrave-MacMillan.

Gracia, J. J. E. (2007). Race or ethnicity? An introduction. In J. J. E. Gracia (Ed.), *Race or ethnicity? On Black and Latino identity* (pp. 1–16). Ithaca: Cornell University Press.

Gramley, S. (2012). *The history of English: An introduction*. New York: Routledge.

Gurak, L., Antonijevic, S., Johnson, L., Ratliff, C., & Reyman, J. (Eds.). (2004). *Into the blogosphere: Rhetoric, community, and culture of weblogs*. Minneapolis: University of Minnesota.

Herring, S. (1993). Gender and democracy in computer-mediated communication. *Electronic Journal of Communication*, 3(2). Retrieved from http://www.cios.org/www/ejc/v3n293.htm

Herring, S. (2003). Gender and power in on-line communication. In J. Holmes and M. Meyerhoff (Eds.), *The handbook of language and gender* (pp. 202–228). Maiden, MA: Blackwell Publishing.

Herring, S. (2010). *Who's got the floor in computer-mediated conversation? Edelsky's gender patterns revisited*. Language@Internet (7). Retrieved August 14, 2014, from language atinternet.org

Herring, S. C., Kouper, I., Scheidt, L. A., & Wright, E. (2004). Women and children last: The discursive construction of weblogs. In L. Gurak, S. Antonijevic, L. Johnson, C. Ratliff, and J. Reyman (Eds.), *Into the blogosphere: Rhetoric, community, and culture of weblogs*. Minneapolis: University of Minnesota. Retrieved from the University of Minnesota Digital Conservancy, http://hdl.handle.net/11299/172825

Herring, S. C., & Martinson, A. (2004). Assessing gender authenticity in computer-mediated language use: Evidence from an identity game. *Journal of Language and Social Psychology, 23*, 424–446.

Hill, J. H. (2008). *The everyday language of white racism*. Oxford: Wiley-Blackwell.

Jackson, P. (1968). *Life in classrooms*. New York: Holt, Rinehart and Winston.

Kachru, B. (1983). *The Indianization of English: The English language in India*. New York: Oxford University Press.

Lacan, J. (1966). *Ecrits*. London: Tavistock.

Lippi-Green, R. (1997). *English with an accent: Language ideology and discrimination in the United States*. New York: Routledge.

Lynch, K. (1989). *The hidden curriculum: Reproduction in education, an appraisal*. Sussex: The Falmer Press.

Margolis, E. (Ed.) (2001). *The hidden curriculum in higher education*. New York: Routledge.

Motter, J. (2011). Feminist virtual world activism: 16 days of activism against gender violence campaign, guerrilla girls broadband, and subrosa. *Visual Culture and Gender, 6*, 109–118.

Nakamura, L. (2002). *Cybertypes: Race, ethnicity, and identity on the Internet*. New York: Routledge.

Nakamura, L. (2008). *Digitizing race: Visual cultures of the internet*. Minneapolis: University of Minnesota Press.

Pedersen, S., & Macafee, C. (2007). Gender differences in British blogging. *Journal of Computer-Mediated Communication, 12*(4), article 16.

Romaine, S. (2001). *Language in society*. Oxford: Oxford University Press.

Tannen, D. (1990). *You just don't understand: Women and men in conversation*. New York: Ballentine.

Tannen, D. (2001). *Talking from 9 to 5: Women and men at work*. New York: William Morrow Paperbacks.

Trudgill, P. (2000). *Sociolinguistics: An introduction to language and society*. New York: Penguin Books.

William, D., Cosalvo, M., Caplan, S., & Yee, N. (2009). Looking for gender: Gender roles and behaviors among online gamers. *Journal of Communication, 59*(4), 700–725.

Chapter 7

Truthfulness and access in online communication

This chapter will help you understand that:

1   There is a difference between invention, knowledge construction, and knowledge fabrication.
2   Anonymity online has resulted in significant challenges to our habitual patterns of interaction.
3   Politeness, a construct explored by sociolinguistics and pragmatics, is context-dependent.
4   Grice's Maxims and the Principle of Cooperation have been challenged by virtual communications.
5   A number of new words have appeared to describe the less desirable "side effects" of online communications.
6   Linguistic practices of politeness have also been challenged by virtual communication.
7   The terms appropriacy, appropriation, and reappropriation have particular meanings in relation to sociolinguistics.
8   The dynamics of flame wars have linguistic elements.
9   Besides questions about anonymity and accountability, the Internet has brought us questions about truth and truth-telling.

Innovation, English, and the side effects of change

For a large portion of this book, we have been writing about the linguistic innovation and advancement that the digital age has helped propagate, and at the same time arguing that the linguistic dynamics that allow these phenomena to happen have always played a significant role in language change and linguistic innovation. While we have tried to keep a descriptivist point of view combined with our analysis, some of the information we relay does show that we are neither afraid of what the Internet will do to language dynamics/the dynamics of English, nor are we critical of language change, which we see as a usual, common aspect of language in all its incarnations. If we study the history of languages – the English language, for example – we see that innovation and change are always a part of linguistic dynamics. To be alarmist and think that there is something about this place and time that does not speak at any level to the linguistic reality of other times would be naïve, the uniqueness of digital communications notwithstanding. As we mentioned before, each new medium of communication, be it the telephone, the telegraph, or the computer, has brought with it concerns regarding human interactions, linguistic standards, and other aspects of interaction among people. They have also resulted in linguistic and social "side effects" that we do not always approve or find adequate and helpful.

While at times in this book we may have sounded optimistic about the many prospects of new media, we acknowledge that they are not without problems – some of them quite big and impactful. For each advancement and process of linguistic inclusion made possible by the Internet and forms of digital communication, several challenges can also ensue. In addition, the possibilities of any new medium are only as fruitful as their users can imagine it to be, and can only be fully realized if the users make sound decisions about such use. If the choices are geared toward inclusion, access, respect for others, education, and advancement, we see improved communication, knowledge generation, community building, and ultimately stronger social and linguistic networks. If, on the other hand, users choose exclusion and disrespect, the media cannot fulfill their complete communicative potential.

In short, we do not sail through innovation and change without obstacles and hurdles. Sometimes they come in the form of less-than-helpful linguistic and social practices; other times, they are simply the result of linguistic experimentation in newer environments (as, for example, when we are inadvertently curt in an email message even though we were just going for speed or directness). In this chapter, we will tackle some of the more undesirable consequences of global communications, including instances of communication failure, here represented by such Internet phenomena as cyberbullying, trolling, and flame wars. We will also deal with issues of access and age, and the relationship between anonymity and a breakdown in commonly accepted rules of politeness, and a challenge to the principle of cooperation in conversation. We will start with the very idea of anonymity and the continuum between knowledge construction and knowledge invention, and we will ultimately reflect on the idea of truthfulness and how it plays out online. By the end of the chapter, we will have returned to the more encouraging developments in digital communications.

The construction and invention of knowledge

Social constructionism

If you try to think critically about several of the actions you take every day that have possibly become invisible to you, you might realize the large degree of social construction that sustains these actions and our everyday lives. For example, you might be going to a young niece's party and, in the process of selecting a gift, end up choosing the pink tee shirt without even noticing. You might have never considered the possibility of eating grilled vegetables for breakfast because "breakfast food" includes only such items as pancakes, breads, waffles, or bagels (if you live in the US). You might have accepted the medicalization of life as the only way to approach the idea of health, or you might have as the first reference to the word *work* the 9-to-5 job. Even highly agreed-upon behaviors can pass for "right." For example, it is not uncommon to hear an American comment on how, in England and Australia, people drive "on the wrong side of the road," even though a more accurate description would be "opposite side of the road" or even "the left side of the road" (it is really hard to argue for one being right and the other being wrong).

There is nothing wrong with any of these perceptions of reality. The fact, however, is that they are, to a large or small extent, the concretization of social beliefs about reality that might be so engrained in us that they pass for natural phenomena. By "natural," we mean the opposite of social-mediated, that which occurs in nature without our intellectual or social intervention. To put these assumptions in perspective, all we have to do is find a time, a culture, or a context where they do not hold true. For example, if you do some research, you will discover that pink and blue only became associated with gender in the Western world in the twentieth century; if you interact with other social and linguistic networks, you will realize that many plant-based vegans advocate for the consumption of cooked and raw vegetables and fruit-vegetable beverages for breakfast; and while the full-time office job still has its place in our social order, many people now work from their homes through flexible schedules made possible by virtual interactions and file sharing. Finally, holistic approaches to health usually can, alongside medications, include a significant change in eating and exercise habits and the practice of meditation or yoga, and should you stay long enough in a culture where driving is done on "the opposite side of the road," you, too, will start feeling that such a practice is "normal." All of a sudden, what seemed natural, we realize, is mediated by our beliefs about reality and therefore liable to change and revision, or in the very least questioning.

In their 1966 classic work *The Social Construction of Reality*, Peter L. Berger and Thomas Luckmann formalized the realization that

> The world of everyday life is not only taken for granted as reality by ordinary members of society in the subjectively meaningful conduct of their lives. It is a world that originates in their thoughts and actions, and is maintained as reality by these.
>
> (Berger and Luckmann, 1966:33)

So what we have assumed as reality, objective and even fixed, is actually often created and mediated by us and our ideas about the world. Change those thoughts, and reality can change as well; is that not part of the whole process of invention? This is the case in "real life," and we can intuit even more so in virtual life. In a way, the reality of the virtual age is very much constructed; this technology, after all, was born out of our imagination and mental maps, and concretizes our representation of the world and what should be in it in many different ways. Imagination and invention have allowed us to create Internet-building tools and e-translators, forge the alternative virtual universes of video games, and given us the option of choosing our own avatars or fragments of self to share. As we have discussed before, linguistically, the virtual world gives us an opportunity to represent ourselves in languages we do not really use otherwise, to contribute to the further construction of knowledge and language by adding information to online encyclopedias and dictionaries, and to become a part of literary culture by writing fan fiction and blog posts, or critiquing the work of others.

The fabrication of reality

The opportunities for perceived anonymity and freedom afforded by this newer, less-regulated flow of information, this ability to be and represent the world and self without many constraints, also result in a process that is different from construction: that of the fabrication of reality.

What we are calling fabrication of reality here is different from construction. By construction, as we have seen previously, we mean the mediation of reality by our cultural and social beliefs. Fabrication, on the other hand, is the making up of information by taking advantage of the open flow of it in virtual reality. Many of us may have already seen that phenomenon in action online, be it in the meme with a quote by a celebrity who has never said what the meme claims, or the making up of data and statistics that cannot be substantiated (not unlikely in the form of the generic "studies show that . . . "). In more traditional media (e.g., newspapers, books, academic papers), a series of steps provide attempts to safeguard the accuracy and origin of information (fact check, editorial input, peer review processes); and while it can be argued that they also add a gatekeeping element that emphasizes the existing power dynamics, they do curb the multiplication of "fake" information. Because there is little gatekeeping in virtual environments, the possibilities for spreading fabricated information are very great.

Another interesting case in need of further investigation is that of satirical news which, in dealing with current events, is sometimes hard to tell apart from actual news (some commentary on the nature of "entertainment news" may also be warranted). As a result, while the Internet has caused a democratization of knowledge and expanded the population that gets a say in the construction of knowledge (consider collective encyclopedias, wikis, and dictionaries), it has had as a side effect the possible spreading of deliberately fake information. This new reality might also require that we increasingly engage critically with our sources, with the medium, and with information itself. It might also mean that we should further consider the nature of what we call "truth"; we can argue that there is more truthfulness to construction – after all, it contains fragments of our beliefs and value system – than fabrication, which is not necessarily mediated by such forces or by a belief in the information provided.

Internet etiquette

Part of the reason for the proliferation of the fabrication of reality has to do with accountability and anonymity. The Internet has allowed the participants in interactions to achieve degrees of (perceived) anonymity that are beyond what generally applies to other forms of linguistic interaction. A series of peculiarities, for which we have created **neologisms** (new terms and vocabulary items), are connected to the breach of etiquette and linguistic conventions that happens once accountability is perceived as lacking: "trolling," "flame wars," "doxxing," and "cyberbullying" are but four of them. While they can and do occur in multiple languages, the predominance of English use online, including its presence in communities of multilingual users, makes a discussion of these phenomena in the content of digital Englishes necessary.

Trolling, or the act of purposefully offending or provoking online interactants, often has the goal of eliciting a reaction or simply causing confusion and anger. Interestingly, one of the historical definitions of the verb "to troll" is to "wander, to go in quest of game without purpose,"[1] and this seems to fit the behavior of online trolls very well; they seem to roam chat rooms, comment areas, and other public online spaces with no goal other than to aggravate interactants. Notice how the word *troll* might have come into use: when we need new linguistic terms we have a few options, the most common of which are to create a term from scratch, borrow from another language, or expand the uses of an existing word (many times with a certain metaphorical element to it). The latter applies to *troll* as a neologism.

What *trolls* post does not necessarily represent their view of the world, so in that sense, they are not engaging in cooperation or being truthful, but are also not invested in the points of view they express. Many times, their only agenda is to see what happens when they make outrageous, offensive, or tension-generating posts. Sometimes trolling results in *flame wars*, when unsuspecting or rattled interlocutors respond to trolls, a reaction that can cause an escalation of tension and a back-and-forth of offenses. Flame wars are heated discussions, often times involving *ad hominem* attacks, resulting from online provocation. In many cases, the original topic of discussion is abandoned while two or more posters "flame" one another.

As it happens with trolling, flame wars are an unfortunate side effect of the perceived anonymity and inconsequence of these new modes of communication. Flame wars, however, can also happen among non-anonymous interlocutors, even among people who know each other, a fact which would require an explanation other than obscurity to account for its proliferation online. That is, something about the nature of computer mediation should explicate why people do things online that they would not do or say in face-to-face interactions. Now it seems that besides anonymity (which can lead to a sense of inconsequence) and invisibility (which can mediate introversion), researchers have been able to establish that lack of eye contact plays a significant role in the breech of social and linguistic conventions common in face-to-face interactions.

Noam Lapidot-Lefler and Azy Barak (2012) have been able to demonstrate that what has been called *online disinhibition effect* can be manifested both through traits considered desirable (such as a pull toward philanthropy and a wish to disperse help) or undesirable ones (e.g., bullying, flaming, and trolling). Furthermore, they have discovered that in controlled studies, the number of behaviors considered rude and threatening doubled in situations of no eye contact, resulting in a very high flaming effect. Citing Turnage (2008), the authors also explain that besides the often-mentioned linguistic features of rude language, flaming behavior can also include such textual elements as capital letters, more question marks and exclamation points, bold face, and even red font. These are the written equivalent of rude tone, intonation, and stress that can occur in impolite oral interactions.

Social inaptitude and breech of politeness, however, are also mediated by other elements. A separate study by Markus Appel and colleagues (2014) has found that verbal aggression is lower for teenagers who reveal high-quality parent-related communication, which means that if the teens can rely on their parents to deflect some of the tension generated by online communications, they themselves present fewer flaming traits. Notice that there seems to be an interaction between these variables relating to anonymity and lack of the kind of rapport that interlocutors get in face-to-face interactions. Moreover, if one controls for two of the variables, the effects of the other can be clearly noticed. Remove eye contact, however, and a parcel of the population starts showing behaviors that can be construed as flaming and trolling. As with other social behaviors, it is to be expected that a part of the populace will behave undesirably even in the presence of strong social constraints (e.g., laws), another part will keep behaviors in check even if those constraints were removed (guided by some internal moral, ethical, or motivational force), and another, perhaps sizable part of the population will show different degrees of conformity and defiance when they perceive rules are not present or irrelevant. This is what we usually see on the Internet as well.

But flaming and trolling are not the only phenomena that defy a sense of social order in digital universes. *Doxxing*, for example, is the transference of shaming to the realm of online communications. Doxxing (derived from "document-dropping") is the public outing of a person's address, real name, or other personal information online. Like trolling and cyberbullying, doxxing has the goal of disrupting the life of others, and also like them, it is yet another side effect for which speakers of English (we expect equivalent phenomena in other languages) have had to create a neologism and devise coping behaviors. It is a more localized behavior than our next topic of discussion.

While educators have known and mentored students and parents about the dangers of bullying and the negative impact such behavior has on the victims, society now has to contend with the spread of bullying to electronic media in the form of *cyberbullying*. This is a significant development because of the reach and scope of virtual phenomena. In addition, curbing such behavior when it happens online can be very challenging. According to Patchin and Hinduja (2012:14), cyberbullying is characterized by the bully's intent to harass, use of technology to bully, infliction of negative social and psychological impact on the victim, and engagement in a repetitive pattern of the behavior (which we can expand to include linguistic behavior). Because the phenomenon happens in virtual environments, **threats to face** (challenges to a person's public image; see Brown and Levinson, 1987, for theories of face) can be even greater in online environments, that is, there is an audience that goes beyond the intended bullied person to make matters worse.

A portion of the literature in computer technology, computer science, and information systems has now turned its attention to working and reporting on the creation of programs and software based on linguistic features and vocabulary items commonly associated with cyberbullying to try and detect posts associated with the practice.

Politeness

When we think of these Internet phenomena, breeches of politeness quickly come to mind. The phenomena described earlier can be said to be, among other, more serious charges, challenges to polite behavior. Politeness can be thought of both in a more layperson term as synonymous with *etiquette*, or in more clearly linguistic terms. The seminal work of Penelope Brown and Stephen Levinson inaugurated, in a way, the linguistics and pragmatics preoccupation with a theory of politeness. In *Politeness: Some Universals in Language Usage*, the authors explain that:

> In the case of linguistic pragmatics a great deal of the mismatch between what is 'said' and what is 'implicated' can be attributed to politeness, so that concern with the 'representational functions' of language should be supplemented with attention to the 'social functions' of language, which seem to motivate much linguistic detail.
>
> (Brown and Levinson, 1987:2–3)

This statement appears to also significantly endorse the work and analyses we do in sociolinguistics and in World Englishes. That also means to us that politeness can only be assessed in context, and that politeness is an integral part of the construction of meaning. Consider this example:

Example 1: Would the princess like to have breakfast in the morning room?

Now imagine three different contexts where the question might be uttered. In the first, an actual princess is being addressed by a member of the staff of the palace, who truly wants to know where the royal family member would like her meal sent to. Then think of a completely different scenario where, for example, a roommate, tired of a peer's lack of commitment to keeping their common space tidy and organized, shows dissatisfaction by suggesting through that question that the friend is acting in a spoiled manner. Finally, consider the question being uttered in a play, where the audience and the actors all understand that these are not the words of the actual actors but rather of the people (characters) they represent. Once we know the contexts, we can probably agree that while the first case will likely be decoded as a polite request for information, it is unlikely that the second will be taken in that same fashion. In the third, on the other hand, the lack of truthfulness is not a problem because it is agreed-upon and therefore does not present consequences for the public face of the actors; in this last case, the question can only be considered polite or impolite in the context of the story – not in real life – very differently from the first instance.

In a very simplified way, therefore, politeness aligns with **face wants** while impoliteness can cause **threats to face**. Going back to the example, in the first instance, face is enhanced when the princess realizes that her station is upheld by the way the staff member interacts with her (which includes addressing her in the third person); in the second, the sarcastic comment presents a threat to face, and the roommate will have to decide whether to apologize and start helping more, denounce the comment as exaggerated, reply with an equally mocking comment, etc. (here the third-person use makes the point even more salient). The same will be true of computer-mediated communications: contextuality will help determine if something is said in joust, sarcastically, in friendly banter, disapprovingly, as part of a fantasy universe, etc. Therefore, trolling and flaming, for example, need to be examined in the environment they occur, because it is the nature of those environments and of the interactants involved that causes the behaviors to be affecting or not.

To say that impoliteness online includes such elements as capital letters and exaggerated punctuation is not the same as to say that every case of those uses is rude. Jo Angouri and Theodora Tseliga (2010:66) explain that strategies employed online are context-dependent and can be used for exactly opposite purposes depending on where they appear. We offer you another example. Consider the use of capital letters in this first instance, where a political flame war has erupted between supporters of two political parties:

Example 2A: YOU ARE SOOOO CLUELESS!

In Example 2A, the upper-case letters are used to enhance a sense of harshness and are the written equivalent of shouting at someone; that is, together with the content of the utterance, they point to impoliteness. The repeated letters emphasize the sense of disapproval and criticism.

Now consider the next example as a response to a social media posting in which a teenager announces they are leaving to take an important exam:

Example 2B: HANG IN THERE! WE ALL LOOOOVE YOU!

In Example 2B, the capital letters enhance a sense of support. They are the written equivalent of cheering. The repeated letters further highlight the good feelings and well-wishing. To equate the capital letters with impoliteness would therefore be a hurried generalization.

Whereas punctuation and fonts need to be disambiguated in context, one other element of impoliteness is more straightforward: the use of features of *ad hominem* attacks. That is, escalation of tension can result from a personal attack coming in place of a disagreement with an idea or premise. For example:

Example 3A: You're such a fake!

In this type of utterance, the implication is often that what is being addressed is an immutable, permanent personality trait of one of the interactants, which is then being highlighted and/or publically revealed as undesirable. An *ad hominem* attack poses threats to face and usually represents an exaggerated, distorted interpretation of the issue at hand. Compare the statement in Example 3A above with this example:

Example 3B: I'm sorry, but I am not sure that statement represents your ideas fully.

In Example 3B, **hedging** and **softening** – politeness strategies used to minimize threats to face (e.g., apologizing, or showing uncertainty through "not sure" and gradation through "fully") – make the statement much less hostile. Here the focus is also on an act (the uttering of a statement) and the shortcomings of the act itself rather than on the person as a whole. However, when people get upset on the Internet, especially in open forums, they can quickly resort to personal attacks. Usually in superficial forms of interaction, that is, those where there is a supposition that there will not be further interactions in the future, it is less likely that people will be worried about **saving face**, and that is when escalation can happen more quickly and to greater degrees.

Trolling complicates the matter of politeness, or better yet impoliteness, even further, because in some respects it does not display the characteristics associated with the concepts that have so far defined the parameters of one and the other. Claire Hardaker (2010:237) explains that we really do not yet have a term in politeness theory to express what trolls do because "mock impoliteness" implies that the interlocutors know it is all part of a game (as when two friends are teasing each other). The term "malicious impoliteness" also falls short of explaining the dynamics, because this form of impoliteness presupposes that an overt revelation of the intention to be impolite should take place (and part of the troll's "success" lies in *not* revealing they are actually a troll). It seems that the lack of truthfulness in either intent or disclosure complicates the application of known politeness parameters in this case.

On the other hand, Hardaker explains that there are four dimensions to trolling: 1) Deception, since one pretends to be a real person expressing real ideas and beliefs; 2) Aggression, since the languages and the posts are meant to attack unsuspecting interactants; 3) Disruption, because aggravation is often directed at the whole chatting/commenting community with the purpose of simply causing a disturbance; and finally 4) Success, if the troll manages to upset interactants, elicit a brusque response, and cause disorder. We therefore must come up with a description that encompasses these four aspects. Since the parameters for "achievement" in this kind of interaction is so counterintuitive – after all, we usually measure success in communication by assessing whether information was transmitted, something was learned, or good rapport was established – we will likely need new theoretical elements to account for these phenomena where success means not cooperating, and indeed causing a breakdown in communication.

Cooperation

In 1975, Paul Grice wrote about the **Principle of Cooperation** in conversation. The principle is explained through a series of **maxims** that interact with one another: they are the maxims of quality, quantity, relation, and manner. That means that when people engage in conversation cooperatively, they should try to make contributions that are helpful (but only as informative as necessary), reflect the truth, are pertinent given the situation, and are presented in good order, briefly, clearly, and unambiguously. We can also defy the use of the maxims for a variety of reasons. For example, we might not have the needed information, or we might, to be good-mannered, tell a white lie (as when someone asks if we like their new clothes, but we really do not). We may also try to send a message by flouting the maxims. For instance, if a friend asked another friend, "How did your dinner date go?" and the latter responded, "Look at that dress in the shop window! Isn't it gorgeous?" and thus clearly not abiding to the maxim of relation, the intention might have been to indicate that the information requested is somewhat private and that the person does not want to talk about it. So we can abstract that, even in cases of disrespecting the maxims, there is often intent to cooperate (however loosely defined), be it by avoiding conflict or threats to face or by not telling a lie. In the real world, nevertheless, when people do not want to cooperate, that intent tends to be more obvious.

What happens, however, when people engaged in supposed cooperation do not want to cooperate in the first place? It seems that several phenomena of the Internet age require a revisiting of this principle of cooperation, or in the very least the acknowledgement of the intentional cessation of collaborative modes in some environments by some interlocutors. The afore-mentioned perceptions of anonymity and lack of accountability have led to a breakdown of interactive patterns in several realms of communication. Likewise, linguistic politeness needs to be reexamined in light of the nature of some interactions online, especially the ones that escape our intuitive patterns of interaction or of denial of helpful interaction.

Code-mixing, Englishes, and politeness

Politeness issues are made more complex by the transposition of politeness strategies across Englishes or across linguistic boundaries online. Because different cultures have different views about how features of discourse pose threats to or enhance face, the use of a lingua franca such as English does not guarantee that even under the best of intentions, perceived impoliteness will not result. If members of a given high-context culture (Hall, 1966) believe that to be polite, one must engage in small talk for several minutes before "talking shop" or dealing with business, a member of a high-content culture (Hall, 1966) might be considered impolite or too direct for not honoring such practice. Because, within virtual environments, we cross those linguistic boundaries often, the risk of perceived impoliteness is high.

Imagine, for example, a very short email with a request such as, "Bring your report to the meeting on Tuesday. Thank you." At face value, this is a simple, straightforward message and, although somewhat neutral in tone, the text is softened by the *thank you* at the end. This might be enough to fulfill the expectation of high-content-oriented interlocutors. However, even in something that simple, unmet expectations can play a significant role in communication clashes. Those readers with a cultural preference for high-context orientation, for example, might be taken aback by the lack of an introductory message and other contextual cues. For example:

> Good morning everyone. I hope that you had a wonderful weekend and that you are looking forward to our upcoming meeting. So that we can make the best of our time together, I would like to ask that all participants please bring their reports with them. Thank you for your help.

For similar reasons, or even more compelling ones, when one mixes different languages or varieties, they are not simply juxtaposing linguistic elements; the social expectations and social norms of different cultures are also being brought together. If you mix, for example, English (more traditionally associated with high-content orientation) and Spanish (commonly associated with high-context cultures), what rules apply? Is the language base, the purpose, or the listener the decisive element in mediating directness? What if the three elements do not align? That is part of the reason why code-switching and code-mixing require more than linguistic competence: sociolinguistic and strategic competence play a significant part in the success or failure of the interaction.

Therefore, high- and low-context orientations should be considered together with the many other elements we have presented so far as impacting online interactions, code-mixing, and virtual communication. Next, we will introduce age as another variable of importance in the virtual universe.

Ageism and the Internet

In chapter 6, we wrote about the need to add disability to the other often-cited dimensions of identity, namely gender, race, and ethnicity (for sociolinguistics, class and class **stratification** matter, too). Here, we would like to add one more component: age. David Divita (2012:585) calls our attention to the limitations that have been common in sociolinguistics of considering age to be somewhat of a "fixed chronological fact." Age, it appears, can be as crucial as the other elements, since it "functions as a dynamic interactional resource in more ways than generally thought" (Divita, 2012:586). In investigating the interactional patterns of computer literacy and Internet use among a group of senior citizens in France, Divita identified "talking to grandkids" and "being curious about the Internet" as two important motivators for Internet use.

However, we would also like to consider that alongside the motivators, there are certain barriers to entrance in these linguistic communities. First of all, the same way that languages themselves can be a deterrent (if you do not know Japanese, it would be hard to participate in a community that uses that language), so can variations in dialect and unfamiliarity with a medium-specific language. That is, because so much linguistic innovation on the Internet is spearheaded by youth language and youth culture, age can become a factor in interaction and participation. Sometimes language does not even stay still long enough for latecomers to acquire it. In addition, knowledge of ever-changing technological tools can also present a barrier to entrance. However, these are not insurmountable difficulties, and we can find groups of individuals of different age ranges forming their own networks and speech communities online as well. Attitudinally speaking, the absence of ageism (ageism can be defined as prejudice based on age) greatly facilitates the presence and the thriving of all age groups online, so this acceptance of diversity in age is a characteristic that we should cultivate in ourselves and in our communities. As with other populations, Internet communications can, when thought of strategically, offer greater mobility, opportunities for continuing education, and a bridge across physical space.

Linguistic appropriation, appropriacy, and reappropriation

If you remember earlier in the book, we spoke of many cases of hybridization, code-mixing, and code-switching. But we also spoke of instances where a sort of linguistic theft is involved. Two of those cases entailed lingo-piracy and the appropriation of a minority's linguistic expressions due to a difference in power. We exemplified those with "no problemo" (often used by a group not familiar with Spanish and not representing a form of reverence to the language) and an instance of trademarking abroad of Portuguese terms for everyday foods. These examples, both of them forms of linguistic theft, have nothing to do with a similarly named linguistic concept – that of **linguistic appropriacy**. Appropriacy has to do with how suitable a grammatical or linguistic use is in context. As explained by Suzanne Eggins (2004:139), appropriacy belongs to the realm of descriptivism, since grammar in this sense is about

> . . . making statements and assessments not about good/bad, right/wrong, but also appropriacy or inappropriacy. Degree of appropriacy is assessed not in terms of arbitrary blanket statements about inflexical grammatical 'rules' but as statements about grammar as a set of choices for use in context.

In that sense, because we are in the world of description and observation rather than *a priori*, static prescriptive judgments, we can only decide if a string of language is appropriate given knowledge of the situation and an estimation of our available choices. But appropriacy is also about more than grammar. Dell Hymes (1972), one of the fathers of modern sociolinguistics, coined the term **communicative competence** as a reaction to Noam Chomsky's (1965) **linguistic competence** to evidence that knowledge of strings of language alone could not guarantee successful communication. When assessing the suitability of a particular linguistic form, sociolinguists oftentimes evaluate the **context of situation** (Halliday, 1978:21), or "the set of meanings, the configuration of semantic patterns, that are typically drawn upon under the specific conditions, along with the words and structures that are used in the realization of these meanings." To say "You must shut up!" may show evidence of linguistic competence, that is, knowledge of the syntax of English, word order, vocabulary, modal verbs, and other exclusively linguistic items. However, uttered at an inappropriate context (to a professor, for example, during a formal lecture), the phrase will likely elicit a negative response and will evidence a gap in communicative competence, since the latter also includes knowledge of the sociolinguistics of the context and strategies to make up for such items as imperfect knowledge (i.e., we often err on the more formal and respectful side when we are unsure of the level of formality of a situation).

As another everyday example, speakers of such languages as Portuguese and Spanish are often surprised at the common American response "I don't care" to questions such as "Would you mind if I moved this chair?" Because the sentence translates into an expression of disregard in those languages, what would be a casual and non-face-threatening response in the American context is often taken as inappropriate by interlocutors with a different cultural orientation.

To ask a related question regarding digital language, we could enquire: Is "C u l8r" appropriate? We posit that, just like in the other examples, we will not know until we consider the context of situation. Should it appear as a text message or a post in social media, it will likely be appropriate. If it is used in an academic paper or in a formal email to a potential client, it will likely be deemed inappropriate by several recipients (although even that is not static and absolute). If you remember another early example, we deemed it appropriate to ask a small child if their dinner is "yummy," but it is likely less appropriate to ask your boss at a company dinner the same question (unless it is part of some form of inside joke). So appropriation and appropriacy are not to be confused; they point to very different phenomena, even if both can be of a linguistic nature.

Finally, we want to remind the reader that if there is appropriation, there is also **reappropriation**, or the reclaiming of linguistic form by the very linguistic communities from which they were "stolen." In that case, if speakers of Spanish reclaim "no problemo" (and use it in banter), that might help the term lose the power to disenfranchise them. Members of a Spanish-speaking speech community might find it inappropriate for an outsider to that community to use the term, yet they might find it appropriate if members of their own community reappropriate the term and use it inside the speech community.

A short note on trolling is also relevant here: as it happens with a theory of politeness, we also must question what communicative competence and knowledge of context of situation mean in this online universe of pretend commentary and real offense. In a way, the troll is relying on their communicative competence and knowledge of the situation to gauge what would be an *inappropriate* response in those cases and then proceeds to do exactly that. He or she is relying on sociolinguistic knowledge to make their strategy "work," however undesirable to those on the receiving end those practices might be.

When being unidentifiable is put to good use

Although phenomena such as flaming and trolling are undesirable side effects of anonymity, lax accountability, and lack of eye contact online, not all is gloom. There are instances where this invisibility is put to good use to explore aspects of one's identity, to be less shy, to interact with others for the purpose of self-help, or to help an equally anonymous individual in need – or yet, more broadly, to develop what researchers have been calling "online mobility," (Cruz, 2008: 110–111), that is

> . . . the possibility to travel through the virtual world of the Internet and of its communication spaces, breaking barriers imposed by the lack of knowledge of its codes and languages.

Every day, the users of digital languages are coming up with new ways to use the media to achieve their goals, to build community, and to learn. An endearing project by a Brazilian language school, for example, pairs up English language learners with residents of a retirement home in the US for video chat opportunities[2] (in an oral, synchronic version of the traditional "pen pal"). The students have an opportunity to practice their language skills, while the retired Americans have a chance for social interaction that is also mediated by a piece of technology they might be wanting to understand better (in a great way to address ageism, as well). It is these practices, the ones that foster inclusion, learning, and understanding, that we need to study more and highlight. Our hope is always that the more common virtual communications become, the more we learn to use them for dignified purposes.

Questions for discussion

1 What are some linguistic practices that you have encountered in computer-mediated communication that surprised you? What are some examples of Internet linguistic practices that you find rude?

2 What do you think are appropriate individual and collective ways to deal with trolling?

3 Have you tried to engage people of different ages in Internet communications? If so, what strategies have you used to cater to the linguistic needs of these different age groups?

4 If you are able to code-mix or code-switch, create a simple exchange between two friends in some form of digital medium (an inbox chat, for example). While you were writing it, what elements were more salient in helping you make decisions about tone, directness, word choice, etc.? Explain.

5 What are some online linguistic behaviors that you believe enhance face? Conversely, which practices can you think of that threaten face? Give specific examples (you can provide sample dialogues, too).

6 Write a short email message aimed at a high-content recipient. Then revise it so that it would appeal more to someone who would be more context-oriented. What if you don't know the preference of the recipient? What would you do?

7 If you could write the basic premises for an anti-bullying campaign based on its linguistic features, what would those premises be? What would the campaign be like?

8 What creative ideas for language learning can you envision for digital communications?

Notes

1 See the Online Dictionary of Etymology at http://www.etymonline.com/

2 Williams, R. (2014). Brazilian students learn English through video chat with retired Americans. *The Guardian*, May 12. Retrieved from http://www.telegraph.co.uk/technology/news/10824993/Brazilian-students-learn-English-through-video-chat-with-retired-Americans.html

References and suggested further reading

Angouri, J., & Tseliga, T. (2010). "You have no idea what you are talking about!" From e-disagreement to e-impoliteness in two online fora. *Journal of Politeness Research*, 6(1), 57–82.

Appel, M., Stiglbauer, B., Batinic, B., & Holtz, P. (2014). Internet use and verbal aggression: The moderating role of parents and peers. *Computers in Human Behavior*, 33, 235–241.

Berger, P. L., & Luckmann, T. (1966). *The social construction of reality*. London: Penguin Books.

Brown, P., & Levinson, S. (1987). *Politeness: Some universals in language usage*. Cambridge: Cambridge University Press.

Chomsky, N. (1965). *Aspects of the theory of syntax*. Cambridge, MA: MIT Press.

Cruz, M. (2008). Intercultural cybercommunication: Negotiation of representations of languages and cultures in multilingual chatrooms. *Journal of Multicultural Discourses*, 3(2), 98–113.

Divita, D. (2012). Online in later life: Age as a chronological fact and a dynamic social category in an Internet class for retirees. *Journal of Sociolinguistics*, 16(5), 585–612.

Eggins, S. (2004). *An introduction to systemic functional linguistics*. New York: Continuum.

Grice, P. (1975). Logic and conversation. In P. Cole and J. Morgan (Eds.), *Studies in syntax and semantics III: Speech acts* (pp. 183–198). New York: Academic Press.

Hall, E. T. (1966). *The hidden dimension*. New York: Doubleday.

Halliday, M. A. K. (1978). *Language as social semiotic: The social interpretation of language and meaning*. London: Edward Arnold.

Hardaker, C. (2010). Trolling in asynchronous computer-mediated communication: From user discussions to academic definitions. *Journal of Politeness Research*, 6(2), 215–242.

Hymes, D. (1972). On communicative competence. In J. B. Pride and J. Holmes (Eds.), *Sociolinguistics: Selected readings* (pp. 167–179). Harmondsworth: Penguin.

Jamet, D. L. (2010). What do Internet metaphors reveal about the perception of the Internet? *Metaphorik.de*, 18, 7–32.

Lapidot-Lefler, N., & Barak, A. (2012). Effects of anonymity, invisibility, and lack of eye-contact on toxic online disinhibition. *Computers in Human Behavior*, 28(2), 434–443.

Patchin, J. W., & Hinduja, S. (Eds.) (2012). *Cyberbullying prevention and response: Expert perspectives* (pp. 13–35). New York: Routledge.

Tokar, A. (2007). Internet metaphors: A cross-linguistic perspective. *Culture, Language and Representation*, 5, 209–220.

Turnage, A. K. (2008). Email flaming behaviors and organizational conflict. *Journal of Computer-Mediated Communication*, 13, 34–59.

Chapter 8

Culture and webs of significance

This chapter will help you understand that:

1   Culture can be represented through webs of significance, whereby peoples signify their knowledge and experiences in the world and share them socially.
2   Language is intrinsically related to the concept of culture, as it is itself a symbolic system, and because it is used to share and transmit cultural meanings and values; thus, we may view language *as* culture.
3   The contemporary context of globalization has challenged our traditional understandings of the nation-state and of cultures and languages as inherently linked to different countries and other geopolitical divisions.
4   In the current context of globalization, increased cultural flows have happened (i.e., movements of people, images, symbols, sounds, and so on) through which cultures and people have come into contact with one another, and cultural concepts have become increasingly modified and/or mixed.
5   English (its fragments included) is one of the cultural symbols that has flown across space.
6   Cultural flows in general, and the flow of English in particular, have increased significantly with the advent of the Internet.
7   The new ways in which Englishes have been used online have reflected the structures of a newly emerged cyberculture (in the general sense) and of individual cybercultures.
8   The metaphors of "Web" and "net" work in more than one way, including a linguistic one.

What is culture?

To understand language in context, one has to also understand the pervasive role culture(s) play(s) in our lives. In fact, many are the linguists and academics in other areas (e.g., anthropology, sociology) who consider the association between language and culture to be an intrinsic one, and who use one of the concepts to explain the other. Just like identity plays an important role in sociolinguistic phenomena, so does culture. Our first difficulty, however, is to narrow down culture to the few words of a definition. In fact, as explained by Raymond Williams (1983:87), culture is one of the most complicated terms in the English language:

> . . . partly because of its intricate historical development, in several European languages, but mainly because it has now come to be used for important concepts in several distinct intellectual disciplines and in several distinct and incompatible systems of thought.

In spite of such difficulty, and despite intuitively knowing what we would label as a cultural manifestation, we must still seek to explain the concept. What exactly is culture anyway? One manner in which culture has been positioned is in a binary relation to nature. This understanding differentiates between elements that are already naturally part of an environment (e.g., flowers, rivers, animals), and elements resulting from human activity (e.g., physical, intellectual, spiritual, and so on) upon or within this environment (e.g., a greenhouse, a sculpture, a book). This view also presupposes that while some of our traits are genetic and thus posed as natural (such as one's original hair texture or eye color), others are cultural (such as our religion, social habits, technological advancements, dishes, etc.). Although this binary of nature and culture may be helpful for one to begin conceptualizing culture, it may also be too broad and not complex enough to encompass the rather messy aspects of human interaction with the environment. When one begins to wonder about how race and ethnicity are so intertwined, and of what they might (or might not) mean for many groups of people in terms of their cultural identities, or of how much of what we produce and believe is closely linked to our natural necessities and resources, we may begin to question or at least seek to elaborate more on the supposed dichotomy of nature versus culture.

Perhaps a better way of seeing the interaction of these two concepts is to understand them as complementary in terms of human development and existence. An interesting way to observe such relation is thus to look at how we have advanced – as a species – throughout history. As explained by Carol Delaney (2011), culture, and the capacity for culture, are human universals, and we humans have developed along with them. To illustrate such claim, Delaney uses (among other examples) the insight that anthropologist Franz Boas had, during his fieldwork in Baffinland, where the local people talked about colors of seawater that they could see but that were imperceptible to him. This led Boas to the conclusion that the eye is not merely a physical organ, but it is also a means through which we perceive the world visually; and such perception is conditioned by one's culture and tradition.

While this understanding of culture and human nature as intrinsically interwoven is very helpful, it still does not in and by itself give us a path to how culture can be defined. In order to come to such a definition, we must consider what we believe to be cultural. This would generally include artistic manifestations – such as music, paintings, and dance – and intellectual achievements, habits, and social institutions of a particular group of people (an ethnicity, a nation-state, a region, etc.).

While even a more inclusive conception may fall short of being encompassing of all culture, if we begin to reflect on most of the aspects of any given culture, we will start to see that what they have in common is that they make a statement about how people signify and interpret their own experiences, those of others, their environments, and the world as a whole. The example cited by Delaney, of Boas's inability to perceive certain colors that were easily identifiable to the members of the local community in Baffinland, for instance, shows that they had signified (i.e., conceptualized, grasped) their environment in ways that were unfamiliar to the researcher. Similarly, the institution of marriage in a society (another example given by Delaney) shows how its members signify or symbolize not only emotional and sexual attachment, but also property rights, household organization (e.g., in families), etc. If we think more specifically of the practices involving last names in many marriages, we will also see significations of power relations between men and women in a society, family affiliation, and so on. Hence, culture can be viewed as *a system of symbols* (visual, auditory, behavioral, and so forth), *significations*, and *meanings* that are constructed and transmitted socially. This understanding, we believe, is in line with Yamuna Kachru's (1982) understanding of culture as shared knowledge that enables people to behave as they do, create different artifacts, and structure their knowledge as a whole. It is also in tandem with Clifford Geertz's (1973:5) definition of the term culture as *webs of significance*:

> Believing, with Max Weber, that man is an animal suspended in webs of significance he himself has spun, I take culture to be those webs, and the analysis of it to be therefore not an experimental science in search of law but an interpretive one in search of meaning.

Here, such concept of *webs of significance* will be a central tenet in our discussions of culture, language, and cyberspace, as you will see in the following sections. Important, too, is the idea of a search for meaning, which can be applied to analytical texts (such as this book) but also more encompassing to the whole enterprise of technological development. Human beings engage in a constant process of imagining and re-imagining their surroundings in part to give meaning and purpose to their very existence.

Language and culture: An intrinsic relation

What does language have to do with culture? The quick and straightforward answer to this question is *everything*. Although many have seen language as either an entity in and of itself (detached from anything else), and have tried to study it based on such terms, it is undeniable that actual meanings in language only occur within a sociocultural context. As explained by Claire Kramsch (2002) – based on the work of Vološinov, Rommetveit, Bakhtin, and others – language does not exist in a vacuum:

> ... without historically situated language users or meaning makers in the local context of their communicative practices. Every word uttered or written is addressed by someone to someone about something and for someone's benefit at a particular juncture in time.[1]

Not only that, but it is also mostly – if not entirely – through language (be it verbal or non-verbal) that we construct and pass forth (from a generation to the next, for example) our sociocultural symbols and significations. Hence, while language does not exist outside of culture, it is also the case that culture could not exist and could not be diffused without language. Yamuna Kachru writes of how a "grammar of culture" (i.e., the structures of a particular culture) is closely related to a grammar of language, including linguistic competence and the acquisition of a language itself. The example given by Y. Kachru – of written varieties of Indian English reflecting the same cultural meanings of other Indian languages – illustrates that very well, as it shows how "English in India has truly become an Indian language" (Kachru, 1982:347). Therefore, as proposed by Kramsch in some of her work and also by other scholars, we must look at language *as* culture[2] rather than seeing them as separate entities.

In fact, the connections between language and culture have been considered by a number of scholars in different disciplines for many years. In linguistics, two of them were Edward Sapir (who was himself a student of Franz Boas) and his student Benjamin Whorf, who hypothesized that one's language influences how one perceives or thinks about the world – a theory that is referred to as the **Sapir-Whorf hypothesis**. In a few words, the hypothesis claims that the language of a particular group can affect the way the speakers of that particular language signify and/or categorize certain phenomena. In a way, the theory positions language in a causal relation with thinking itself.

Today, most linguists distinguish between a stronger and a weaker version of the Sapir-Whorf hypothesis. The former (also known as **linguistic determinism**) suggests that our languages actually determine our conceptualizations of the world. The latter (**linguistic relativism**) proposes that different languages have different sets of categories for different phenomena in the world, and thus their speakers perceive the world differently. It is this second and weaker version that is more accepted in current academic circles, although not universally endorsed.

The theory as a whole is widely questioned and considered controversial, particularly its stronger form. If languages really did determine or affect our thoughts and perceptions of the world, it would be (nearly) impossible to translate between different languages or to learn second/foreign languages, for instance.

Peter Trudgill (2000) explains that the one-way hypothesis that operates in the opposite direction (i.e., that society and the environment have an effect upon different languages) is much less controversial. For Trudgill, there are three types of examples that illustrate this claim. First, that the *physical environment* of a particular society is generally reflected in its language – a good example being that some languages have more than one word for a particular object or animal, and others have only one (or none) depending on how specialized the knowledge of the concept has to be for better operation in the society. Second, that language can also reflect the *social environment*, as in the case of kinship vocabulary in different languages – where the one-word items (such as *father* and *uncle* in English) often signal the important relationships for a particular culture (other languages, such as Australian Aboriginal Njamal, for instance, may have a single word for father, uncle, father's cousin, and so on, signaling a difference in how these people are perceived in that culture, as opposed to many English-speaking cultures). Third, that the *values* of a society also affect its language(s) – for example, dictating what subject areas can be spoken of directly and what are usually communicated through euphemisms. In this matter, our language morphs to serve the societies and the people who are a part of social and linguistic groups, where having conceptual terms for those constructs is necessary.

These examples, however, do not eliminate the possibility that the possession of linguistic concepts and terms affects the ways (that might not be causal but rather correlational) we think about the world. For much elaboration in this regard, see the work of Ian Hacking (1995:238) on *semantic contagion*, that is, the fact that having terms to name a certain phenomenon might correlate with our ability to think of phenomena and of the world in those terms.

Sociopolitical issues

Factors other than purely linguistic ones also attest to the close, indivisible relation between language and culture. One of them is that language has been so strong in defining culture (and vice versa) that it is often cited as a type of glue that can hold people together. In his work on the origins and workings of nationalism, for instance, Benedict Anderson (1983:6) makes the case that the idea of the nation-state is one that is imagined rather than real. Imagined, he states, "because the members of even the smallest nation will never know most of their fellow members, meet them, or even hear of them, yet in the minds of each lives the image of their communion." And at least two of the main factors that have enabled the emergence of such nationalist feelings are language-related: a) literacy and commercial printing, which led people who spoke the same language to read the same things (e.g., newspapers and books that became accessible to them) and to think about themselves and others as closely related; and b) the spread of certain vernaculars as a tool of administrative centralization by some monarchs (i.e., the standardization of these vernaculars), having become what Anderson (1983:44) calls print-languages, that is those that "laid the bases for national consciousness." To put it briefly, then, what Anderson says is that these two factors (among a few others) played a major role in defining our thoughts of nationally defined cultures – thoughts that are still quite strong in today's age.

It is not surprising, then, that nowadays many people usually associate nations with specific cultures and with their (official) languages, such as French culture and French (the language) to France; Spanish culture and language to Spain; and Japanese culture and language to Japan. Such associations, however, are usually essentialist and overly simplistic. Cultures and cultural identities are not defined solely based on the territorial boundaries of nation-states, and neither are languages and linguistic identities. Furthermore, many individuals will identify, to different degrees, with more than one culture and language, as explained by Pennycook (2010:64):

> Although the control that nation states have taken over the regulation and construction of languages and cultures has had a great influence over them, especially in the ways in which standard languages and national cultures have been produced, it has never been the case that nations have been good ways of thinking about language and diversity.

If we look at the United States, for instance, we will see that, in spite of the fact that nationalist feelings do exist and may be considered quite strong there, the numerous varieties of English found in the country (e.g., African American Vernacular, Southern English, Chicano English, and so on), as well as the large number of other languages spoken by many of its citizens (such as Navajo and Spanish), reveal a much more complex cultural and sociolinguistic profile than the simplistic association between the country as a whole, including all of its citizens, and its most widely spoken language (English, which – surprisingly for many – is not its official language).

The same can be said about France, Japan, Spain, or any other nation-state. The case of Spain, in particular, is quite interesting, given its complex political and sociolinguistic reality, which includes Basque, Catalan, and Galician (spoken in three of the country's regions: Basque Country, Catalonia, and Galicia) as co-official languages – all of which have very strong identity associations with their respective regions. As anyone who has ever been to Barcelona can attest, for example, the **linguistic landscape** of the city (that is, the salience of languages in signs across its region) reveals an intricate arrangement of Catalan, Spanish, and English.

One of the main challenges of this association between language, culture, and the nation-state in the contemporary moment of globalization, according to Pennycook, is the influence of new media and the new flows of people, cultures, and languages worldwide. Such a view seems highly based on (or closely related to) the work of cultural anthropologist Arjun Appadurai (1996), who made the claim that trying to understand cultures based solely on the notion of nation-states is not enough to account for **diasporas** (movements from one's original homeland) of people, of images, and ultimately, of cultures. This, Pennycook states, does not mean that the nation-state has declined, as it still plays a central role in the regulation of much sociopolitical and economic activity, "but rather that it has become increasingly clear that it is not a very useful construct for thinking about language and culture" (Pennycook, 2010:64–65).

In brief, what Appadurai and later Pennycook and others have meant is that the current context of globalization (where people, images, sounds, ideas, and so on move so fast) results in **cultural flows** through which cultures and people are coming into contact with one another, and cultural concepts have become increasingly indigenized, hybridized, changed, resisted, displaced, and so forth, making it very difficult to analyze them based on static notions of nation-states. As we will see in the following two sections, this understanding has been very important for analyses of how English has spread throughout the world and turned into Englishes; it has also been particularly crucial for discussions of how such spread has taken place in the Internet era.

Englishes and cultures

In chapter 1, we explained that the spread of English worldwide has been historically and sociolinguistically described by the field of world Englishes in a model of Concentric Circles that accounts for the ways the language has extended its reach. That model also makes room for the many varieties of English worldwide to be profiled, documented, and legitimated. As we have explained before and reiterate here by way of a review, the Concentric Circles model establishes that there are three circles of English based on the historical pattern of English spread: **Inner Circle** countries, in which English is often acquired as a first language and has official or default official status (e.g., the UK, Canada, the US, Australia, New Zealand), having been established by a particular pattern of colonization; **Outer Circle** countries, which are those where English was introduced through a second wave of colonization, and generally has official status alongside other languages (such as India, Nigeria, Pakistan, Bangladesh, and Kenya); and **Expanding Circle** countries, where English continues to expand in different degrees and to fulfill different functions (e.g., China, Peru, France, etc.), many of which involve international interaction, travel, and communication (i.e., very limited intranational functions).

The model has been of paramount importance to the understanding of English on a global level and has had a strong impact on its teaching and learning worldwide. It has particularly been praised for its significance in challenging beliefs that varieties other than those from the Inner Circle are deficient; instead, it proposes that they are different due to **nativization** – the process whereby a language becomes acculturated to the people and places to which it expands. An interesting consequence of an understanding of this diversity was the realization that Inner Circle countries are full of different Englishes within themselves.

In terms of language and culture, more specifically, a more pluralistic understanding of English-speaking cultures starts to take shape, one that not only includes the cultures of Inner Circle countries, but that also looks into those of Outer and Expanding Circle countries as significant and active in the process of language change. In this context, literary works in English written outside of the Inner Circle, for example, are believed to bring a "new dimension of English literature and its linguistic, cultural, and literary implications" (Lowry, 1982:2838; see also Thumboo, 1982). **Post-colonial Englishes**, how they have evolved, and their unique properties (Schneider, 2007) have also become a focus of attention. Finally, we can understand communicative competence not in terms of what is "right" or "wrong," or "native" versus "nonnative," but with regards to cultural differences, where appropriacy is defined based on cultural contexts (Nelson, 1982). Still, the main criticism of the Concentric Circles model is related to its emphasis on the idea of the nation (the homogeneous nation, to be more precise), which at present does not alone encompass language variation when these geopolitical demarcations are challenged by virtual media.

World Englishes scholars have not disregarded these additions and amendments to the model – especially because the Concentric Circles came into being before some of these paradigm-changing innovations – to represent a historical movement that has now reached a turning point. World Englishes began as a field of study that changed the way we look at English from a monocentric to a polycentric view. As a field and an orientation, it has constantly evolved to make more and more space and draw more attention to issues of cultural hybridity, multiculturalism, intercultural communication, and multilingualism in the contemporary age of globalization, and of the role that English plays in each of these aspects in many contexts around the world. Our insistence in permeating all the discussions in this book with world Englishes awareness stems from our strong belief that, rather than an appendix to the study of English, a world Englishes approach is a *sine qua non* element for the understanding of language relations in our contemporary world.

In this manner, growing numbers of studies focusing on pop culture, and the role that English has played in many cultural manifestations worldwide, have come to supplement the theoretical bases on which world Englishes stands. These include but are not limited to discussions on instances where English is claimed as one's own and nativized, and where it functions as a signifier of hybridity beyond a Western (mainly American) symbol of cultural identity. These discussions allow us to question gender and racial stereotypes, to reflect local realities, and to re-evaluate cases where the very concepts of language, culture, and territory are central to our understanding of human relations. In turn, new creative possibilities of identity construction and language use can be offered.[3] In all of this work, we see English functioning as a cultural symbol, one that is not bound by territorial borders but that flows easily across space. In fact, in many of them, the concept of territory, as well as the idea of English belonging to specific nations or peoples, is highly contested.

Another interesting way in which the field has addressed issues of multiculturalism, multilingualism, and so on is manifested in the number of scholars who have sought to deconstruct the taken-for-granted, essentialist assumptions about certain types of English and their respective cultures. A good example in that case is Matsuda and Duran's (2013) discussion of how problematic the construction of US Americans as monolingual English speakers is. Such conceptualization, the authors claim, brings an inaccurate representation of the linguistic repertoire of US Americans and disregards the **diasporas** of people who have moved and continue to move into the country. It also reinforces the ideology of English monolingualism in that context, ultimately having consequences in terms of language policies and practices, including the marginalization of multilingual, multicultural speakers, and of multilingualism itself.

Finally, it is crucial that English has come to be treated not as a "foreign" or "other" language, but as an international one that is utilized as a lingua franca to serve the communicative needs of many individuals across the world. That is, English is a language that belongs to all of its speakers (native and nonnative alike), independently of territorial boundaries. As explained by Matsuda and Friedrich (2011), this understanding has clear implications for the ways in which culture is perceived and addressed, especially in English language classrooms. In a few words, Matsuda and Friedrich state that instead of thinking about English as related to the cultures of native-speaking countries, we now have to look at it in terms of the cultures of those learning the language, of the cultures of different types of interlocutors they may encounter, and of global cultures (i.e., issues that pertain to the global community as a whole, such as world peace). This brings a more pluralistic and holistic view of cultures, one that can be more macro or micro depending on the actual needs and realities of the users and learners of the language.

That is not to say that the epistemological unit of the nation-state has been losing force in world Englishes or in sociolinguistics, or that it is no longer important/valid. What we claim is that the understanding of Englishes and their relations to different cultures has gone beyond the limitations that such an approach may have. Scholars are now engaged in grasping how Englishes function to enact and portray local as well as global identities (within macro or more micro spaces), how it interacts with other languages in different settings (again, macro and micro), how it is itself a cultural symbol that flows across territorial boundaries, and all of the sociolinguistic, pedagogical, and cultural implications that these phenomena have had.

Even though the nation-state unit may still be useful in the understanding of cultures and languages (as well as language varieties), we need to move beyond this perspective alone. This means looking at cultures not only based on territorial (mainly national) boundaries, but also in terms of social and linguistic networks, of shared interests, and of multiple perspectives and webs of significance, whereby a person can be more than simply American, or Brazilian, or South African, or Russian.

In regards to Englishes, more specifically, understanding its function as a lingua franca, as well as the endless possibilities of cultural encounters that can take place precisely because of this role, is essential. This implies developing **multicultural awareness** (sensitivity and appreciation for a plurality of different groups, defined not only in terms of territory, but also in regards to gender, ethnicity, sexual orientation, socio-economic status, religious affiliation, mental/physical conditions, etc.) and **intercultural communication** when using the language. It also means digging deeper into the symbolic meanings that the language has in different cultural settings, and how such meanings can bring us new insights into these settings and the language itself. It includes trying to understand discourses *about* English around the world (i.e., what people actually say about the language) in order to see what cultural and linguistic feelings and attitudes have been caused by its global spread. Finally, it requires investigating the boundaries that are actually *created* or *perpetuated* by English, such as educational and socio-economic ones – based upon which some people (from privileged backgrounds) will have the chance of learning and using it, and others will be excluded for not knowing it.

Englishes and culture: The online version

When we look at the online world more specifically, even more complex ontologies (i.e., realities) of Englishes and cultures appear. These new realities require that we look back at **cyberculture**, which we defined in chapter 2 as the cultural practices, beliefs, instruments, and so on that have been formed along with the Internet on a global scale. We also explained in that chapter that the emergence of cyberculture has brought with it new language practices, such as the use of emoticons (or emojis), new abbreviations, vocabulary, and the formation of new cultural subgroups (Web-based), with their own distinctive language uses and repertoires, as well as new modes of communication between people who may or may not know one another outside of virtual spaces.

Given cyberculture, the possibility for people, ideas, and cultural symbols (to name a few) to move across spaces has dramatically increased. Today, for instance, even if one cannot physically relocate to a different place, one can still have friends, acquaintances, and partners (in business or in video games, for example) from around the globe. A person can also spread their ideas on a worldwide scale with the use of the Internet. It has also become much easier for anyone to come into contact with and access cultural symbols that were once considered foreign, unachievable, or even completely inexistent to them.

These cultural symbols have included different languages and what we can call **bits of languages**, in tandem with what Jan Blommaert (2010) has described. In brief, bits of languages refer to parts of a language (e.g., a word, a phoneme, a letter, etc.)

that are used semiotically (symbolically) by those who do not necessarily speak it to communicate their ideas (thus being very close to the concept of borrowing or loanwords). Examples of this phenomenon can be found in Friedrich (2002) about uses of English in advertising in Brazil, where bits of language serve the symbolic purpose of signaling modernity, or technological advancement, or yet status. If these symbolic fragments of language were already in circulation before the advent of new modes, such instances have become more and more widespread on the Internet. Diniz de Figueiredo's study (2010) showed moments when English words were either used online by Brazilian speakers in combination with Brazilian Portuguese morphemes, or had their meanings and/or lexical categories changed when used in that language. These borrowed terms were not necessarily linguistically meaningful in English; instead, their meanings were symbolic, and referred specifically to the context in which the terms were being used (Brazil), in particular to certain (cyber)cultures within that context.

Other interesting points follow. One of them refers to how the study of global English may be accommodated to the use of the language in online communicative encounters. When trying to investigate this issue, Seargeant and Tagg (2011), for instance, raise the question of whether a **post-varieties approach** (i.e., one that goes beyond the notion of language varieties that are associated with communities of speakers) might be necessary to account for English on the Internet. Their questioning is mainly based on the difficulties that one may encounter when attempting to use the concept of linguistic varieties to explain virtual communicative events on the Web, such as online chats, social media entries, and so on.

In order to investigate this matter, Seargeant and Tagg looked at computer-mediated discourses (Herring, 2001) via social media and the Microsoft Network (MSN) communications on smartphones between native speakers of Thai (who either lived in Thailand or in an Inner Circle English-speaking country), all of whom had studied English at least up to a higher education level. Their findings revealed a number of factors. For instance, they showed that English was quite extensively used between these speakers in online communication, even though they were all native speakers of the same L1 (Thai) – whereas in oral, offline communication it was likely that they would use Thai exclusively, as explained by one of their participants (whom they later had the chance to interview). Another interesting issue revealed had to do with the fact that the English being used by them was not oriented towards any Inner Circle, norm-developing variety. Quite the contrary, their English discourse was characterized as *sui generis*. Yet another factor that proved noteworthy was that the use of English by these speakers had other motivators, such as creativity, convenience (characterized by the participant who was interviewed as "laziness"), and/or communicative clarity.

Seargeant and Tagg (2011:509–510) interpreted their results as evidence of three main phenomena: 1) that the use of English has become an intrinsic element of the speakers' online literacy practices, and "offers a broader range of semiotic opportunities (such as the indexing of different degrees of social distance, and the flexibility to overcome the limitations of available technologies) than Thai alone would"; 2) that although Thailand is an Expanding Circle country, "there appears to be little compulsion amongst these interlocutors to comply with Inner Circle norms as these are codified as teaching standards"; and 3) that the practices of digital literacy "act as a site for unregulated and individualised vernacular linguistic expression . . . rather than one in which the participants replicate an offline vernacular variety."[4]

Seargeant and Tagg offer two main conclusions in their study. First, the type of language they encountered does not fit precisely within the Concentric Circles model of the spread of English proposed by Kachru, or with the idea of discreet, easily identifiable languages and linguistic varieties (mostly based on nations and/or regions) that is generally commonplace in sociolinguistics. Second, their data have shown a paradox in terms of language studies. On the one hand, they can identify which features belong to English or Thai (distinct languages), or to a particular variety (Thai English); on the other, they cannot consider the phenomenon as a whole – the discourses themselves – under the category of a variety. In the words of the authors themselves, such a phenomenon "exhibits too much diversity [and] does not have obviously identifiable systematic regularities" (Seargeant and Tagg, 2011:511). When it comes to online language use – and particularly online English use in this case – the authors claim we are at the intersection of what is systematic and what is free-flowing, and thus "it would seem counter-productive to *begin* with a varieties approach" when documenting this type of English use on the Web (Seargeant and Tagg, 2011:511).

Seargeant and Tagg, posit, and we would concur, that these new findings do not invalidate the concept of a variety itself or the Concentric Circles model. For them, while an analysis of certain types of data – such as online encounters that code-switch between English and other languages – may not be best achieved by these frameworks, and the actual notion of varieties may be "more appropriate for the description of a community's language use in contexts where the focus is not simply on strategies of communication but also on cultural and political identity" (Seargeant and Tagg, 2011:512). Hence, as we have previously explained, scholars in sociolinguistics and world Englishes have moved beyond the exclusive use of a perspective based on nations, regions, and varieties, but these have still been very useful in the study of cultures and languages, including Englishes.

The ease with which flows of symbols, messages, and images (to name a few) take place in digital environments, and the central role that language and bits of language have had in such flows, have allowed people to shape their cultures in varied, expanded ways, and to have access to a myriad of other types of culture that have become available for them. Through the Internet, many young people worldwide have, to name a few: 1) organized social movements that have had an impact on urban landscapes in many cities; 2) had access to different types of music and other cultural manifestations on a larger scale, and used music devices and online media to socialize in novel ways; 3) promoted new genres of music and other arts; 4) engaged in life writing, fan fiction, and other powerful narratives with accounts of themselves and of how they perceive the world; and 5) reshaped spaces in terms of private and public in accordance to their own necessities, wishes, and tastes.[5] In a few words, then, we can say that online cultures, especially those of youth groups, are more flowing, less stable, more fluid for one to navigate across, and harder to conceptualize in terms of easily identifiable categories than our traditional understandings of territorially bounded cultures.

Are these new identities and cultures exclusive to speakers (native and non-native) of Englishes? Of course not. Yet, it is undeniable that English has been central to many of these changes, not only because of its communicative, lingua franca function, but especially due to its symbolic meanings of globalism, cosmopolitanism, mobility, modernity, fashion, and coolness. These meanings can surely be contested, but have nevertheless been prevalent in many circles around the globe.

Some controversial issues

While much of this discussion has focused on the increased, improved, and freer flow of people, ideas, and language in this virtual age, not all is without problems and complications – a point that we hope we have made obvious by our discussions in chapter 7. For example, Delaney (2011:online version) has considered whether virtual relationships and cultures reinforce meetings and bonds only between those who think similarly, and thus exclude the possibility of people having to face those who are different or think differently from them. In the words of Delaney herself, the concern is that cyberspace "limits rather than expands our cultural horizons, by consolidating people of common outlook and effectively creating new versions of the gated community." This concern is not unfounded. However, even if this type of situation does exist (and it indeed does), it is also true that there seems to be more cultural communities available for one to join online than there were before (when one was limited by physical space), and more possibilities for one to see and meet people who think differently than ever before. In other words, if many are indeed staying within their social bubbles, many times they are not doing so for lack of other options, but because they choose to do so.

Another of Delaney's concerns, and one we mentioned previously in chapter 4, is that the Internet is not a universally public medium, since access to it is still limited to certain sectors of the world's population based mostly on socioeconomic status and cultural capital (also explained in chapter 4) but also on language (especially languages of wider communication). This is particularly relevant when we think of Englishes and of how a lack of proficiency in the language can many times limit the access one can actually have to information and opportunities online (for publishing, being read, etc.).

Still, English in and by itself does not grant or constrain access to computers, to the Internet, or to digital literacy, even if it does have strong influence on what one can or cannot use, understand, and do online. Instead, then, English can perhaps be seen as an additional segregating factor to an already separated cyberspace. Even then, we must once again remind the reader that power and access are not absolute or totally inherent to knowing or not knowing English (or to any other factor for that matter), as a number of other aspects may actively determine how much can actually be done with such knowledge. Furthermore, we must also restate that there are increasing numbers of tools being developed to solve difficulties that may be caused by language barriers, such as online dictionaries and translators.

One final concern regarding Englishes online is whether the prevalence of the English language in cyberspace, both for communicative and symbolic purposes, brings with it the sociocultural values, attitudes, and beliefs of certain places – in this case, more specifically, of countries such as the United States and United Kingdom – to the detriment of cultural manifestations and beliefs of others. Perhaps the most precise answer to this question is "yes, but only to a certain extent." We have to answer at least partially in the affirmative because it is undeniable that these two areas are still highly associated with English by a large number of individuals worldwide (even if uncritically); and also because the US, especially, is highly associated with the technology industry, as many of the major companies involved in it are based there. But accepting that statement *only to a certain extent*, on the other hand, refers precisely to the flexibility of cyberspace and of cyberculture, and the strong flow of other Englishes on the Web – flows that have allowed a large number of people to come into contact with them, claim them as their own, and use them. These language users are not necessarily abiding to the norms of Inner Circle countries, as Seargeant and Tagg have shown, because the Internet has helped us de-essentialize our uniform notions of Inner Circle (and also Outer and Expanding Circle) cultures, and to question cultural assumptions we used to make in the past, even if we are just beginning to do that. And finally, as more and more linguists have argued, and as we have tried to explain at different moments in this book, there has been a shift of perception in the way we look at English itself. It has gone from a localized language belonging exclusively to specific countries, to a globalized language that can be adopted and claimed by many – either communicatively or symbolically. In this case, the semiotics of Englishes have started to move from "symbol of the US or the UK" to symbol of internationalism, intercultural communication, mobility, and so on; and we begin to see a shift in notions of center vs. periphery, to a broader understanding of how individuals can challenge dominant discourses of English use through the ownership they can take of the language in their various social, cultural, and linguistic contexts. The Englishes and the cultures of the Internet age are polycentric.

Englishes and the new webs of significance

Earlier in this chapter, we explained how Yamuna Kachru shows that English in India has become a true Indian language, since the structure of the language has reflected the "grammar of culture" of India, which is also present in other

Indian languages. A question we may raise in analogy, then, is whether English has become a truly digital language; that is, whether the grammar of online English echoes the grammar of cyberculture.

To answer this question, we must look at two different aspects of this inquiry. Indian English – even when we consider its different varieties instead of looking at it as a single one – is somewhat localized, with relatively easily identifiable boundaries, whereas online English is a far more open concept, one with no clear limits, and which exists in a space that is already hard to define – a "space that is no space," to cite Carol Delaney (2011) once again. By the way, this is what complicates a formal description of English as a lingua franca in its world-wide manifestation: the lack of boundaries makes the formal features negotiable in context rather than *a priori* determined. Moreover, the diversity and lack of systematicity of online uses of English, so appropriately pointed out by Seargeant and Tagg (2011), and the expanded uses they have when compared to Englishes in the real world (such as Indian English) would make the comparison seem difficult. However, even in the case of Englishes in the real world, we do face the complication that original geopolitical boundaries exist only to be challenged. How many users of Indian English now live outside of India and form communities whose "linguistic glue" happens to be Indian English? Probably many. How many of these users of Indian English code-switch between their communal varieties and other varieties of English associated with the physical spaces where they now live? Certainly quite a few. And how many of these users of Indian English expand the boundaries of this variety by adding to it, creating new terms, and borrowing language from other Englishes and other languages? Likely all of them.

When we think of Geertz's (1973) assertion at the beginning of this chapter that culture refers to webs of significance we ourselves have spun, we may then see cybercultures as new webs that are undergoing the very process of spinning at this very moment. Metaphorically, isn't that how the idea of the "Inter*net*" or "Web" works anyways? We have just started to make sense of the Internet (a couple of decades is historically just a little point in a long line), of what it means to us as individuals and as a collective, of the power it has and that it can bring us, and of the implications it has had (and may still come to have) for our social relations, identity construction, and so forth. And thus, we have only just begun to spin the webs of cyberculture as a whole, and of the many individual cybercultures that we currently have and that will come to exist. But we know what spinning these webs means, because we have continuously done that in the non-virtual world.

Language figures as one of the main elements in the construction of these webs of significance in cyberspace. This means that creating new genres, merging spoken and written varieties, building new forms of symbolism, and code-switching and code-mixing in different ways, is intrinsic to the process of spinning these webs. In other words, we can re-conceptualize language use as a whole based on the characteristics of the cyberculture(s) we have been developing since the mass popularization of the Web. And at the same time, these new forms of using language have helped us in the very construction of these new cultures.

It may seem that such re-conceptualization has taken place exclusively in the realm of language online. That is, many may still believe that language use online and language use in "real life" are completely separate things. This is not the case. The way we have used language digitally has influenced the way we use language outside of the Internet in many occasions (think, for example, of words that came up in cyberspace, that were thought of as youth **slang** or some other type of fad at first, and that have ultimately been incorporated into a language). Even more crucially, the dynamics of change that underline the processes are the same. It is for that reason that we can teach you established sociolinguistic concepts through the narration of digital phenomena.

Hence, as we have shown, the grammars of online Englishes (the forms the English language has taken when expanding into the online realm) have reflected the grammars of cyberculture and of individual cybercultures (i.e., the new webs of significance we have been spinning on and through the Internet) in the same ways that the grammars of everyday life reflect those users and realities, but the porosity between these universes is very great. In a way, we can say that this is no surprise, given the intricate relationship between language and culture. Still, it will be interesting to see the novel ways in which this relationship will develop in years to come, as the Web itself advances and becomes more and more part of our lives and of our selves, in whatever shape it comes to have.

Questions for discussion

1 How does (do) the language(s) of your community(ies) reflect its (their) culture(s)?

2 What do you think about the Sapir-Whorf hypothesis that one's language influences how one perceives or thinks about the world? Can you justify your answer using real-life examples from your own experience?

3 What do you think about Benedict Anderson's claim that the idea of the nation-state is more imagined than real? (Think of your own national identifications when answering this question.)

4 Can you think of cultural products, images, sounds, etc. (other than English) that have also flowed across space and that have impacted different cultures? Has the Internet had an important role in such flows? If not, what other media may have impacted them?

5 What bits of language do you know that have flowed from English into other languages? How about from other languages into English?

6 Start a table in which you list characteristics of Internet phenomena and their linguistic equivalents in "real" life.

Notes

1 Electronic article. For more on this matter, see chapter 2.
2 For instance, see Kramsch (1995).
3 See, for instance, Chan (2009), Dimova (2012), Diniz de Figueiredo (2015), Lee (2006), Moody (2006), Omoniyi (2006), and Stanlaw (2000).
4 See Androutsopoulos (2011) for more on vernacular linguistic expressions and vernacular practices of digital literacy.
5 Bennett and Robards (2014). For more on these and other illustrations on how the Internet has changed cultural configurations among youth, see also the edited volume by David Bell and Barbara Kennedy (Bell & Kennedy, 2000) for an earlier account of changing cultural patterns in the virtual world. See also Avdeef, 2014; Bird, 2014; Jung, 2014; Lincoln, 2014; and Robards, 2014.

References and suggested further reading

Anderson, B. (1983). *Imagined communities: Reflections on the origin and spread of nationalism.* New York: Verso.

Androutsopoulos, J. (2011). Localizing the global on the participatory web. In N. Coupland (Ed.), *The handbook of language and globalization* (pp. 203–31). Oxford: Wiley-Blackwell.

Appadurai, A. (1996). *Modernity at large: Cultural dimensions of globalization.* Minneapolis: University of Minnesota Press.

Avdeef, M. (2014). Young people's musical engagement and technologies of taste. In A. Bennett and B. Robards (Eds.), *Mediated youth cultures: The internet, belonging and new cultural configurations* (pp. 130–145). New York: Palgrave Macmillan.

Bell, D., & Kennedy, B. M. (Eds.). (2000). *The cybercultures reader.* New York: Routledge.

Bennett, A., & Robards, B. (Eds.). (2014). *Mediated youth cultures: The internet, belonging and new cultural configurations.* New York: Palgrave Macmillan.

Bird, S. (2014). Flash mobs and zombie shuffles: Play in the augmented city. In A. Bennett and B. Robards (Eds.), *Mediated youth cultures: The internet, belonging and new cultural configurations* (pp. 213–232). New York: Palgrave Macmillan.

Blommaert, J. (2010). *The sociolinguistics of globalization.* Cambridge: Cambridge University Press.

Bruthiaux, P. (2003). Squaring the circles: Issues in modeling English worldwide. *International Journal of Applied Linguistics, 13*(2), 159–178.

Chan, B. (2009). English in Hong Kong Cantonpop: Language choice, code-switching and genre. *World Englishes, 28*(1), 107–129.

Delaney, C. (2011). *Investigating culture: An experiential introduction to anthropology* (Kindle DX version). Malden, MA: Wiley-Blackwell. Retrieved from Amazon.com.

Dimova, S. (2012). English in Macedonian television commercials. *World Englishes, 31*(1), 15–29.

Diniz de Figueiredo, E. H. (2010). To borrow or not to borrow: The use of English loanwords as slang on websites in Brazilian Portuguese. *English Today, 26*(4), 5–12.

Diniz de Figueiredo, E. H. (2015). English identity and Manguebeat in Brazil. *World Englishes, 34*(3), 456–470.

Friedrich, P. (2002). English in advertising: Sociolinguistic considerations and the case of Brazil. *English Today, 3,* 21–28.

Geertz, C. (1973). *Interpretation of cultures.* New York: Basic.

Hacking, I. (1995). *Rewriting the soul: Multiple personality and the sciences of memory*. Princeton, NJ: Princeton University Press.

Herring, S. (2001). Computer-mediated discourse. In D. Tannen, D. Schiffrin, and H. Hamilton (Eds.), *Handbook of discourse analysis* (pp. 612–634). Oxford: Blackwell.

Hinkel, E. (Ed.) (1999). *Culture in second language teaching and learning*. Cambridge: Cambridge University Press.

Jung, S. (2014). Youth, social media and transnational cultural distribution: The case of online K-Pop circulation. In A. Bennett and B. Robards (Eds.), *Mediated youth cultures: The internet, belonging and new cultural configurations* (pp. 114–129). New York: Palgrave Macmillan.

Kachru, Y. (1982). Culture, style and discourse: Expanding noetics of English. In B. B. Kachru (Ed.), *The other tongue: English across cultures* (pp. 340–352). Urbana and Chicago: University of Illinois Press.

Kramsch, C. (1995). The cultural component of language teaching. *Language, Culture and Curriculum*, 8(2), 83–92.

Kramsch, C. (1998). *Language and culture*. Oxford: Oxford University Press.

Kramsch, C. (2002). Language and culture: A social semiotic perspective. *Association of Departments of Foreign Languages Bulletin*, 33(2). Retrieved from http://www.adfl.org/bulletin/v33n2/332008.htm?ref=ARKADASBUL.NET

Kubota, R. (2012). The politics of EIL: Toward border-crossing communication in and beyond English. In A. Matsuda (Ed.), *Principles and practices of teaching English as an international language* (pp. 55–69). Tonawanda, NJ: Multilingual Matters.

Lee, J. S. (2006). Crossing and crossers in East Asian pop music: Korea and Japan. *World Englishes*, 25(2), 235–250.

Lincoln, S. (2014). Young people and mediated private service. In A. Bennett and B. Robards (Eds.), *Mediated youth cultures: The internet, belonging and new cultural configurations* (pp. 42–58). New York: Palgrave Macmillan.

Lowry, A. (1982). Style range in new English literatures. In B. B. Kachru (Ed.), *The other tongue: English across cultures* (pp. 283–298). Urbana and Chicago: University of Illinois Press.

Matsuda, A., & Duran, C. S. (2013). Problematizing the construction of US Americans as monolingual English speakers. In V. Ramanathan (Ed.), *Language policies and (dis)citizenship: Rights, access, pedagogies* (pp. 35–51). Tonawanda, NJ: Multilingual Matters.

Matsuda, A., & Friedrich, P. (2011). English as an international language: A curriculum blueprint. *World Englishes*, 30(3), 332–344.

Moody, A. J. (2006). English in Japanese popular culture and J-pop music. *World Englishes*, 25(2), 209–222.

Nelson, C. L. (1982). My language, your culture: Whose communicative competence? In B. B. Kachru (Ed.), *The other tongue: English across cultures* (pp. 327–339). Urbana and Chicago: University of Illinois Press.

Omoniyi, T. (2006). Hip-hop through the world Englishes lens: A response to globalization. *World Englishes*, 25(2), 195–208.

Park, J. S., & Wee, L. (2009). The three circles redux: A market-theoretic perspective on world Englishes. *Applied Linguistics*, 30(3), 389–406.

Pennycook, A. (2010). Nationalism, identity and popular culture. In N. H. Hornberger and S. L. McKay (Eds.), *Sociolinguistics and language education* (pp. 62–86). Tonawanda, NJ: Multilingual Matters.

Robards, B. (2014). Mediated experiences of 'growing up' on Facebook's timeline: Privacy, ephemerality and the reflexive project of self. In A. Bennett and B. Robards (Eds.), *Mediated youth cultures: The internet, belonging and new cultural configurations* (pp. 26–41). New York: Palgrave Macmillan.

Schneider, E. W. (2007). *Postcolonial English: Varieties around the world*. Cambridge: Cambridge University Press.

Seargeant, P., & Tagg, C. (2011). English on the internet and a 'post-varieties' approach to language. *World Englishes, 30*(4), 496–514.

Stanlaw, J. (2000). Open your file, open your mind: Women, English, and changing roles and voices in Japanese pop music. In T. Craig (Ed.), *Japan pop! Inside the world of Japanese popular culture* (pp. 75–100). Armonk, NY: M. E. Sharpe.

Thumboo, E. (1982). The literary dimension of the spread of English. In B. B. Kachru (Ed.), *The other tongue: English across cultures* (pp. 255–282). Urbana and Chicago: University of Illinois Press.

Trudgill, P. (2000). *Sociolinguistics: An introduction to language and society*. New York: Penguin Books.

Williams, R. (1983). *Keywords: A vocabulary of culture and society*. Oxford: Oxford University Press.

Chapter 9

Conclusions

In this concluding chapter, you will:

1 Revisit some of the crucial concepts in sociolinguistics presented in previous chapters;
2 Understand that theories have been proposed to try and represent the current state of English;
3 Question whether deterministic views of language power stand up to scrutiny;
4 Reflect on our condition as human beings living in the digital era as both subjects and researchers of linguistic phenomena;
5 Review the relationship between changing Englishes and the changing nature of digital communications; and
6 Be invited to consider what the future may hold.

Liquid language, liquid times

For years now, sociologist Zygmunt Bauman has been conceiving of our contemporary times as what he calls *liquid modernity*. What Bauman means by the term *liquid* is that our behaviors, relationships, trade negotiations, wants, and wishes transform so fast in present society that we do not have time to strengthen them enough for them to become robust and durable. In the words of Bauman (2007:1) himself, this liquid modernity consists of the following:

> . . . a condition in which social forms (structures that limit individual choices, institutions that guard repetitions of routines, patterns of acceptable behavior) can no longer (and are not expected) to keep their shape for long, because they decompose and melt faster than the time it takes to cast them, and once they are cast for them to set. Forms, whether already present or only adumbrated, are unlikely to be given enough time to solidify, and

cannot serve as frames of reference for human actions and long-term life strategies because of their short life expectation.[1]

According to Bauman, such liquid property of our contemporary lives is related to the loss of power of the nation state, to increasingly frail interhuman bonds, to the weakening of social structures, and to the great amount of responsibility that is ultimately placed onto individuals' shoulders to solve new, volatile issues that change so easily and quickly. Ultimately, Bauman's description of this new liquid condition of our times is a criticism of the unregulated nature of neoliberalism, whereby the concept of an open society – once conceived based on the "self-determination of a free society cherishing its openness" – now brings with it "the terrifying experience of a heteronomous, hapless and vulnerable population confronted with, and possibly overwhelmed by forces it neither controls nor fully understands" (Bauman, 2007:7).

Bauman's criticisms, while an important point for reflection, give away what has always been a constant amid change in the history of the world: that life is becoming harder, that things were more under control before, and that people were happier and had fewer problems. Each society always seems to think that things were easier in the past, perhaps because the past is already done with, and so it is hard not to conclude that nostalgia is an active aspect of any living society. In a way, in our time, the "liquid nature" of digital communication may have contributed to these fears, but we should not exaggerate those into pessimism: we have been given tools that, combined with linguistic expressions, could help us devise a world with more inclusiveness, respect, and opportunity, dreams that many societies historically have also desired to make into reality.

While these issues can be seen from a number of perspectives (sociological, psychological, urbanist, economical, ecological, to name a few), and of course there may be many who will find them problematic for one reason or another, still we believe they serve as a good starting point for a final discussion over the object of our study throughout this book. Hence, there are some questions we wish to address in this final chapter: 1) Have languages become liquid in our contemporary world, and if so, how? 2) Have Englishes (also) become liquid, and if so, how? 3) If both of the previous questions (or at least one of them) have (has) an affirmative answer, what has been the role of the Internet in this liquefaction process? As we seek to answer these questions, we will return to some of the main concepts we have presented throughout the book. We will then engage with a discussion over the sociolinguistics of globalization, and how a look at the Internet and Englishes can be helpful to us in that sense. We hope this final discussion over this topic is clarifying, and that it can contribute to further enquiries over languages and Englishes on the Web and in contemporary society as a whole. Yet, we know that our accounts here may be only one small part of the full picture, one that includes innumerous "webs of significance," as we related in chapter 8, with connecting threads of complexity and variation. Thus, we invite readers to join the conversation and bring contributions to it, especially now that you have the language and the linguistic concepts to engage more fully with the subject matter of this text and with your experience online.

Liquid times, Englishes, and the Internet: The nature of digital Englishes

In order to address the three questions we posed in the previous section, we must again consider that there are different ways of using language in our contemporary world. As explained by Gee and Hayes (2011), there are three different social formations in our present context, and each one of them encompasses different ways of using language. The **oral social formation**, the first one we developed in our history as a species, involves oral **genres**, which usually have highly interactive exchanges, flexible interpretation, the possibility of instant clarification, and negotiation of meaning, among other characteristics (of course, this varies from genre to genre). The historical problem we faced here was that there was little or no possibility of confirming one's statements as true or correct.

The second social formation we developed – **literate social formation** – solved that problem. We could now produce and refer to records, and find written evidence of what had been previously stated; and our messages could now travel across space and time and be received by others in distant locations and ages. However, other problems emerged from this type of communication. For instance, texts had to be interpreted outside of their original contexts, many times leading to misinterpretations or other types of problems, and there was little or no room for meaning negotiation between the producers of a certain text and their readers. This fact led to the appearance of what Gee and Hayes (2011) call *fixed interpretations of texts*, generally provided by bureaucrats, technical experts or specialists, and institutions – which also sought to certify those whose interpretations actually counted.

The most recent of the social formations is the **digital social formation**, which came with the development of digital technologies, including the Internet. In this new type of formation, written and oral genres seem to merge and create yet newer genres, and individuals use written language in ways that resemble oral language. In addition, many people have gained more interpretive **power** – as well as the power to create and disseminate new messages – which in turn has caused the authority of those who provide fixed interpretations of texts to dwindle. The issue we may be facing, on the other hand, is that this new formation "lends itself to many fragmented 'discourse communities' or passionate affinity spaces setting their own norms and enforcing their own rules and values" (Gee and Hayes, 2011:126), which may lead to more chaotic social configurations and less protection for minorities by nation-states.

This information is not new, and we have addressed it in previous chapters, although not with the exact same terms we have been using here. However, we will revisit these ideas since they are, we believe, at the center of the questions we proposed at the beginning of this chapter. Let us explain how.

As far as oral uses of English are concerned, we can say that a number of established **varieties** exist (such as Indian English, American English, Australian English, New Zealand English, Singaporean English, British English, Jamaican English, and so on), both in the Inner and Outer Circles proposed by Kachru,[2] and that there are multiple varieties of each one of those varieties as well (such as Cockney, African American Vernacular English, etc.). In fact, some scholars working with English in Expanding Circle contexts have claimed that we can now even speak of established Expanding Circle varieties as well, like Japanese or Chinese English (see Hino, 2009 and 2012, for example). In this way, people who speak Japanese or Chinese English, for instance, do not always rely on native-speaker norms, and instead can express local values through their own forms of English use. They can also engage with code-mixing and switching in innovative and language-changing ways. Note that although Expanding Circle varieties do exist and are in no way substandard or deficient, scholars still do not have comprehensive accounts of their purposes and functions intranatioanally, for example, and some still doubt whether they have become systematized enough to be considered established. Many, for example, do not have markers of such institutionalization, such as a literature of their own or a described grammar (in the form of grammar books) of their own characteristics. For more, see Matsuda and Friedrich (2011).

Careful! Under construction

For our purposes here, it matters that readers understand that the existence of these different variations of English in the world today – in other words, these Englishes, including the Expanding Circle ones – does not imply that the language has become *liquid* or less robust in any way, even if some can argue that English as a whole and its multiple varieties are in fast, constant change. The same is also true of written Englishes, which are actually even more solid and less susceptible to change than their oral counterparts due to their more standardized nature – although **language change** does take place in them as well. In fact, the "rules" of standard uses of Englishes promoted by prescriptive grammars and purists are still – at least for the most part – heavily based on formal, written forms, which shows the strength that written varieties have in portrayals of the language, its documentation, and spread.

In other words, then, when it comes to the oral and the literate social formations, and to their respective genres in Englishes, we can say that they remain quite strong, and have not reached a *liquid* state (in the sense defined by Bauman), even though it is the case that they are malleable, susceptible to change, and have received influences from several contexts, including the online world and its ways of using languages. And that is why, as we stated in chapter 8, the Kachruvian Concentric Circles model and the variety-based notion of English remain useful for us to understand the spread of the language worldwide – even if, as we have also stated, we have had to go beyond them in recent years in order to explain more recent phenomena and/or to take into consideration other social and linguistic issues we have encountered.

What can we say about the digital social formation, then? Here we have a different story. First of all, English has been very adaptable in digital genres, and many of its terms have been **borrowed** by other languages to refer to novel technological advances (be them physical, as in the case of computers and smartphones, or virtual, such as vocabulary for things that exist in digital space, such as *blogs*). Second, in digital media, power shifts have allowed for phenomena such as the increasing influence of nonnative uses of the language over native-speaker uses, the emergence of new spoken and written genres, high degrees of code-mixing and switching, and the creation of alternative references to Englishes, such as online dictionaries. These and other similar phenomena have made the language more malleable, and have even exerted some influence over how people use the language outside of the online world. The example of the *Urban Dictionary* given in chapter 5, and of how it has destabilized traditional, prescriptive lexicography (both online and in the "real" world), is a great illustration of such fact.

And third, as stated in chapter 8, we have encountered more and more instances of English being used online for communicative purposes in ways we had not witnessed very much in face-to-face interactions: as an intrinsic (sometimes predominant) element of **digital literacy** practices among nonnative speakers who share (or not) the same native language – at times with little or no reference to Inner Circle varieties (as has been normally expected in oral and written genres) – with high instances of **code-mixing** and individualized linguistic expression, and with a true reflection of globalized, cosmopolitan **identities**.

These factors could lead us to the conclusion that Englishes in the digital social formation (i.e., **digital Englishes**) are indeed in a liquid state, as they do not seem to have a regular shape that is based on specific norms and institutions, or regular patterns that can be expected. Moreover, when we consider that the language has been **flowing** across spaces, it could seem natural to think of it as entirely fluid or *liquid*, in Bauman's sense of the word. However, such a conclusion may be only part of the whole picture of digital Englishes today. For one, it must be said that it is still too early for us to determine whether these digital uses of the language are simply taking place now and will soon decompose or melt, or if they are here to stay (as seems to be the case), and we will at some point be able to account for them with new frameworks and models of analysis (such as the post-varieties approach proposed by Seargeant and Tagg, described in chapter 8). When we study phenomena that took place through the history of the English language – the multiple invasions to the British Islands, the plague epidemic that may have triggered the Great Vowel Shift, or the effect of the formation of the first urban centers – we do so from the vantage point of the future. When we study language and the processes taking place in the digital era, we are immersed. We are, ourselves, catalysts of the changes taking place, and these processes are not done with. Our conclusions are a bit of an educated guess, a bit of a transposition of the known dynamics of language, and a bit of futurology.

Other questions still remain: has this relative fluidity of English in particular, and languages in general, and the expanded opportunities of language use, had an effect on attrition (i.e., the loss of fluency in an original or first language after a move to a different country where other languages are spoken)? Are our linguistic choices made online more impacted by emotional connections or functional needs? What is the degree of influence of online linguistic behavior on behavior outside digital media?

We also need to consider that Bauman's conceptualization of the term *liquid* seems to imply a very negative sense to it, a criticism of contemporary modernity and globalization, a sense of weakness, whereas the way in which Englishes have evolved on the Web is not – at least in our view – necessarily problematic; nor has it weakened the language, which seems to continue getting stronger (especially after its digital expansion). This does not mean that we cannot see the problems pointed out by Bauman with issues of economics and social relationships, for instance, in our contemporary realities, such as issues of inequality, lack of protection for the lower socioeconomic classes, access, and so on. In fact, as shown in chapter 4, similar problems may exist in relation to English, especially to many of those who do not speak the language, and who may for this very reason have less mobility (by which we mean desired mobility, and not forced mobility) to navigate across different spaces. And that is precisely why debates about English **linguistic imperialism** have been so prominent among language scholars – with various different takes on the issue, but with some degree of agreement that such kind of imperialism does exist, even if balanced out by stakeholders' own transformation of languages to fulfill their own. Because we believe that power is diffuse (remember our short discussions on Foucault's work), we do not agree with any unidirectional linguistic force, however, and therefore we posit that imperialist forces are counteracted by decisions, actions, and resistance by language users and their claiming of linguistic rights and linguistic ownership itself (for a great demonstration of this, refer to Canagarajah, 1999). In that sense, languages such as English simply belong to those who use it, and they change and morph given such uses.

What we *are* saying then is that we do not necessarily see *digital Englishes* as something which, by themselves, have caused damaging consequences to their users (old or new) and to the language – whether it be because of their fragmented nature or for any of their other traits. Actually, as we hope to have shown, something quite different may be taking place: that is, the digital expansion of Englishes may have brought with it more possibilities of learning the language, more power to both native and nonnative speakers, and more potential for shaping the language based on speakers' actual use of it. Furthermore, the language seems to have gained strength and breadth with its digital expansion rather than lost it, and examples of creativity are all over the Internet.

We can thus say that digital Englishes are somewhat *liquid* – in the sense of being fluid and not in the sense of being frail – but that we still need many more research accounts about their nature and their uses in order to make stronger claims about the issue. In any case, it is probably safe to say that digital Englishes are more liquid (again, meaning fluid) than many (if not all) digital versions of other languages, such as digital Germans, digital Spanishes, digital Portugueses, digital Japaneses, digital Chineses, and so forth, given the magnitude of their reach and the numbers of people who use English online around the globe (even if we could probably argue that some of those, too, are more liquid than others). English also has a history of much hybridization, which has transformed its very structure and use into one that allows much innovation. And it is also probably safe to say that the changeability of digital Englishes has reflected the change-ability of the Internet itself, and of cyberspace and cybercultures – which are also still under construction.

Education and the role of the classroom in a liquid language environment

Because of the scope of this book, we only touched briefly on the role of educa-tion, both in its digital incarnation as well as in its more traditional format, in helping people learn languages and gain awareness of the issues of our time and the virtual world. This came mostly in the form of discussions on large online course offerings and the not-yet-optimal use of digital media to teach foreign and second languages (given how some traditional approaches have simply been transferred to the digital environment, but not revolutionized). We hope much more scholarship comes into being in the next few years to describe and analyze the impact of digital modes on classroom language, standard variety use, as well as language teaching itself. Classrooms have been deemed as places of conformity and maintenance of the status quo (Pennycook, 2001, for example) or resistance and rebirth (Canagarajah, 1999). With the democratization of knowledge on the Internet, but also with its lack of formal structure, it is important to revisit these beliefs in light of new modes of interaction – even because, to a degree, we can say that any encounter with language is a potential learning opportunity. As the educators we are, we believe in the power of education, awareness, intention, and action in changing people's lives for the better, and it is up to us to seize the education opportunities that the digital era affords to make the best of these newer media. We look forward to the ideas and insights that are forthcoming.

The sociolinguistics of digital Englishes

In his book *The Sociolinguistics of Globalization* (which we have cited in previous chapters), Jan Blommaert (2010) argues that in the current context of globaliza-tion, sociolinguists need to account for language use in ways that are not static, with fixed notions of territory, but that can encompass movement and the dynamics of our contemporary world. He then proposes the notion of **sociolinguistic scales** to address the mobility of messages, people, languages, and so forth around the world, and to address issues of power as it relates to languages in different contexts.

In brief, Blommaert's sociolinguistic scales refer to the idea that when something moves (a language or a linguistic variety, for instance), it moves not only across spaces but also across what he calls **orders of indexicality**, which are "stratified normative complexes that organize distinctions between, on the one hand, 'good', 'normal', 'appropriate', and 'acceptable' language use and, on the other, 'deviant', 'abnormal' etc. language use" (Blommaert, 2010:6). He goes on to explain that these orders of indexicality "define the dominant lines for senses of belonging, for identities and roles in society" (Blommaert, 2010:6). In other words, they have to do with how much prestige and power are assigned to something in different contexts.

For example, when Indian English (or one of its varieties, to be more precise) moves to another space (say, the US or South Africa), it is hierarchically ranked differently in that new context from what it was in its original place. In other words, although a certain variety of Indian English may enjoy a lot of prestige in India, when such variety moves to the US, for instance, it will most likely be ranked in a different way with different levels of power and prestige. This will ultimately affect people in the way they express themselves, and it will have an impact on **intercultural communication**, among other things; and thus, such types of movement must be examined not only horizontally (across space), but also vertically, across hierarchical positions in different spaces.

A third element in Blommaert's (2010) model is called **polycentricity**, which indicates the existence of several different norms and indexes at the same time over the use of language in a certain space. Thus, in the example of Indian English used in the US, it could be the case that the use of this variety would be assigned power based not only on the macro-context in question – that is, the United States – but also on those involved in the communicative act, their socioeconomic and cultural realities, their contexts of origin, and so on.

The framework proposed by Blommaert (2010) has been quite influential in recent years, and it is particularly interesting for its critical aspect. However, it has also received some criticism by scholars – criticism which is worthy of attention. Most notably, Suresh Canagarajah (2014) has criticized it for being over-deterministic, as according to Blommaert, some norms (of which American English, especially Standard American English, would be a good example) will always prevail across contexts. For Canagarajah, then, Blommaert's model presupposes – among other things – that scales, and language statuses and norms, be predefined; that there is little or no room for renegotiating statuses; and that, consequently, there is no possibility for resistance, renegotiation, or reconstruction of norms by people themselves. However, in the real examples provided by Canagarajah (2014) of immigrants living in different parts of the world, we find exactly that resistance, renegotiation, and power relations are reconstructed at the local level.

The arguments we have made in this book about digital Englishes are more in line with those made by Canagarajah. We have made the case that the Internet has made Englishes even more malleable than before; that users in different domains have taken ownership of the language and shown how they themselves can reconstruct it, and exert that diffuse power that we have talked about, so as to renegotiate and redefine their relationship with languages such as English. The language has been used by individuals to cross identity barriers created by space limitations, and the new ways in which Englishes have been used online have reflected individual conceptualizations of it. Moreover, Englishes are now probably more polycentric than ever. Even the use of the term *normal* in relation to language use (or any other such human institution, for that matter) is context-dependent, given that a normal curve can only be drawn with data from a particular population. Thus, in the case of digital Englishes, we have suggested, at least to a certain degree, that sociolinguistic scales and orders of indexicality are being negotiated by individuals most – if not all – of the time, in spite of the negative consequences of the language's digital expansion, which we have also mentioned at different parts of the book. These processes of renegotiation are continuous or continual, and for that reason, to us they defy determinism.

More interesting even, perhaps, is the fact that the online space is already in and by itself a different type of space, a "space that is no space" as defined by Carol Delaney (2011), and mentioned in chapter 8 (remember also the many metaphors that we used to help us understand and anchor this new reality). How, exactly, can we account for sociolinguistic scales, orders of indexicality, and polycentricity, and how they operate in relation to Englishes in such a different type of realm? Should we consider the different physical spaces where people are located as separate, and look at how the language moves (both horizontally and vertically) through the Internet to each of these spaces? If we choose to do that, the Web becomes a mere medium through which languages can move. Or should we look at people's interactions in cyberspace and consider this space alone, as a location (albeit a metaphorical one) in its own right? By choosing to do so, we may miss important factors in people's communicative practices that come from their local, physical contexts. The plausible answer here, then, especially if we consider how polycentric power has become too, is that we should most likely do both.

A look at the sociolinguistics of digital Englishes is crucial to the understanding of the sociolinguistics of globalization, since Englishes and the Internet are such a big part of how we experience globalization in today's age. The present book has been an attempt to look at how sociolinguistics and world Englishes theory may (or may not) help us understand the phenomenon as a whole, and to help students and (novel) scholars grasp the concepts we consider important in relation to it. As we move forward, we need to do more. To bring more depth to the study of the sociolinguistics of digital Englishes, we will probably have to gather more and more empirical data, looking more closely at how individuals themselves (more specifically) have used Englishes online, and at how they have constructed and/or negotiated power relations, identities, cultures, and so on in their new **linguistic networks** and online practices. We will also have to see how much more fluid Englishes will become in the digital world, but also how other languages will redefine their space in this new reality, and the implications that such fluidity (be it multi-language or multi-variety, or both) will have upon the English language itself and its users. And our feeling is that we – scholars, teachers, students, and world citizens – have just begun this captivating conversation. We hope that our readers will join it.

Questions for discussion

1 What did you understand by the concept of *liquid modernity* proposed by Bauman? What do you think of it? Can you think of examples that illustrate it in your context?

2 Do you agree with the authors when they say that oral and written Englishes have not reached a liquid state, but that digital Englishes are currently somewhat liquid? If you do, do you think the language will become even more liquid in the future? Why (not)?

3 Consider the history of the English language. What milestones in that history could have prompted the same kind of pessimism regarding the state of English that we sometimes find in relation to the Internet and languages? What is different about those examples? What is similar?

4 How do you think researchers could further investigate the sociolinguistics of digital Englishes? For example, what types of online contexts, activities, and users could they research?

5 Can you think of situations that support our hypothesis that linguistic power is determined in context and can be renegotiated by users of language? What examples of this (or its opposite) do you have?

Notes

1 See also Bauman 2000, 2003, 2005, 2006, and 2011.
2 For great accounts of different English varieties, see journals such as *English World-Wide*, *World Englishes*, and *English Today*.

References and suggested further reading

Bauman, Z. (2000). *Liquid modernity*. Malden, MA: Polity Press.
Bauman, Z. (2003). *Liquid love: On the frailty of human bonds*. Malden, MA: Polity Press.
Bauman, Z. (2005). *Liquid life*. Malden, MA: Polity Press.
Bauman, Z. (2006). *Liquid fear*. Malden, MA: Polity Press.
Bauman, Z. (2007). *Liquid times: Living in an age of uncertainty*. Malden, MA: Polity Press.
Bauman, Z. (2011). *Culture in a liquid modern world*. Malden, MA: Polity Press.
Blommaert, J. (2010). *The sociolinguistics of globalization*. Cambridge: Cambridge University Press.

Canagarajah, S. (1999). *Resisting linguistic imperialism in English teaching.* Oxford: Oxford University Press.

Canagarajah, S. (2014). Agency and power in intercultural communication: Negotiating English in translocal spaces. *Language and Intercultural Communication, 13*(2), 202–224.

Delaney, C. (2011). *Investigating culture: An experiential introduction to anthropology* (Kindle DX version). Malden, MA: Wiley-Blackwell. Retrieved from Amazon.com.

Gee, J. P., & Hayes, E. R. (2011). *Language and learning in the digital age.* New York: Routledge.

Hino, N. (2009). The teaching of English as an international language in Japan: An answer to the dilemma of indigenous values and global needs in the Expanding Circle. *AILA Review, 22,* 103–119.

Hino, N. (2012). Endonormative models of EIL for the Expanding Circle. In A. Matsuda (Ed.), *Principles and practices of teaching English as an international language* (pp. 28–43). Tonawanda, NY: Multilingual Matters.

Matsuda, A., & Friedrich, P. (2011). English as an international language: A curriculum blueprint. *World Englishes, 30*(3), 332–344.

Pennycook, A. (2001). *Critical applied linguistics.* Mahwah: LEA Inc.

Index

Page numbers in *italics* refer to figures and tables. Page numbers followed by n refer to notes.